interplay
of
things

anthony b. pinn

# interplay of things

## RELIGION, ART, AND PRESENCE TOGETHER

Duke University Press  Durham and London  2021

Designed by Aimee C. Harrison
Typeset in Portrait Text and Canela Text
by Westchester Publishing Services

Library of Congress Cataloging-in-Publication Data
Names: Pinn, Anthony B., author.
Title: Interplay of things : religion, art, and presence together /
Anthony B. Pinn.
Description: Durham : Duke University Press, 2021. | Includes
bibliographical references and index.
Identifiers: LCCN 2021002639 (print)
LCCN 2021002640 (ebook)
ISBN 9781478013532 (hardcover)
ISBN 9781478014461 (paperback)
ISBN 9781478021766 (ebook)
ISBN 9781478091769 (ebook other)
Subjects: LCSH: Art and religion—United States. | Religion and
culture—United States. | African American art—Social aspects. | Art
and race. | Performance art—Social aspects—United States. | BISAC:
RELIGION / Philosophy | SOCIAL SCIENCE / Ethnic Stud-ies /
American / African American & Black Studies
Classification: LCC N72.R4 P56 2021 (print) | LCC N72.R4 (ebook) |
DDC 201/.67—dc23
LC record available at https://lccn.loc.gov/2021002639
LC ebook record available at https://lccn.loc.gov/2021002640

Cover art: Robel Temesgen, *Untitled*, 2017. Acrylic, ink,
permanent marker, 60 × 40 cm. Courtesy of the artist and
Tiwani Contemporary.

This book is freely available in an open access edition thanks to
TOME (Toward an Open Monograph Ecosystem)—a col-
laboration of the Association of American Universities, the
Association of University Presses, and the Association of
Research Libraries—and the generous support of the Fondren
Library at Rice University. Learn more at the TOME
website,availableat:openmonographs .org.

WITH

FOND MEMORIES

OF

APRIL 27–28, 2017

I can therefore say that the Absurd is not in man (if such a metaphor could have a meaning) nor in the world, but in their presence together.—ALBERT CAMUS, *The Myth of Sisyphus and Other Essays*

# contents

# acknowledgments

This book has developed over the course of roughly seven years, and it has involved support and assistance from a variety of people. First, I'd like to thank my editor, Miriam Angress, and Duke University Press for helping me refine my ideas in a way that made this book more compelling. I must also acknowledge the insights and critiques offered by the external reviewers. Attention to their reports went a long way in improving and refining my argument.

Prior to it reaching Duke, a good number of people helped me move from rough ideas to more fully developed arguments by reading pieces of the book or responding to presentations of some of the ideas. This isn't a complete list, but I want to thank Mayra Rivera for her critique and suggestions. I also want to thank Peter Paris, James Cone, Katie Cannon, Eddie Glaude, Jeffrey Kripal, April DeConick, Elias Bongmba, Mark Ryan, William Hart, Mike Hogue, Sharon Welch, Stacey Floyd-Thomas, Juan Floyd-Thomas, Cornel West, Jonathan Walton, Juergen Manemann, Stephen Tuck, Eli Valentin, and Benjamin Valentin.

My students over the years, through their questions and insights, have helped me develop my thinking—and I am grateful to them for the ways in which they pushed me toward this project. In addition, one of my current students, Hassan Henderson Lott, prepared the bibliography for this volume. Maya Reine, the assistant director of the Center for Engaged Research and

Collaborative Learning, has been an outstanding colleague and friend over the years. Her hard work and generosity afforded me larger blocks of time to work on this project. She also was generous enough to prepare the final manuscript for publication. Thank you.

I am also thankful to various organizations, institutions, and universities that offered opportunity to work through some of the ideas contained here. They include the Hannover Institute for Philosophical Research (Hannover, Germany), the Rothermere American Institute at Oxford University, Harvard Divinity School, the University of South Africa, the University of Mississippi, Material Secularisms Symposium at the University of Pennsylvania, Claremont School of Theology, Winston-Salem State University, Society for the Study of Black Religion, Indiana University–Purdue University (Indianapolis), the University of Humanistic Studies (Utrecht, Netherlands), Global Studies Conference (Singapore), the University of Paderborn (Paderborn, Germany), and the University of Kablenz-Landau (Koblenz, Germany). Support in various forms from my home institution, Rice University, provided time and resources needed to complete this book. Thank you to my department colleagues and staff, the dean's office, and the provost's office.

Family and friends provided time away from the computer that offered opportunity to catch my breath and put my "work" into context. Thank you all.

Finally, I appreciate permission from Angelbert Metoyer and the Zi Koolhaas-Metoyer Trust to use images found in chapter 3. Also, the Pennsylvania State University Press granted permission to include the article upon which chapter 7 builds.

# introduction

## DEFINITIONS AND CONSIDERATIONS

But one day when I was sitting quiet and feeling like a motherless child, which I was, it come to me: that feeling of being part of everything, not separate at all. I knew that if I cut a tree, my arm would bleed.
—ALICE WALKER, *The Color Purple*

I no longer think of religion as a quest for complex subjectivity.[1] There is *something* underneath the quest for complex subjectivity that prompts particular patterns of thinking and doing. Hence, the quest for complex subjectivity is a second-order arrangement—that is, patterns of thinking and doing—but there is something behind it (prior to it) that constitutes religion proper.

Mindful of this, *I now understand religion as a technology* (or one might also reference it as a religious technology, although I prefer the former). In using this term, I am not appealing to the mechanics of scientific advancements marking life in the twenty-first century; I am not attempting to highlight new economic and social capacities that entail a new understanding of production and the human. Rather, in using the term *technology*, I mean to identify a method of interrogation and exposure, with an archaeological quality to it. Put differently, I am arguing that *religion is a technology; it is a method of interrogation and exposure. And this interrogation takes a variety of forms—such as exploration of places, presentation of the performance of activities, noting of the positioning and workings of bodies.* Religion *is* the exploration as opposed to being what one finds through the exploration of cultural production, for instance. Again, this is a push against a sense of religion as a "thing"—a set of beliefs, practices, and/or institutions.

## On Religion and Technology, and Religion as Technology

I should clarify what I mean by religion and by religion as a technology, and it might be helpful to do so through contrast—by briefly discussing alternate framings of these two concepts.

A relationship between technology and religion is present in a variety of texts, including work by Susan George and Jacques Ellul.[2] For George, the primary concern is the "synergistic" relationship between religion and technology—that is, the manner in which religion is enhanced by technology and how technology is informed through exposure to a range of sociocultural considerations. Regarding the former, George has in mind the ways in which technology enhances (or transforms) how, for instance, the religious gather—such as virtual churches. Furthermore, regarding the latter, George repositions the conversation regarding the impact of technology on human life by arguing technology, such as artificial intelligence (AI), could benefit from theological considerations, theological frameworks by means of which AI is equipped to better understand the nature and meaning of the human identity and humanity—both of which are fundamental to the workings and intent of AI. And so, both facets considered—technology's influence on religion and religion's influence on technology—this synergistic relationship connotes for George a complex enhancement of the form and dynamics of life.[3] In presenting this argument, George suggests religion and technology are similar if for no other reason than both promote modalities of "transcendence"—or a push beyond current arrangements and circumstances.

While the terminology is the same—religion and technology—my meaning is significantly different.[4] George acknowledges that religion is difficult to define and tends, therefore, to speak more generally about religion as often considered to reflect "a social construction, as wish-fulfillment, and as alienation."[5] She highlights a concern for meaning and meaning making but implies a somewhat standard attention to religious traditions—for example, Christianity—and their vocabulary.[6] In this way, at least implicitly, religion is understood in terms of traditionally recognized markers such as doctrines and institutions. Its relationship to embodied beings connotes a standard mode of transformation and "transcendence" by means of ritualized performance. My aim is to challenge such perceptions of religion as pointing to a distinct material-spiritual reality arranged in time and space. Hence, I push for theorization of religion as a hermeneutic of sorts (a mode of interpretation or interrogation)—not a "substance" but rather an approach, a particular framing. And with respect to technology, George has in mind "applied knowledge that impacts daily life." This understanding is discussed in relationship to four possibilities. These are (1) "information and communication technology . . . providing the infrastructure upon which other technologies can sit, (2) AI—artificial intelligence" meant to act in the human world, (3) "ubiquitous computing and ambient intelligence" promoting flow of "information and communication between the human and computer world, and (4) virtual AI, enhancing internet ICT with intelligence and sophistication, merging with ubiquitous computing to make a world where the interface between the virtual and real are continually blurred."[7] Technology as discussed by George certainly has impact and importance, but what I mean by technology here is not tied to modalities of scientific engagement; rather, technology speaks to a more theoretical consideration. My aim, put another way, is not to apply the categories traditionally associated with the religious—for example, God, salvation, and sin—to a secularized and (technologically) enhanced world. Nor is my concern to bring to religiosity a clear and consistent engagement with scientific development. The theorization of religion and the framing of technology undergirding *Interplay of Things* does not involve either of these approaches.

Jacques Ellul has a more expansive sense of technique/technology by which he names more than machines, pointing instead to something that extends at this point in history well beyond mechanics.[8] For Ellul, technology better describes any means used to render "rationalized" and "deliberate" behavior once ill-defined and sporadic. In this way, it describes a formal concern with the development of greater effectiveness for any task, greater processes for achieving any task related to all areas and realms of life.[9] In his words, it "does not mean machines, technology, or this or that procedure for attaining an end. In our technological society, technique is the totality of methods rationally arrived at and having absolute efficiency (for a given state of development) in every field of human activity."[10] It is an intellectual posture or method, a framing, organizing particular processes; machines are more limited in scope in that they produce and depend on technique for refinement of their work. Conceived as such, then, propaganda serves as an example of a human technique; but also of concern here is organizational technique that has to do with the administration—in some sense containment—of life activities and circumstances.[11] Different names are used, but related methods are geared toward the same goal—efficiency.

There is with this definition—related to technique as a general method but more particularly with respect to organizational and human techniques—a sense of technology having impact on human engagement with the world, with other beings, and with structures. This means to enhance what Ellul categorizes as increased motivation for and attainment of "success" in our activities and ventures. And in a sense, all things related to or interacting with technique become machines—that is to say, primed for greater efficiency. In so doing, human life is altered, framed by distance or estrangement from anything that does not promote greater efficiency in general or success in particular. Technique serves to bring things together, or to harness all. In a word, while humans and machines might be distinguishable—of different substances—technique working on the intellectual level serves to link embodied humans with this general scheme of efficiency. In so doing, technique when considered within sociocultural and political realms might be said to organize existence, which is to say that technique coordinates activities and behaviors so as to make activities more efficient and rational. A consequence of this is the loss of distinctiveness—that is, recognition as valuable what cannot be easily cataloged as promoting the terms of a technological process.[12]

There is with Ellul's definition of technique a sense that the human is penetrated (or impacted), so to speak, by mechanisms meant to enhance and streamline processes of collective life. I share some of this concern; yet for Ellul, technique, which is related to science but distinguishable from it (as science is dependent upon technique), entails a refined and refining process of doing—an all-consuming quest for better ways of doing, a quest that takes on a transcendent quality based on its persistence and all-encompassing reach. My use of the concept of technology speaks not to doing but to examining—of exposing what is beneath and what informs processes of organization. As I intend to employ it, the concept of technology has little to do with naming increasingly effective ways of achieving tasks, but rather with interrogating the very nature of those tasks and arrangements and what they say about the relationship between things. The former understanding of technology, for example, has meaning in terms of politics in that technology perceived as the push for processes of excellence/efficiency seeks to rule out all that hampers such processes. However, my concern is with that which undergirds these moves and countermoves.

Religion—by which Ellul means typical presentation of traditions marked by institutions, doctrines, rituals, and personalities—does not fall outside the reach of technique. Keep in mind that for Ellul, technique impacts all spheres of collective life. *The Technological Society* argues that during the fourth to the tenth centuries in the West there was a "breakdown of Roman technique in every area—on the level of organization as well as in the construction of cities, in industry, and in transport."[13] Christianity during the period held technique, as it related to "judicial and other technical activities" suspect—preaching and theologizing against it.[14] Yet, according to Ellul, after this period of technical decline it is also the case that religious traditions from the East served to revive particular modalities of technique. With shifts in the theological sensibilities and accompanying ethics of Christianity over time came a particular metaphysical framework—including a more accommodating theological anthropology—making possible appeal to technique framed in terms of a benevolent deity committed to the prosperity and well-being of the elect.[15]

This cautious encounter with technique was played out for the most part within the realm of mechanisms—think, for instance, in terms of oceanic exploration that transported European Christianity beyond its initial borders, or the printing press that altered the availability and reach of the Bible. Yet a sense of efficiency, or the larger framing of technique, would have to overcome a more transcendent concern with the will of God as measure of activity and a theological sensibility casting a shadow over rationalizations. In general, religion had little to offer. For Ellul, more "secular" movements and a general optimism served to spark a shift toward more technique.[16] The rigid codes for thinking and doing advanced through religious commitment did little to aid technique in its broad meaning. Moral sensibilities frowned upon any advancement, any change, that could not be accounted for through the arrangement of church doctrine and creeds.[17] In a word, "technique was held to be fundamentally sacrilegious."[18] It is only as these moral codes and theological suspicions give way to alternate modalities of religious thinking and living that the relationship between religion and technique is altered.

George speaks of a relationship between technology (by which she means for the most part machines and scientific advancements less expansive than in Ellul's meaning) and religion that involves mutual engagement and shared alteration. And this involves an understanding of religion and technology as separate realities engaging, which is not the sense of religion and technology I intend. Ellul shifts to an understanding of technique that is expansive and that deals more with attitudes and intellectual postures, but it is distinct from religion. In fact, it is hampered by religion—which has often served as an opponent for technique. Still, like George, Ellul has a sense in which religion is understood in traditional terms (e.g., institutions, doctrines, theological frameworks and rituals) and is brought into conversation concerning structuring or framing of production—either material or intellectual.

For Ellul, technique involves an all-encompassing method seeking advancement, a process for refining methods of life. I understand technology differently, as a hermeneutic—a tool rather than a process for/of refining life practices. Technology, as I understand it, observes intellectual and mechanical processes; it does not constitute a naming for these processes. *The Technological Society* claims, "Technique has taken over the whole of civilization."[19] My framing of technology might suggest that it shapes how we view and hence understand civilization but, mindful of this, Ellul and I could not mean the same thing if we were both to talk about technique/technology taking over civilization. *The Technology Society* reacts against technique and what it seeks to do to and through humans regardless of our assumed intent. Technique is supreme.[20] Even his reference to spiritual techniques entails a relationship to the structures of production, of life—a particular type of efficiency desired—that I do not mean to suggest. Ellul's concept of technique involves "something" that does more and perhaps means more than what I have in mind when discussing technology. In short, my aim in speaking of religion *as a* technology is not captured by discourse on religion *and* technology as represented, for instance, by George and Ellul.

My use of technology entails a loose borrowing from, but not strict adherence to, Michel Foucault's conceptual framework.[21] I mean it as a pattern of practices related to examination—a "technique" by means of which humans interrogate experience and knowledge of experience.[22] While using his conceptual framework, I alter it a bit—highlighting, for example, interaction between contemporary and multiple things, and doing so in ways that challenge assumptions concerning the "solid" and "sealed" nature of things. I privilege a triadic and interrelated structuring of technology over against his four-pronged structure. In relationship to the four types of technology addressed by Foucault—"production," "sign systems," "power," and "self"[23]—what I propose most strongly resembles a synergistic relationship between the impetus of production, sign systems, and self. The omitted technology of power better relates—although the others can certainly bend in this direction—to what I reference in this book as the psycho-ethical impulse to the extent that it involves application on bodies for sociopolitical and economic ends related to confinement in certain forms.[24]

More on that later, but for now it is important to offer a point of clarification: Religion as a technology involves a "technique" of observation, but it is not synonymous with the manner in which the technology of power uses surveillance to control and justify the rendering docile of problematic bodies. Religion as a technology's observation is more consistent with exposure without the political discursive tactics and intents of the technology of power. However, like technologies of production, religion as a technology involves interaction (creation, placement, use) of things. Like the technology of sign systems, religion as a technology relies on structures of recognition and naming (what Foucault might call "signs, meanings, symbols, or significations"). Finally, like technologies of the self that "permit individuals to effect their own means or with the help of others a certain number of operations on their own bodies and souls, thoughts, conduct, and way of being, so as to transform themselves," by its very nature religion as a technology focuses on the flexibility and porous nature of things in (inter)action.[25]

In depicting the mechanics of various technologies, my concern is less in a strict sense with the surface content of interaction and more with what interaction or interplay between things tells us about the nature (i.e., openness) of things. Although highlighting different connotations and contexts of expression, my sense of technology does maintain something of Foucault's sense that technologies are tied to methods of "modification," *I here argue that religion as a technology—in its hermeneutical function—exposes and further amplifies the openness, porousness and interaction of things.*[26] Furthermore, my application of religion as a technology is not interested in, as a primary move, the manner in which interaction improves or diminishes a subject—for example, makes us better people. I am most intrigued by challenges to "habitual" (to borrow another word from Foucault) assumptions of wholeness and integrated selves exposed by the observational activity of this particular technology. Yet I do not intend a large-scale understanding of social dynamics and power relations, nor a type of embodied structuring of cultural forms and skills discussed by figures such as Pierre Bourdieu through the category of "habitus." Religion as technology does not entail content—for example, "cultural capital"—rather, it provides a means by which to view these dimensions of life in various forms and manifestations. By extension, what I reference as this technology does not entail what Bourdieu might label a "feel" for the circumstances shaping life. In and of itself, this hermeneutic offers less in that how it is used might be influenced by sensibilities developed over time, but this technology does not connote those sensibilities. In this sense, religion as technology does not entail a type of "know how" enabling one to maneuver through the world, but rather it is simply an external mechanism for isolating and examining the world—not an internal set of acquired competencies.[27] Furthermore, my interest in interaction points in the direction of concern with understanding openness, the gap, and not in how one might configure the whole—or things together. In this way what I aim to describe is not "assemblage"—an ontological mapped, chaotic arrangement or relationship of things constituting an oddly functioning collective.[28] The very ability to influence and affect expressed in Foucault's presentation of the technology of the self, for instance, surfaces the concern for me: the openness—porousness and penetrated—nature of things. *And this openness is the "disclosure," so to speak, offered by means of religion as a technology.*[29] In this way, religion as technology pushes underneath patterns of thinking and doing. This, however, is without metaphysical claims emerging as a consequence and outside a process of meaning formation.[30] The idea here is that religion is a human technology, that is to say it is a mechanism, a technique—or range of operative strategies—for interrogating human experience.

By way of this shift I want to highlight the inclusive nature of this interrogation and also privilege the manner in which religion simply serves as a "mechanism" for inquisition into the cartographies of life. Yet more than this, I needed to name this theory of religion through focused attention to what it, as a technology of interrogation, reveals. In other words, *interrogation of interplay between things can be a religious matter*. And so rather than attempting to show the presence of the religious in cultural production, this book uses religion as a technology to interrogate cultural production and thereby say something concerning the nature and meaning of those "things" making up our cultural worlds.

While my defining of religion as a technology, a type of hermeneutic, escapes certain problems associated with the presentation of religion as "special" with privileged elements such as rituals and doctrines, I understand that my thinking comes with its own set of issues—for example, the implication that certain sociocultural developments have greater importance than others. True, in isolating particular dimensions of human experience for investigation, one could suggest it encourages, or privileges, attention to certain historical moments and constructions—and makes something unique of what is encountered. However, I mean to simply say that this selection process connected to religion as technology is a matter of circumstantial context and social location without any necessarily "deeper" meaning. Other applications of this technology within other sociocultural contexts will yield a different set of materials. What holds together the elements of experience targeted by this technology is their existence as human, as dimensions of a network of "relationships," lodged within human history. Furthermore, I want to position the last several chapters of this book as an effort to trouble reification of experiences as having increased value and by extension increasing the importance of particular "things" associated with those experiences.[31]

My definition seeks to point out the very historical and socially specific nature of religion—the manner in which religion as a technology points out connection to cultural-historical circumstances and understands the "work" done by religion tied as a type of "precondition" to the vocabulary and grammar of these cultural-historical circumstances.[32] Religion points out and focuses on by highlighting. And so rather than producing meaning, religion, as I understand it, involves the uncovering of such assumptions—or interrogation of such assumptions' historical arrangement, thereby exposing the frameworks that undergird them. It is important to keep in mind that this pointing out emphasizes concern for particular developments or activities. But this does not require a next step of assuming that what is uncovered is all there is. Again, religion as a technology works within particular sociocultural contexts and by means of particular historical circumstances. What, then, is highlighted is conditioned yet informative. Furthermore, something about religion as a technology suggests concern with language and social sensibilities. Yet I am not arguing that religion is first an arrangement of "practice, language, and sensibility set in social relationships rather than as systems of meaning."[33] And so religion is not a matter of "what and how people live," but rather what people view and what moments of experience they isolate for consideration and importance. How they "live" in light of this process, for me, is beyond the category of religion as such and instead involves a system of affective and ethical responses.

Religion as a technology offers no particular set of commitments or responses to what it uncovers; that is left to moral and ethical interventions extending beyond this hermeneutical work. In this way, religion is not the things observed, but rather the very process of observation defines it. My concern is to recognize this sense of the religious and to interrogate the "things" observed.[34] In this manner it can be applied to any modality of human experience (here I privilege historical-cultural experience). This is not to say these areas are religious, but rather that they can be interrogated using the methodological tool of religion as human technology.[35] This is not a special technology, but rather a particular technology—one that exposes contextualized concerns and patterns embedded in the workings of the social world, not unique "domains" or worlds.

So understood, it is only useful in a localized manner to think about religion as connected with particular doctrines, creeds, and ritualization associated with world-recognized (and those not so noted) traditions. In certain ways, these traditions represent what remains—as a type of epistemological residue—when religion as a technology is no longer applied. This is the same way snow is not the blizzard but rather constitutes what remains once the blizzard has done its work. Religion in this manner is not a system of promises related to the human condition, but rather it is a means of categorization and interrogation that promises and assumes nothing in particular regarding the human condition other than offering acknowledgment that tools exist for interrogating the history of these individual and collective experiences.[36] By exposing the nature of things, religion as a technology pushes below the surface of activities, to the things involved in that interaction. Here, then, I am concerned to explore the elements, the "principles," so to speak, at work in what religion as a technology presents.

*My objective is to discuss various modalities of the arts so as to highlight the things exposed through religion as a technology.* To put it another way, while much of the existing scholarship on religion and the arts involves uncovering religion within popular culture through the presence of symbols (e.g., the cross), figures (e.g., Jesus), or the expression of doctrines and creeds,[37] this book is concerned with the application of religion as a technology to art so as to expose what art says about the nature of "things" and their interaction.[38] And so the point is not that cultural production expresses human concerns using the vocabulary and grammar of Christianity and other traditions, but rather that examining cultural production using religion as a technology tells us something about the nature of the embodied human's interaction with other things.[39]

## Things Underneath

To highlight my basic point: I am concerned with the importance and interplay of things exposed through application of religion as a technology. But to further interrogate their placement in time and space as well as their "activity" within time and space highlighted by religion as a technology, I have renamed, or better yet, reconceptualized them.

This rethinking allows me to enhance the nature of bodies, for example, and it does so by pushing beyond the assumption of clear distinctions and "integrity" the concept of a body can easily assume. In a word, through conversation with thing theory and grotesque realism among other theoretical frameworks, I want to understand bodies as *things*.

For the sake of clarity, it is important to say that this is not to reduce them to objects and in this way to accept certain forms of disregard I have spent decades arguing against. Rather, they are things, but things understood as vital and vibrant—impactful. And while I use religion here as a way to think through the nature of humans and other forms, the primary contribution of religion so conceived is not a reframing of the human in relationship to other forms of life so as to disrupt a hierarchy of being. What I offer does not qualify as a sustained interest in or wrestling with—a type of intervention into—what Rosi Braidotti calls "the basic unit of common reference for our species, our polity and our relationship to the other inhabitants of this planet."[40] While what I have in mind pushes against a "nature-cultural" binary that calls into question the distinctive nature of the human, I am less concerned with an intervention into thinking about the structure of living beings.[41] Instead, I am more interested in the interaction between forms—for example, not with the Anthropocene but rather a more general interrogation of openness/boundaries not limited to any particular actors. Furthermore, although not existing in opposition to such concerns if for no other reason than my context as a racialized being, *Interplay of Things* does not engage in debate over humanism, and my primary motivation is not a posthumanist concern with "elaborating alternative ways of conceptualizing the human subject."[42] Subjectivity certainly comes up in the following pages, but mapping out alternate modalities of subjectivity is not the first concern here. This is in part the case because I want to shy away from the implicit assumption within posthumanism that the human can speak for and about all other things. This epistemological orientation, I argue, is held over from Enlightenment humanism; but rather than its concern being the positioning of the human over against others, it is within posthumanism a positioning of other beings in relationship to humans. The naming may blur lines, but the linguistic and epistemological assumptions betray continuity with humanistic thought.

Within the following chapters, some attention is given to the manner in which social coding such as race impacts openness. Yet what I propose offers little advice on how humans and other things might better interact, in a general sense, but rather focuses on the mere existence of that interaction as always and already—despite curious efforts to state otherwise. My concern here is not isolation of the psychological dimensions of human experience, or the discursive grid or imaginative structuring of humanized experiences, and so

I make only limited appeal to the work of figures such as Julia Kristeva. When employing her thought it is to clarify some of my language. And in this vein, I want to mention a particular concept as a way of highlighting something of what I have in mind regarding the human as a thing. One might think of the body—to borrow from Kristeva—as a "naming" thing (a play on her notion of the "speaking being").[43] I use this as one of the characteristics of the (human) body as thing, but rather than simply speaking—as other animals speak—I highlight the human as a bodied naming-thing (a type of "more" thing) thereby again turning to the importance of naming as it relates to religion as a technology.[44] I amplify not only the manner in which the human speaks but also the ways in which speaking involves connection to and interaction with other things. I am concerned with how religion as a technology exposes the bodied naming-thing's interactions with other bodied naming-things as well as non-naming-things or what I here call *thing-things*. In this way I seek to give some attention to the manner in which bodied naming-things create and/or shape other things as well as how bodied naming-things are shaped and altered. This interplay, in turn, points out bodied naming-things as open, porous, engaged, and flooded by other things.

This bodied naming-thing is not meant to suggest a sense of the human "as the measure of all things"—as some humanists have defined the grand sub-jectivity of the human—so as to point out a robust valuation of humanity over against other modalities of life.[45] In distinguishing the (human) bodied naming-thing for investigation, I am not implying a ranking of naming-things. I am not providing this renaming so as to suggest a particular metaphysical quality of being. Rather, I use it simply to point out the "thingliness" of the human—the porous and open quality of embodiment without pronounced attentiveness toward how this has come to be or what this means regarding any transcendental framings of human knowing and being. To be a bodied naming-thing is a shared arrangement, or put differently, it entails moments of not quite amalgamation—but rather short-circuiting the pretense of boundaries. The so-called individual is give and take, so to speak, a micro- and macro-confluence of presences.[46] I want to highlight the significance, primarily through description, nestled in openness and porousness. By open-ness and porousness, I mean to point out more than an emotional and aesthetic sense of openness, as an acceptance of the value of this touch. But rather, I mean openness in a more expansive manner that is affective and material in nature.

In making these claims, there remains a distinction: I do speak of naming-things and other things, and in this way this project does not wipe out difference, or what might be called various modes of activity associated with things. Instead, it neutralizes it (e.g., no advocated hierarchy of importance with respect to interaction) to some degree by amplifying the manner in which difference does not serve as a firm boundary and does not, therefore, suspend interaction. And the ability to name is not all that "matters."[47] On one level, for instance, what I propose here maintains difference between humans and other animals—although both are things, and this situation continues with regard to "other" things with which humans and other animals are in relationship (i.e., interaction or exchange).[48] And so one might argue that binaries remain here, and there is something to this, but these are not stable distinctions when one considers there is already and always interaction, exchange, and influence between things.

These things are active, impinging, informing in significant ways. Such is not the case only for naming-things, although the geography of this interaction is described and presented from the vantage point of these naming-things. In a word, I have no interest in parsing out types of things along the lines of what Jane Bennett describes as the "habit of configuring the world of things into dull matter (it, things) and vibrant life (us, being)." Of more interest is what Bennett calls "vital materiality"—recognition of a world filled with "animate things rather than passive objects." My sense of interplay bears similarity to Bennett's animation by which she means the "capacity of things—edibles, commodities, storms, metals—not only to impede or block the will and designs of humans but also to act as quasi agents or forces with trajectories, propensities, or tendencies of their own."[49] I would not disagree with her assertion that there is something to be said regarding the manner in which the "human being and thinghood overlap" and "slip-slide into each other," and so "we are also nonhuman and that things, too, are vital players in the world."[50] Yet while sharing this conceptual element, my motivation is primarily to recognize, document, and describe using art as the nature of this interplay.

Attention to race and gender at the end of the book suggests a concern with ways in which interplay is problematized, but, unlike Bennett, I frame the conversation in terms of a rethinking of religion and offer little attention to how this descriptive project might lend itself (through attention to this interplay) to the politics of new ways of living—such as consumption and conservation.[51] In addition, whereas new materialism can be seen to suggest rethinking the condition of certain things—such as despised populations— through an interrogation of subject-object thinking producing a greater sense of mutuality and collective well-being,[52] my position (in light of my turn to

definitions and considerations 13

W. E. B. Du Bois and Albert Camus) troubles any assumption concerning the ability to fundamentally change the positioning of the despised.[53] And so my goals are more modest: presentation and examination of openness—the point of convergence between no thing and multiple things—exposed through the interplay of things.

The above, brief discussion points to the manner in which this book shares some sensibilities with new materialism while departing from some of its generally assumed concerns (e.g., grounding in a posthumanist or antihumanist philosophy as replacement for humanism and, in some cases, a more biological focus, as well as broad geopolitical mappings).[54] I am mindful of materiality, and *Interplay of Things* centers on the dynamics and significance of materiality. Yet I am less concerned with exploring materiality so as to challenge the assumptions, for example, concerning language and subjectivity and in this way champion the significance of materialization.[55] On the level of social realities, I am a member of a group, African Americans, who have not had the luxury of forgetting their materiality. In this case, to be a racialized "other" at work in the world is to be a materialist of a kind. And so whereas some materialists are concerned rightly to point out that the agency of matter beyond the human is significant and complex, for some groups the idea that they have agency is still a fight to be fought. With this said, as a matter of contextualization, my implicit concern involves attention to the relationship between things so as to point out the absence—the points of openness—and what recognition of those points of no-thing and things at the same time has generated with respect to social difference.

Put another way, my concern involves an effort to wrestle with the nature and meaning of openness by way of the "art" of things. My name for this interplay between things—*presence together*—is drawn from Camus. Expressed more fully, he writes, "the absurd is essentially a divorce. It lies in neither of the elements compared; it is born of their confrontation. In this particular case and on the plane of intelligence, I can therefore say that the Absurd is not in man (if such a metaphor could have a meaning) nor in the world, but in their presence together."[56] He uses this phrase as a way to present relationship between the human and the nonresponsive world. I broaden it out as a way of "naming" the interplay—without resolution or production of wholeness—between the naming-thing and other things (of which the world is a particular constitution). And I argue in relationship to this investigation that interplay between things is presented by religion as the basic structuring of life. Hence, it is to this interplay that all strategies—social, cultural, political, and so forth—respond.[57] Religion strictly as a technology offers nothing beyond interrogation—no "liberation," no "freedom," no "transformation," no exaltation—and no teleological sense of encounter and exchange.[58]

## After Religion: Psycho-Ethical Impulse

What I have elsewhere described as rituals of reference attempts to endorse closure of certain bodies, to end the porous or open nature of these bodies.[59] This is because awareness of openness can foster discomfort as it brings into question all that social networks assume (or consume?) concerning subjectivity—that is, boundaries, integrity, and distinctiveness: subjects of history, not objects of history. In other words, interplay is often perceived as a problem—a network of relationships that various systems of knowledge (e.g., capitalism and democracy) would rather keep hidden. A strategic and common response to openness is to attempt the filling of gaps, to work to (discursively and materially) close off bodies. Within the context of certain social settings, this can entail inscribing social codes such as race, gender, and class that safeguard those who control the means of placement and display. Openness, as I hope will become clear over the course of this book, is the reality that sociopolitical coding, for instance, is meant to deny or to close off for the sake of existing arrangements of life. I frame this openness as a matter of Mikhail Bakhtin's grotesque realism.[60] This is not to dismiss as viable other approaches. Rather, for the purposes of this project, in turning to Bakhtin I gain a sense of the irreverence marking presentation of openness that lends itself to an understanding of the artists I engage. In addition, Bakhtin's theorization of encounter also points in the direction of sociocultural and political context in a way that helps shed light on the consequences of openness as I attempt to present them late in the book.

My aim is to suggest a general theoretical framework marking out the naming of the moment of interplay. Only then do I see it as feasible or useful to sketch the psycho-ethical sequence or modality of response. I say this because the response is contextualized in that in practice not all these naming-things are the same—understood as constituted and placed in the same manner and with the same sociocultural, political, and economic connotations. And while there are numerous ways in which openness/restriction play out in significant ways depending on the coding attached to particular naming-things, I am concerned here with the manner in which openness and closure are informed and influenced by the combination of gender and class in connection to race.

It is only as a consequence of this particular framing of restriction that attention is given to how whiteness as a source of both openness and restriction informs and impacts those naming-things configured as white.

African Americans—and the same would hold for bodies bounded by other modes of coding—struggle against this closing off at least in socioeconomic and political terms. Some naming-things reject closing off with respect to race, gender, and class, for instance; but this is not to say they struggle to remain open. They simply do not want that closing off to limit full engagement—or, in other words, to limit how, when, and where they interplay with thing-things and other naming-things. They resist restrictions on how they are closed and for what purpose they are closed. Yet this resistance is still modeled on boundaries; marginalized bodied naming-things simply resist particular types of restrictions—such as those that deny them certain markers of status. This is certainly one way to explain homophobia, for example, within African American communities, or sexism exhibited by marginalized men. Openness, while I understand it as a positive (and as I will demonstrate in these pages), is resisted.[61] This is not to say there are no instances in which boundaries are of benefit. But my concern is not with boundaries in a general sense; rather, again, as will become evident through most of this book, I am interested in the function of race (often connected to gender and class) as a type of boundary against openness as well as the ways in which certain naming-things respond to this mode of restriction.

It is not the case that religion as a technology is the only technology to expose the openness of things. From the biological sciences to philosophy and psychology, other technologies suggest the same.[62] However, there is some distinction at least in terms of the psycho-ethical response prompted by religion as a technology. For instance, while the "natural" sciences maintain openness of the body, and philosophy typically articulates it, many psycho-ethical responses understood within theological contexts propose deep (and at times eschatological) punishment for efforts to challenge the legitimacy—if not necessity—of this closer. For example, in theological terms, Adam and Eve and the "apple" can be read as suggesting this interplay between things as problematic. The goal of Genesis's angry God is to prevent a particular type of lucidity, to prevent a certain type of engagement between naming-things and other things. Of course, this requires a reading that is not popular in all circles. And so the study of religion has pushed away from more explicit denouncements of the "natural" body and in fact has given rise to embodied approaches to the study of religion—for example, body theologies. Nonetheless, something remains of this negative impulse or reversion against "things" and the interplay between things to the extent the theological body is typically without body functions and capacities. It is, for the most part, a thought body—one free of the more disturbing (disgusting?) markers of life-death.[63] Or perhaps it is even a corpse, a body that does not consume or expel. I intend to privilege, and center, theorization of religion around this seldom approached body (i.e., naming-thing)—the one marked by abuses born (and living) between urine and feces, as one church father put it.[64]

For the sake of clarity, in discussing theology in this context, I am not implying that theology alone attempts to push toward wholeness, or even that all modalities of theology push toward closure.[65] This desire for closure, for containment, is a feature of numerous discourses and structures of thinking and doing. It is not alone in fostering ways to desire closure or in the presentation of rewards for closure. Political discourses—for example, certain modalities of nationalism—do this as well, and the list goes on. Rather, I mention theology here to provide an example, not an isolated indictment. In a more general sense, I reference theology at points in the book because theology—particularly within racialized contexts—is a dominant vocabulary and grammar for discussing the nature and meaning of naming-things. And making my argument at times requires attention to how theological discourse has worked in this regard.

My goal, by extension, is to detangle the study of religion—a sense of the body's place in theorization of religion—from the shadow of restrictions by means of which interplay is held suspect. Furthermore, I mean to contribute to the study of religion in general and the study of African American religion in particular a way to think about key issues of embodiment and justice that go deeper—to a more fundamental arrangement—than sociopolitical and economic markers of injustice typically highlight. In this way, for example, my attention to religion as technology and restriction/openness offers African American religious thought a sense of embodied bodies occupying time and space outside their presence in political discourse marked by arguments concerning civil rights. Instead, I want to raise questions concerning what religion tells us about the activities and anxieties undergirding these political considerations. In addition, this project pushes against the manner in which African American religious thought and ethics is typically restricted to an understanding of "other" things (nonhuman things) as objects of utility, and in this way reinforces restrictive notions of agency, solidarity, praxis, and so on.

Religion as a technology does not relieve the trauma resulting from acknowledgment of openness. Much of religious studies—particularly so-called progressive and liberation-minded theological discourses—has been preoccupied either with subject/subject relations by means of which they seek to advocate for the full recognition of a particular group as fully human couched in language of the cosmic Other, or with a matter of the subject articulated through the language of stability—such as economic and political equality, or liberation. I am not interested in this framing. Instead, I am concerned with the general receptive nature of this interaction—most notably as presented by artistic expression.

*Rather than reading art through religion, as is often done, my aim is to interrogate interplay of things (exposed by the religion as a technology) through various modalities of artistic production.* In this way, I mean to isolate the frameworks through which religion as a technology engages human experience—that is, bodied naming-things and other things. Artistic work lends itself to an examination of the performance of interaction between naming-things and other things as a type of material-mancy. This is not simply ritualization—a repeating of what has been before.[66] No, in a significant way it is the articulation of arrangements, a fostering of connection and the implications of connection that is new each time. The naming-thing and other things relate to and inform each other.

## Unpacking Things

The first two chapters constituting the first section of this book attend to the nature of things, and they do so with respect to three categories: thing-things, naming-things, and the "art" of things. The goal of these two chapters is to present and explain the context in which the technology of religion is applied—for example, the subjects of interrogation. Each of these chapters benefits from my conversation with thing theory and grotesque realism as well as absurdist moralism. My concern in the first chapter is to unpack and theorize what is meant and constituted by "thing" and to highlight the manner in which life in a general sense organizes interplay between things. The second chapter outlines the ways in which religion as a technology explores art as "arrangement" by means of which openness is made apparent and named. Agreeing with theorists such as Mikhail Bakhtin, I note that some of the "content" and "form" of this interplay is best expressed through the language, vocabulary, and grammar of artistic production—visual, literary and performed (or lived) art.[67]

The second section moves from the "naming" of things to examination of the interplay between things through modalities of visual presentation. The first of three chapters examines the visual art of Angelbert Metoyer. A Houston- and Rotterdam-based artist, Metoyer understands his work to employ created and found things (the waste of life), arranged and presented together in such a way as to urge a rethinking of the nature of those materials.[68] This rethinking pushes viewers to understand materials (and themselves) as transitional. Through this motion viewers uncover something about the nature and meaning of the human condition.

The next chapter explores the interplay between things but gives greater attention to things connected to/with the naming-thing—for example, blood. The open nature of the naming-thing is heightened through performance artists who penetrate the bodied naming-thing or in other ways traumatize the bodied naming-thing through graphic penetration. Through attention to figures such as Ron Athey and Clifford Owens, the open nature of things is amplified as readers are introduced to both naming-things and thing-things altered, shifted, and changed through aggressive contact. Hence, the line between naming-things and thing-things is blurred, and the naming-thing is left exposed or altered through sign/symbol and physical transformation, for example, scars produced by a thing-thing (knife). The "look" of the naming-thing is altered in a lasting manner, and thereby distinction is troubled. What is more, the style or custom by which some performance artists make use of body fluids points out the consistent and persistent relationship of the bodied naming-things to (other) things. Put differently, these artists force a question: Is blood (i.e., a thing) external to the bodied naming-thing, or still of it?

This question and its ramifications for understanding the open nature of things are pushed in the final chapter of this section. That chapter addresses performance art's articulation of openness through the use of shit. As I explain in that chapter, like its employment by Dominique Laporte and others, my use of this term is not a crude pronouncement—although discomfort (and a bit of playfulness) resulting from its use is part of the desired mode of engagement and thereby lends itself to the social connotations of the substance.[69] Still, as some in waste studies have noted, terms such as "waste" are inadequate in that they are too inclusive. My concern here is to explore the manner in which a particular mode of waste—shit—highlights openness but also speaks to the way in which the bodied naming-thing remains in relationship to that which it expels.

The final section explores the psycho-ethical impulse through the example of racialization used to close off naming-things so as to safeguard social and cultural codes of belonging. In other words, as Judith Butler has noted, some marginalized groups are transformed into shit. In saying this and as a basic positioning of my intent in these final chapters, it is important to note that my attention to restriction late in the book and my framing of this in relationship to racialized naming-things is not to imply that there is a universal notion of the human against which this restriction works. Openness is always challenged, and porousness is limited. While I give some attention to a sense of restriction in earlier chapters, I reserve a much fuller discussion until the end in order to situate the discussion within a larger set of assertions regarding the nature of things and the practice of art, and also to highlight the manner in which those considerations move from theorization of religion and openness to what I argue is an ethical response. I aim to provide a sense of two sides of restriction—the effort to trouble closure (chapters 3–5) and then to trouble openness (chapters 6–8). Through this arrangement, I work to make apparent situations in which I believe power relations (always present) between naming and being named are most graphic.

Chapters 6 and 7 present the work of Romare Bearden and Jean-Michel Basquiat for what they offer concerning response to the attempted fixing and sealing off of racialized naming-things. Both say something about the relationship between naming-things and thing-things in ways that point out the manner in which both are "penetrated" by the other: in/between. What is most graphic about their work is the relationship of naming-things placing thing-things in time and space and what this says indirectly about naming-things. There remains a space of separation between the two despite their creative impulse relationship—for example, the ability of naming-things to promote new awareness through the manipulation and presentation of thing-things. Yet both artists promote a different sensitivity to naming-things and thing-things, highlighting their flexibility and fluidity of movement, but this does not require a shift concerning the hierarchy of cultural action: naming-things using thing-things made. Naming-things act on and alter thing-things, and in the process perception and "placement" of naming-things is also affected. Thing-things—for example, Bearden's pieces of material used to make collages or Basquiat's taming of language and signs through application on alternate surfaces of display/communication—are left altered, but naming-things are "touched" also through a shifting of signs and symbols of presentation and representation, or more physically through muscle memory that leaves a shadow of the movement needed to make the work. The same could be said of Metoyer, whose work with the layering and presentation of altered thing-things, while having its own integrity and intent, is akin to that of artists such as Basquiat. With Bearden or Basquiat, the relationship between naming-thing and thing-thing highlights awareness through utility and manipulation of thing-things.

The final chapter rethinks and repositions W. E. B. Du Bois's *The Souls of Black Folk*. I want to avoid any assumption that my turn to this particular text is meant to suggest that Du Bois's substantive work ends with this popular volume, or that his thinking does not change.[70] I am aware of his other significant contributions to theorization and description of race within the United States. However, I see in *The Souls of Black Folk* a framing of racialization in relationship to issues of thing-ness (e.g., his question "How does it feel to be a problem?") that helps to clarify the ways in which naming-things struggle against restriction. In this way, attention to *The Souls of Black Folk* offers an intriguing way to present the psycho-ethical impact of effort to close off and thereby to foster boundaries against certain bodied naming-things.[71] This is done by arguing that his underexplored question—How does it feel to be a problem?—lends itself to a mode of interrogation concerned with the effort to fix blackened naming-things and in the process to render them things of a different sort. That is to say, like Camus, Du Bois offers a way of speaking about the limitations to openness—for example, in light of the racialization and impoverishment of certain naming-things. Both Du Bois and Camus provide a way to think about the power relationships entailed in naming and being named, and the final few chapters of the book speak to such issues in both implicit and explicit ways. Mindful of Butler, Du Bois's question could be rephrased: How does it feel to be cast a different thing, to be made shit?

The book ends with an epilogue meant to do two things. First, it offers readers, who might be interested in context for this book, a way to connect presence together to my earlier thinking on the nature and meaning of religion. Second, it explores the psycho-ethical impulse presented in section 3, and it does so using Camus, Nella Larsen, Richard Wright, and Orlando Patterson to argue for the benefits in guarding openness as the proper positioning of things.[72] My concern is to read openness through absurdist moralism and in this way to push against boundaries and fixity as a mode of "unity," which ties bodied naming-things to delusion and disregard.[73] As these authors reflect, the compelling psycho-ethical response is a position that seeks no ungrounded certainties and assurances but simply struggles to maintain openness to and with the world.

# meaning
## part i

# things                                                    1

"Things"—the word designates the concrete yet ambiguous within the everyday.
—BILL BROWN, "Thing Theory"

Man is the only creature who refuses to be what he is.
—ALBERT CAMUS, *The Rebel*

Having provided in the introduction some attention to key concepts and the presentation of an intellectual map for this project framed in light of the work with which it might be assumed connected, in this chapter I tackle dimensions of materiality—types of things. This attention to things is highlighted here and discussed as representing two fundamental mechanisms at work in my understanding of religion.

## Things

As Daniel Miller rightly reflects, materiality figures into our systems of religion as a benefit or a problem to solve. Either way, matter matters. But there is a difference worth stating for the sake of context. For Miller in what he frames as the "humility of things," the significance of things and their impact on us is most forceful when we do not see them. "The less we are aware of them," he writes, "the more powerfully they can determine our expectations by setting the scene and ensuring normative behavior, without being open to challenge."[1] With respect to materiality, this points to something Foucault says regarding the "power" of discourses found in the disappearance of discussion—imposing parameters, shaping and controlling bodies without being spoken.

My sense of things is different in that I want to highlight what I believe takes place when things are noticed, when we are confronted by things consciously arranged in selected time and space. And within this interplay I want to highlight the flexibility of things, which points out the "thingliness" of things.[2]

Thingliness—having something to do with "duration and presence" recognized and encountered—is not, for me, another way of speaking simply about human intentionality.[3] Sure, humans create and display things, arrange them, and name them—and in this way the human body-thing of concern here is a "naming" thing over against things named.[4] But there is something about this placement in time and space often against the assumed utility of these things (e.g., chairs not for sitting) that calls to the fluidity of things beyond our first observation of them, or in other words our first creation/placement and learning of them.[5] All of this points to things as opposed to objects in that the latter might be understood as pertaining to that which is "relatively stable in form."[6] Objects, in this case, are materials metaphysically flat and lacking dimension in terms of their connection to human life. Things, unlike objects, have a pedagogical quality to them. Things have an interactive, connected quality. As a way of pointing to this "activity" or "presence," I use "thing" as opposed to "object."[7] Furthermore, in speaking of the naming-thing, it should be noted that my concern here is not with the ontology of the human—what the human is. Rather, I am concerned with the body, which I want to understand as a particular type of thing.[8] Unlike the function of things celebrated by religious tradition systems, religion as a technology, as I define it, does not point to some metaphysical some*thing* beyond the reach of our historical grasp.

The thingliness (or openness) of things is the stuff of religion as a technology's use of things.[9] Put another way, things, by means of religion as a technology's interrogation, are pushed beyond them/themselves—beyond what we first notice about them—and offer opportunity to train a different awareness as this is encouraged by recognition of their openness (i.e., their presence together, to borrow from Camus). What do things push us to do, to think, to sense? They are invested by us (with us) in the same way a speed bump "is not made of matter, ultimately; it is full of engineers and chancellors and law makers, comingling their wills and their story lines with those of gravel, concrete, paint, and standard calculations."[10] The thingliness of a thing is constituted in an important way by its ability to push on bodied naming-things—to urge a particular set of questions and concerns about the world as we think we know it, encounter it, and want it to be.

For Bill Brown, things are objects imbued with "a metaphysical dimension."[11] I do not want to go that far. While this might be the intent within the framework of traditional religious systems, again, my concern is with the working premise that religion is not a system as such but a technology and, hence, does not invest things with deep meaning. Still, what Brown and others associated with thing theory posit is of value here in that it offers a lens by means of which to observe what takes place when religion as a technology engages.

The thingliness of a thing is the thing active and impinging beyond its physical space—oozing or seeping beyond the boundaries we had hoped to set for it. This openness of things involves a disruption by means of which material is reconfigured, combined, and put to a work not necessarily intended in the material's borrowed form. Things are also sticky in that they connect beyond themselves; there is fluidity to their interactions marked by an ability to shape change—which is not a quality present in objects despite what importance they might have in the daily workings of human life. "So things," writes Ian Hodder, "are connected by the fact that they work together. . . . In all these ways the material world is connected to our bodies, to other things, to society, to the other parts in the complex networks."[12] Things, therefore: (1) force a confrontation with ourselves in that we are connected to, related to these things with which we have a shared history; (2) prompt us to wonder if there is more to this relationship: Do these things urge other considerations and scopes? Do the production, arrangement, and interrogation of these things tell us all I can know about others, the world? These questions have to do with what we perceive as the fragility but also durability of things over against the particular limits of bodied naming-things in motion.

## Observing Things

Things and/with/against/for naming-things: There are numerous formulations of this relationship. For example, there are the various ways Heidegger represents things: "present-at-hand" or "ready-to-hand," which give a sense of things, including utility. But there are also things thinging as a way of framing the human's (i.e., Dasein or "being there") relationship to things. And as numerous scholars have pointed out, there is a growing move from a strict functional concern with human use of things to some consideration of things as things.[13] I conceptualize the relationship by thinking in terms of the *naming-thing* (i.e., the human as bodied thing/being/doing) and things as thing being thing (or *thing-thing* for short). Over the course of the book, what I mean by and intend to perform by means of this conceptual framework will become clearer.

More will be said on art and things in chapter 2. For now, I want to further clarify the nature of things within the context of artistic work. In exploring the technology of religion's potential relationship to the arts, I highlight particular genres and moments of artistic presentation, in part because art as discussed here is a wide scope in that it incorporates into it other strategies (e.g., other things meant to speak about naming-things such as written texts, images, statues, wood, stones, and music). In offering this argument, I am making a distinction between the technology of the artist and religion as a technology. I am not concerned fundamentally (although this will come up at times) with the specifics of the development of artistic work—the mechanics of putting together an exhibit, for example; instead I refer to artistic production examined through religion as a technology, arguing that this process of exploration does not require the status of, say, a preacher (artist as religious leader), but rather the artist as a naming-thing interacting with thing-things offers opportunity for a particular type of analysis and interrogation of our circumstances. Encounter with circumstances (e.g., the world) is inevitable as a type of "spewing forth" marking the naming-thing-human condition, but *particular* modes of encounter and particular expressions of that encounter are not.[14]

This is not to suggest that things beyond their creation do not impact the naming-thing. To the contrary, naming-things are influenced and affected by all sorts of materiality.[15] There is a mutual orientation and impact between naming-things and thing-things. They are open and, as the title of the book claims, marked by presence together. I do not want to push this point of mutual influence too far in part because my concern with art means a limit on conversation to those things-things manipulated and placed by naming-things; and this might include things not created by naming-things but rather simply placed in alternate spaces (e.g., rocks and wood). In this way, I also give attention here to things not necessarily created by naming-things but impacting naming-things as they (thing-things) are pulled into artistic expression.

Through artistic production and presentation, I mean to highlight the plasticity, the nonfixed quality, or the openness of things so as to better understand the activity of things.[16] Use a chair in this way, or wear a pair of pants that way, and so on is lost as the logic of interaction is shifted by the artist and the placement of things.[17] What naming-things know and understand about thing-things is shifted, and this fosters a productive dissonance by means of a deeper awareness of openness to things. Art, then, involves a particularly useful mapping of the relationship between naming-things and thing-things that shows at one time something about both. Art that highlights what we understand as ordinary things—things that we encounter during the course of mundane dealings—provides an important lesson related to the significant linkages between naming-things and thing-things. There is something important in the effort of figures such as Antony Hudek to demonstrate "the artist's privileged role in rerouting, recycling, deviating, transforming and *deturning* . . . the object." And Hudek continues, "This role is far from one of mastery of 'subjectivity'; rather it hints at a capacity to inhabit the object world, to engage with and translate it for the benefit of other objects and subjects alike."[18] I would make a modification to this assertion, one in line with the work of thing theorists such as Bill Brown, and that is to note the manner in which objects become things—in this context through the arts.[19] By means of artistic production, things are exposed to themselves, naming-things, and to circumstances, and this takes place without the ability of the artistic exhibit location to limit significantly the impact of this scope of openness.[20]

What Arthur Danto says when reflecting on Andy Warhol's *Hammer and Sickle* and other work such as *Campbell's Soup* in a general sense speaks to what I mean by the work of things. According to Danto, "His soups are in sacramental celebration of their earthly reality, simply as what one might call one's daily soup, as what one eats day after day. . . . If this sacramental return of the thing to itself through art is the energy which drove him as an artist to bring into the center of his work what had never, really, been celebrated before . . ."[21] I end this section with this incomplete thought because it is sufficient to frame my point. Religion as a technology often employs artistic production to highlight the thingliness—or openness—of things, and in this way makes possible through interrogation of things in time and space greater awareness of our circumstances (i.e., world) and our place in those circumstances. It provides no answers, just clarity, or what one might call deeper awareness regarding the connotations of our circumstances as naming-things in a world of other things. Before offering more detail regarding art and things, it is important to further explicate what I mean by naming-things.

## Other Things

There are types of things. Here I offer some distinction between things by giving attention to what I above referenced as naming-things. In so doing, the general theme of things presented previously obtains greater detail through this somewhat rough categorization of things in the form of thing-things and naming-things.[22] While the potential scope is expansive, in this book I limit myself to a particular naming-thing—the bodied naming-thing.[23] Through attention to the bodied naming-thing, I mean to highlight a particular structure of the naming-thing (i.e., body) and its relationship to other things.[24] In this way I provide a discursive mechanism for framing the interplay between things that undergirds chapters in the remaining two sections of the volume. I entertain the perception of the body as signifying or "naming" thing akin to what John Frow has in mind when arguing, "Persons, too, count or can count as things. This is the real strangeness: that persons and things are kin; the world is many, not double."[25] And recognition of—perhaps even naming of—circumstances (i.e., world) and human/circumstances amounts to a moralistic awareness or lucidity in relation to the conditions of life.[26] Hinted at here, but more fully expressed later, is the notion of things—including bodied naming-things—as "open."[27]

Naming-things are bodied, and other things—still other things. They have "form," but they ooze into each other, inform each other. "Abjection," one might say, works in the shadow of an assumption, an assumption of a difference as possible—cleanliness, for instance.[28] This said, and in light of the scope of my argument, the most compelling depiction of bodied naming-things and their interplay is found in Mikhail Bakhtin's theorizing of grotesque realism.[29]

## On the Grotesque

Before addressing what Bakhtin's sense of the grotesque offers my thinking on open-bodied naming-things, I provide contextual comments on what I consider a negation of a Bakhtin sensibility. This negation takes place through a theological taming of the grotesque that reduces it to service on behalf of a theistic sensibility tied to immaterial hope. In offering this discussion, I am not suggesting all theology works in this manner and produces a desire for closure framed by an energetic appeal to transformation in the form of wholeness or union with something greater. I am not interested in grotesque as a theological category—or even aesthetic category—but rather as a way of theoretically capturing the nature of the open body—the body put on view by religion as a technology. And so my purpose is not a critique of theology per se as if it uniquely lends itself to matters of wholeness—for example, closure through bounded life. Rather, I use this discussion in a more limited fashion as a helpful counterpoint in that it also provides a direct reading of Bakhtin in light of a traditional definition of religion (e.g., highlighting institutions, doctrine, and ritual). And by means of this contrast I offer a way to further mark out and clarify my application of his theorizing of the grotesque in line with my sense of religion as a technology and over against traditional notions of religion. To make this point, I turn to Wilson Yates's reading of *Rabelais and His World*.[30]

The open body, Yates acknowledges, is for Bakhtin a vital and vibrant body—whose eating, pissing, and defecating is not to be denounced or hidden.[31] "The grotesque," writes Yates, "refers to aspects of human experience that we have denied validity to, that we have rejected, excoriated, attempted to eliminate and image as a distorted aspect of reality."[32] Yet he narrows the scope of the grotesque by reading it through the "perspective of the Christian mythos" and in light of a series of questions: "Does the grotesque take on a different meaning for one who creates and looks at it from within a faith stance and from within a world already well-formed by its own mythos? And . . . what does the grotesque have to say to us about basic Christian perspectives such as the nature of creation, the human condition, the possibility of transformed life?"[33] These questions posed and, more to the point, the answers Yates provides entail a taming of the grotesque—an effort to confine its reach and implications for the messy nature of life. Yates forgets the context of carnival—of an antichurch moment in certain respects—within which Bakhtin finds and celebrates the grotesque. The grotesque is not simply physical deformity, monsters, as Yates seems to think. Bakhtin presents it as a description of the state of being porous, open, exposed.

Some of what Bakhtin has in mind, I believe, has been demonstrated recently in exhibits by Tori Wrånes (*Ældgammel Baby*) and Ovartaci (*Ovartaci and the Art of Madness*), both at Kunsthal Charlottenborg in Copenhagen, Denmark.[34] The former involves several rooms set apart and marked off by darkness except for a few dedicated lights illuminating various objects accompanied by the haunting sound of a voice. Projected on the walls are figures wearing bright-colored outerwear and with faces disturbing in their proportions, colors, and exaggerated features that resemble the extremes of the grotesque discussed by Bakhtin. They are suspended in space and seem to come toward the viewer. In another room is a figure without a head, with shoulders penned to the ground and legs outstretched, with another character balancing with one foot atop the bottom figure's foot. The body seems in motion, but this is not the odd component. Instead, the grotesqueness is expressed through the replacement of much of the top figure's face with two birds emerging from/as the face of the figure. This is not a monster, but rather the blending of "things," pointing to the porous nature of bodied naming-things. Ovartaci provides an even more graphic depiction of this porousness giving way to blending. This is captured through the presentation of figures that intermingle various life-forms and in the process create something novel, something new—such as an eye in the palm of a hand or the head of a "creature" whose large eye is composed of (or houses) smaller creatures and whose other orifices contain bodied things that have penetrated the head.[35] Neither artist rejects penetrated and penetrating figures; instead, they seem to endorse or assume the normative status of such open things.

The mimicking of the bodied naming-thing through technology can further create dissonance-prompting recognition of the blending of things (e.g., video, plastic, and the characteristics of the naming-thing) as a sign of mutability. Ed Atkins's *Ribbons*, part of the Louisiana Museum (Copenhagen, Denmark) *Being There* exhibit, provides a graphic example of what I have in mind.[36] In a room, there are three large video screens with the avatar Dave speaking (in the voice of the artist), drinking, farting, urinating, bleeding, "all signifiers of a physical body leaking with imperfection." And while the artistic statement calls into question the ability of technology to capture a "physical being's vulnerability and imperfection," I would suggest the discomfort fostered by Atkins's use of technology to ape the bodied naming-thing is enough to suggest the nature of this naming-thing is without clear boundaries; it is without an integrity that prevents disruption.[37] That is to say, it can be aped, and through technology the aping renders the limits and vulnerabilities of the bodied naming-thing perpetually present.

Returning to my read against Yates, the porous and penetrated nature of the bodied naming-thing (with all the accompanying sights, smells, sounds, and activities) is not rescued by the myth of salvation premised on the lingering image of God contained in and by that bodied naming-thing. Yates claims his depiction does not cause the grotesque to lose its edge. But to use a musical analogy, Yates positions the grotesque as a hymn of sorts complete with a desire for closure from the world, while I argue that a more useful framing involves the grotesque sung through the blues—for example, the graphic and celebrated interaction with and exposure to the workings of life. In other words, Yates sees the grotesque as a condition of life to be resolved through faith and the workings of divine forces.[38] According to Bakhtin, and I follow his lead here, nothing is gained by attempting to overcome grotesquery; to think so is to paint it as a negative and to fail to recognize the nature of embodied life. This is not to say that values are missing from human thinking and doing; they are present. However, there is no reason to assume such values bend to the will of Christian doctrine. Rather, these values might just signify doctrinal-theological assumptions concerning embodied and material life. They are bluesy values that relate porous thing to porous thing, rather than porous body to its "fix" called "god."

For Yates, the grotesque speaks a theological language framed by a grammar of "sin" and "judgment."[39] Hence, grotesquery might on the surface disturb or create a certain type of dissonance, but according to Yates, "the horrifying character they take can itself speak, both to and out of the context of the church."[40] Yates notes that the grotesque upends "our world view and moral codes," but he does not have in mind the worldview and moral codes of the religious in relationship to the church. Yates means unproductive— nonfaithful moral codes and worldviews—codes or values that will not bend to staid Christian doctrine and that refuse priority of the church over against the "folk."[41] He wants to understand the moral codes and worldview under threat as being those that do not point in the direction of the will and eternal truths of the divine. The grotesque, he would have us believe, is a rejection of efforts to turn humans into gods.[42] I would not assert divinity as the agenda for Bakhtin; no, the goal is to render humans more fully material—porous and unfixed. This is what Bakhtin means by the value of the degraded. Grotesque realism is content with this world and projects little concern for unseen realms populated by more perfect beings. This is because it refuses to see oozing, defecating, urinating bodied naming-things as a problem to solve. With Yates's Christianization of the grotesque a wager is established: one can have one's theology or one's bodied naming-thing.

Yates fails to note that the activities—the defecating and pissing in public— Bakhtin's sense of the grotesque highlights (without judgment) were roundly condemned by the Christian church as oppositional to its theological-ethical sensibility. He believes imagery of the grotesque "in the drama of religious life" takes us "out of everyday life and provides us with a different way of seeing the center—the center in its demonic manifestation and the center as the place alone where we can know the grace of God."[43] However, it is the stuff, the activity of everyday life, that is highlighted by the grotesque in that these are the activities pointing to the porous and open nature of the body and thereby its capacity for mutuality. Christianity, to the contrary, seeks to seal off the body for the love of God and only allow its penetration (on special occasions) by the divine. The Christian tradition, among others, is notorious for its suspicion concerning the body—preferring the clean soul to bodies so easily soiled. Mindful of Bakhtin's presentation of the defecating body, what Coco Fusco says concerning the "West" (i.e., the West as a posture or mindset as opposed to geographic location) in general is applicable to the religious "West" in particular: "Excrement derives its subversive power within the history of Western art as the least abstractable substance in a society with a prevailing modernist aesthetic that privileges transcendence over the material."[44] Yates truncates the body whose openness is addressed, and to some extent ended, through relationship with God: communion, pain, and suffering (as exemplified by the Cross) resolved through hope and redemption. In this sense theodicy, sacrology, and eschatology are intertwined. And in this theological framework, religious tradition and practice are in fact a betrayal of religion to the extent it turns a technology into a substance.

So much religious studies and theological work assumes the body and claims a paradigmatic attachment to embodied bodies. Yet this is visual, metaphoric, and symbolic in nature. Yes, in some cases it is acknowledged that these bodies eat, they cum—but they do not defecate or piss without shame. To the extent traditions like Christianity dominant through a figure of excellence (i.e., Christ) that evacuates waste only in the form of ethical sin, how could it be otherwise? To the extent body waste is "eliminated" from discussions of bodies in theology and religious studies, they are discourses of mythic bodies addressing a range of ideas but without sufficient material grounding and premised on a rather sterile logic—an idyllic Christian formulation of life and embodiment honoring a shadowy figure of Christ. Followers of the figure expel waste, but their Christ does not—although he eats and drinks. He is the fulfillment of the law, as they note, but not with respect to its acknowledgment of human waste and other fluids.[45] This has had conveniences for a Christian sense of bodies: "And that he died for all, that they which live should not henceforth live unto themselves, but unto him which died for them, and rose again. Wherefore henceforth know we no man after the flesh: yea, though we have known Christ after the flesh, yet now henceforth know ye him no more. Therefore, if any man be in Christ, he is a new creature: old things are passed away; behold all things are become new" (2 Corinthians 5:15–17). Through Bakhtin, *imago Dei* is exposed as a lie. The human body, unlike the exemplar Christ, is known to be porous—with openings that expose it. Human waste, for instance, announces the deception of the life of *imago Dei*. Christ did not defecate, although those in his line of

chapter one

descent, as the Hebrew Bible points out, did. Artists have pointed out this open and grotesque body whereas so many religious thinkers have attempted to overcome it.[46]

As Yates demonstrates, the effort to posit a Christianized grotesque theology loses something. It loses the "realism" in Bakhtin's grotesque realism and pushes for an altered perception of the bodied naming-thing—one that loses its openness through a fixed *imago Dei* perception of being. Thereby the more graphic and earthy dimensions of this grotesque body, as Bakhtin presents it, are sanctified. Rather than being degraded (in Bakhtin's sense of the word— e.g., materiality and integration into the world), the human body—as I read Yates—is exulted and freed from the urine and feces between which it is born, according to St. Augustine, and through which it speaks to the life-death binary that is its frame of reference. Yates and others working within traditional theological discourses might agree with Bakhtin that the human is "becoming," but they would mean something different by that statement. Bakhtin points to the dualism of life-death, food-waste, and so forth, framing the movement of the grotesque body. For some theistic theologians, on the other hand, this is a becoming that pushes in a cosmic direction with the intent of freeing the bodied naming-thing from more troubling dimensions of that porous status.[47] This, according to these theologians, entails a vertical dynamic of growth and increasing closed-ness. For Bakhtin, the better read involves openness to horizontal development by means of which the embodied (and oozing) nature of embodied life is not lost but is amplified.[48] In terms of the role of religion in this: religion as a technology probes and turns back on the bodied naming-thing and exposes its grotesque nature.

Maintaining a focus on *Rabelais and His World*, I now want to offer a different read of the grotesque, one less constrained by the theologized body of Christ and traditional framings of religion.

## Grotesque Realism

The folk practices of carnival—intriguing to Bakhtin—undercut the authority of the church, belittle its awful proclamations, and highlight those activities of the body long held with distain by many Christians.[49] Think in terms of carnival's rejection of "grand unity" of any kind that pushes beyond what is tangible about the world: "it," in fact, "was hostile to all that was immortalized and completed."[50] For instance, carnival replaces ritualized penetration by the divine with the open naming-thing defecating in public. Grotesque realism, a grand theory of collective engagement emerging out of the practices of embodied "folk culture," is for the open-bodied naming-thing a safeguard against theological efforts to pretend the integrity of boundaries. The church, and what Yates wants to claim from the grotesque (salvation for the individual soul), works against the very nature of the grotesque: it rejects efforts toward individualization that cut off naming-things from other open naming-things and thing-things. Instead, grotesque realism arranges material life in terms of groups—of collectives.[51]

Such framing of life in terms of the "people" gives the activities of naming-things a more significant presence, which is difficult for theological organizations and their teachings to undo. Grotesque realism by means of a carnivalistic impulse is something of an existential centripetal force resulting in the centering of the defecating naming-thing exposed to and in the world. For Bakhtin, eating and drinking are two of the most significant illustrations of the naming body as open. It is through these activities, for example, that the world is taken into the body whereby "the body transgresses here its own limits: it swallows, devours, rends the world apart, is enriched and grows at the world's expense."[52] And of course, this open naming-thing pushes itself back into the world as it urinates and defecates. This is not to suggest that the naming-thing has no distinctiveness; rather, it is to say this distinctiveness is superseded and countered by its openness and by its "points of intersection."[53]

Whereas Christian theologizing cannot resist a grammar of transcendence, the grotesque represents a different register in that "the essential principle of grotesque realism is *degradation*, that is, the lowering of all that is high, spiritual, ideal, abstract; it is a transfer to the material level, to the sphere of earth and body in their indissoluble unity."[54] Degrading in the theological language of thinkers such as Yates is a negative, but for Bakhtin it is a positive: it connotes a reminder of flesh, that the earth is the naming-thing's place, and it is a reminder that the naming-thing that eliminates waste is significant and the openings that allow for the oozing of thing-things are to be celebrated. In crude terms, degradation means acknowledging without shame the importance of the mouth and the anus. How could Christian theologizing do this when it finds it hard to even acknowledge that the figure of Jesus had a penis? If that organ cannot be named, what is to encourage belief that the anus can be named? Both the penis and the anus mark openness in and to the world, and the interplay between the bodied naming-thing and other things gets expressed in human waste. Is this proper church talk? It certainly verbalizes a claim beyond "We are born between feces and urine." The latter encourages movement away from both; the grotesque embraces them: "The grotesque body is not separated from the rest of the world. It is not a closed, completed unit; it's unfinished, outgrows itself, and transgresses its own limits. The stress is laid on those parts of the body that are open to the outside world, that is, the parts through which the world enters the body or emerges from it, or through which the body itself goes out to meet the world."[55] This is the nature of interplay in that the naming-thing which "swallows the world . . . is itself swallowed by the world."[56]

Bakhtin gives to the material world and its functions a type of sacred emphasis that destroys the sacred as an individualized and individualizable revelation or specialness.[57] In this case, that status involves recognition of incompleteness, porousness. One might frame it as a type of lucidity geared toward the protecting, safeguarding, or fulfilling of the naming-thing. Through this grounding in naming-thing thingliness, circumstances are brought to earth and thereby are resolved through the workings of materiality and not left to the vague cosmic claims of theological traditions. As Bakhtin notes, folk culture and grotesque realism stem the flow of "cosmic fear" resolved through abstract theological claims and religious ritualization that isolate the individual.[58]

The grotesque is often referenced as a way (within artistic production, for example) to outline a challenge to normative notions of beauty and life, thereby rendering the familiar unfamiliar. It centers a particular "disjuncture and shifting," or "lack of fixity," as well as "unpredictability and . . . instability" as awakened through a privileging of what was once despised or at least hidden and reassessing its context and content.[59] Abject/abjection speaks to a discomfort and effort to remove openness or in-between status, whereas the grotesque seeks to amplify this openness. The grotesque body is the quintessential open naming-thing entangled and entangling the world of things. It is a naming-thing content to be exposed and to be penetrated while it penetrates. It is associated with the stuff—the things—of life and death.

I am intrigued by that moment when the bodied naming-thing and thing-thing fain affrication.

The naming-thing through this presentation of openness is "purged" of its illusion of stable distinctiveness, the pretense of being bounded and closed. Again, the bodied naming-thing defecates! The public presentation of this body function is not limited to the world described by Rabelais and celebrated by Bakhtin. For example, Yoko Ono alludes to this process through the "Toilet Thoughts Film No. 3," which includes a close-up shot of a buttocks poster to be hung in public toilets and then photographed over the course of time. Images were shot of the poster in public restrooms in various stages of disarray.[60] Or one might think in terms of the song "Sympathy for the Devil" (*Beggars Banquet* album)—with which the Rolling Stones celebrate, so to speak, the "degraded" and ethically alternative dimensions of historical engagement—attached to an (rejected by Decca) album cover containing the image of a soiled and well-used toilet against a wall marked (penetrated?) by written sayings and images.[61] And while these—Yoko Ono's art and the rejected cover image of the toilet—are not the same graphic arrangement of public defecating present in Bakhtin's description of openness, they nonetheless highlight and normalize the removal of waste and in this way highlight, both through the image and the location of the image, the relationship of naming-things to thing-things.

The grotesque appeals because it rests in the moment of interplay, and in this way it maintains the playful and played-out intersectional nature of bodied naming-thing and thing-thing engagement.[62] This moment of interplay is an "undoing"—pointing out the organizing deception; the subject is not whole, guarded, and fully distinct. It is never bounded because it is porous and marked by fractures and fissions by means of the various normativities "arranging" the socially situated and coded (e.g., race, gender, class) bodied naming-thing.

The naming-thing is framed in accordance with an open system of movement, geography of activity, and processes, as the cultural and social codes shaping and guiding discourse of an epistemological, existential, and ontological nature shift and change. Furthermore, there is entailed here a system at work, in action—the flow of blood, the shifting of chemical languages, the development and death of cells, and so on. Naming-things involve movement, and they move. Religion as a technology assumes this movement, depends on this movement, informs and is informed by this movement in that the trail of this bodied naming-thing's flow constitutes the human experience manipulated by religion as a technology.

### Brief Examples of the Grotesque

To further clarify what I have in mind, I want to give some attention to a reading of Nella Larsen and Richard Wright through Bakhtin.[63] I do this in part because I perceive a similarity of insight in Bakhtin's sense of a carnivalistic viewpoint and the moralist (Larsen and Wright) sense of lucid rebellion. Hence, art—in this case literature—provides a description (to play off Bakhtin) or a dynamic cartography of sorts regarding the interplay between naming-things and thing-things.[64]

In making this argument, I highlight Nella Larsen's *Quicksand*, a novel published in 1928—shortly before the Great Depression but during the reign of "Jim and Jane Crow," as popular and deadly restrictions on the life circumstances of African Americans meant to reinforce the power of whiteness after the end of formal structures of dehumanization in April 1865.[65] It tells the story of Helga Crane, a mulatto moving between the southern and northern United States and Europe. Yet it is not the typical story of the tragic mulatto. While the racialized and gendered process of being named is certainly in play, circumstances framing life for her are beyond traditional markers of social identity and instead reflect issues of a metaphysical quality. There is, of course, what one might expect regarding critique of social status, class dynamics, educational attainment in a racist-sexist society, and many of the other troubling circumstances of life for African Americans—particularly those whose light skin color places them between worlds. But there is more to Crane's story than this. Through a process of signification and performance—such as offering alternate naming for things and alternate relationship to other things—she resists the limitations of Harlem classed interactions and refuses to be the "exotic" other in Europe. Instead, she signifies all expectations by surrendering to a religious force and marrying an unlikely "suitor" in a southern preacher. He takes her from Harlem to the South, where she encounters a radically different environment—yet one like the others in which even her best efforts did little to break down her outsider status. She, as a naming-thing, is impacted, altered, and shifted. In certain ways her ability to name as a naming-thing is reduced through contact with other things. Religious doctrine fails to provide resolution to her metaphysical concerns and instead tries to seal her up in a framework of racial and sexual restriction. And the demands of her home life eat away at her physical being. She is consumed; child after child has sapped her strength, and a husband who values only her ability to please him has robbed her of dignity. Combined, these forces bring her to a breaking point—a point at which she denounces transhistorical assumptions of aid and instead plots for her well-being, which does not come. But still she rebels—pushes against circumstances despite circumstances.

Richard Wright's "The Man Who Lived Underground" shares Larsen's sense of the manner in which naming-things naming and being named can have deadly connotations regarding openness and closure.[66] And, as in Larsen, Wright's main character moves through a process of performed rebellion. This short story is from a collection titled *Eight Men*—each "man" representing a particular narrative.[67] Initially published in 1961 (a year after

Wright's mysterious death), this collection reflects Wright's rehearsal of racialized life in the United States from his self-imposed exile in Paris. While many of its themes reflect his philosophy of life graphically expressed in best sellers like *Black Boy* and *Native Son*, it has received little of the recognition and commentary reserved for those books published while Wright was immersed in the turmoil of life as a U.S.-despised and blackened named naming-thing—impacted and named in relationship to economic, sociocultural, political, and psychological "things."[68] Yet Wright also speaks to the manner in which all naming-things (not just blackened naming-things) are impacted by circumstances; things interact with things, often in unaccepted ways. Or as Paul Gilroy describes the text, "Wright," for instance, "demonstrates that some of the supposed beneficiaries of white supremacy are no less likely to be unhinged by its operation than its black victims."[69] Furthermore, the interplay of things—the grotesquery of this interaction—is performed in this collection through Wright's attention to the proximity of things.[70] Racial disregard and its mechanisms of deployment might suggest distance, but the actions and the thinking of Wright's characters suggest that interaction—impact of things—is an ever-present dimension of collective life, a marker of power dynamics often at play in the arrangement of things. This is surely the case with the main character in the story I highlight in this chapter, where even in the relative isolation faced, he is always exposed to and mindful of the ways in which he encounters other things—things that have consequence for his understanding of himself and his relationship(s) to the larger world. Even segregation, or more generally confined space, as Wright reflects in this story, entails a particularly antagonizing mode of encounter. In describing an underworld of decay and darkness, Wright crafts literary situations pulled from lived circumstance that involve the grotesque as performance of the impossible possibility of openness—as, if nothing else, a defiant signification.

Bakhtin highlights the folk realm of carnival as a location where the grotesque body takes center stage. Of course, it is not the only context for the presentation of the grotesque. In "The Man Who Lived Underground," Wright offers the sewer as another, urban, locale. Having gotten away from the police who tried to hold him for a crime he had not committed, Fred Daniels makes his way to the sewer, where "he snatched the cover far enough off to admit his body. He swung his legs over the opening and lowered himself into watery darkness."[71] Inside the sewer his body is confronted with thing-things. The world is turned inside out, and its elements penetrate him, affecting and influencing him—demonstrating the manner in which he as a naming-thing is unfixed and exposed. The water washes against him, urging the question of life or death. Water is significant in religious culture, performance, and teachings—but this is different. Daniel's interplay with water seems a mode of degradation whereby going down into the sewer, as Bakhtin might explain, involves an entering into flesh. It is a pushing into the world through denouncing its codes and structures. Bakhtin, in discussing Rabelais, remarks on the manner in which traditional religious thought on bodies tends to position them as down (toward hell) or up (toward heaven). He rejects this normalizing narrative, as does Fred Daniels, for whom down is life. He vertically enters into the sewer, but vertical entering points to a horizontal reality of material place occupied by bodied naming-things. Daniels leaves the "upperworld," where restrictive encounters question his humanity, and enters the lower world of penetrated material being; the underworld enters Fred as he fills "his lungs with the hot stench of yeasty rot."[72] Life gains a different materiality for Daniels in the sewer; even time is knowable through materiality. As Wright narrates, "He heard the noise of the current and time lived again for him, measuring the moments by the wash of water."[73] Everything revolved around the interplay of him as an exposed naming-thing with other things found within the waste passages below the city.

This situation promoted for Daniels a different perspective, one which might be named a kind of grotesque realism: living and dying occupy the same space, and this space is a location marked by life in fleshy bodies that are open to the world. For instance, smoking points to this openness—the manner in which a thing-thing penetrates and infuses while also being expelled:

[Daniels] crept down and, seeing with his fingers, opened the lunch pail and tore off a piece of paper bag and brought out the tin and spilled grains of tobacco into the makeshift concave. He rolled it and wet it with some spittle, then inserted one end into his mouth and lit it: he sucked smoke that bit his lungs. The nicotine reached his brain, went out along his arms to his fingertips, down to his stomach and over all the tired nerves of his body.[74]

Wright also spends time describing the proper use of the mouth. And he does so in a manner I argue would appeal to Bakhtin. The mouth marks penetration, the movement of food into the naming-thing—the extension of the grotesque body beyond itself. Daniels, continuing to devour the food he had stolen, "ate the other sandwich and found an apple and gobbled that up too, sucking the core till the last trace of flavor was drained from it. Then, like a dog, he ground the meat bones with his teeth, enjoying the salty, tangy marrow."[75] This is interplay with things that heightens materiality. In so doing, flesh is privileged in a way those in the church he overheard could not muster. The failure to recognize this embodied, fleshy, open body on the part of church people he hears singing songs of "Zion" constitutes misuse of the mouth and denial of the rest of the body.[76] The same is the case for those in the theater, whom he watches denying degradation as they "were laughing at their lives." This, if one follows Bakhtin, is a misuse of laughter in that it closes off the body rather than conquering fear. This is not laughter of the grotesque body—a laughter that "degrades and materializes," but rather the whimper of those who refuse to embrace the unimaginable who "were shouting and yelling at the animated shadows of themselves."[77]

Daniels's is the grotesque body (i.e., the open, bodied naming-thing) that takes in from the world and expels a bit of itself into the world. Wright, like Bakhtin, sees body waste as a sign of this interplay; regarding that, Wright describes the following as Daniels breaks through the sewer into a room:

> He went to the sink and turned the faucet and water flowed in a smooth silent stream that looked like a spout of blood. . . . His bladder grew tight [after drinking the water]; he shut off the water, faced the wall, bent his head, and watched a red stream strike the floor. His nostrils wrinkled against acrid wisps of vapor; thought he had tramped in the water of the sewer, he stepped back from the wall so that his shoes, wet with sewer slime would not touch his urine.[78]

The notion of the grotesque body played out in Wright's story is also highlighted through the blending of forms—naming-things and other things in a state of mutuality: like the old man comfortable in the dark like a sightless worm. Into the room—entered through the sewer—where Daniels has located himself, the old man enters to shovel coal into the furnace but he does not turn on the light. Wright says, "The old man had worked here for so long that he had no need for light; he had learned a way of seeing in his dark world, like those sightless worms that inch along underground by a sense of touch."[79]

At the end of the story, Daniels leaves the sewer to confront the police and bring them into his "truths," but instead they murder him and throw him back into the sewer. This time, rather than encountering life, he "sighed and closed his eyes, a whirling object rushing alone in the darkness, veering, tossing, lost in the heart of the earth."[80]

Helga Crane, the protagonist of Larsen's *Quicksand*, also knows water—the way in which it penetrates the open body, exposes it, but is also exposed by it. In fact, the major transitional moment of her life, the point at which one might say she is most aware of the grotesque nature of her body as open to the world and penetrated by the world, takes place after an encounter with water. She stumbles into a church lured by the sounds but also wanting to get out of the heavy rain. In that loud room, there are moving bodies, penetrating bodies involved in what Larsen describes as a performance that "took on an almost Bacchic vehemence."[81] That is to say, the church scene is a display and interplay of bodies marked by riotous energy and excitement— as if in honor of Bacchus, the god of wine and revelry. If read in light of Bakhtin, Crane encounters a carnivalistic gathering marked by blending of things (i.e., women slithering on the floor like reptiles) and a general heightening of the flesh. The consequences are the same for Rabelais and Larsen— the flesh is highlighted, and the body is known for its openness. Like the "folk," Crane embraces this situation: "She remained motionless, waiting, as if she lacked the strength to leave the place—foul, vile, and terrible, with its mixture of breaths, its contact of bodies. . . . And as Helga watched and listened, gradually a curious feeling penetrated her; she felt an echo of the weird orgy resound in her own heart; she felt herself possessed by the same madness she too felt a brutal desire to shout and to sling herself about."[82] She was penetrated by a sensibility that pulled her from the city to the rural world—where the smell of manure lingered and sweat on bodies confronted her.[83] She was a preacher's wife, having married the minister from the carnivalistic gathering. And while the openness of her body brought her into the collective, the social codes within that collective sought to close her off. Church could not accept this openness despite its efforts to co-opt it. Her body had to be consumed, just as she was told Christ had surrendered his for her salvation.[84]

Sadly, this is not the degradation Bakhtin writes of and celebrates. The religious tradition—practices, rituals, theological formulations and so on—that points beyond the human to some cosmic mystery or comfort is actually a shortsighted surrender by means of which the unity of a being without pores and openings—or at least its potential—is desired. Bakhtin claims that laughter opens to this realization of shortsightedness. Perhaps something of the embodiment of this laugher is found in the defiant impulse undergirding Crane's embodied rebellion against herself, other bodies, and the world. There is an impulse to render material that typically has been situated as abstract or above. This is certainly the case with Crane, whose body is ravaged by children. Crane discovers the deception with each child she delivers: The body is not whole, fully formed, fixed, and nonporous. It is porous, open to the world, open to itself, and prone to release itself in such a manner that the things produced are both of the naming-thing and foreign to it. This is the realization that with each birth she is pushed closer to death.

In either case, Daniels or Crane, the grotesque nature of the bodied naming-thing is highlighted, and its interplay with other things is performed. As Bakhtin reminds us, it is within this context of mutuality, the realm of "presence together," as Camus might name it, that naming-things are most vibrant.

# the art of placement                           2

The meaning, if I have it right, is philosophical, and internally related to its viewers. It [art] put their lives in perspective. It tells them what, really, they already
know.

—ARTHUR DANTO, *The Abuse of Beauty*

Having given attention in chapter 1 to the nature of things in relationship
to the conceptual framework of grotesque realism, I mean in this chapter to
provide a sense of the relationship between things and art through the process of construction or creation and to do so by first briefly reflecting on
Robert Fuller's sense of bodies reconstituted. In *Spirituality in the Flesh*, Fuller
explores the body by means of an interdisciplinary perspective with a particular aim in mind. He writes, "I am exploring the intriguing thesis that many
aspects of religion can be understood in terms of the body's efforts to reconstitute reality as part of its ongoing adaptation to the environment."[1] Fuller
is concerned with the biological nature of the body and what that means for
understanding religion. While related to a certain degree, my concern is with
the mechanics of the naming-thing, not its constitution as such other than
to say it might be framed as a "thing" or as Hans Belting names it, "a living
medium" that speaks to the fact that these naming-things relate to, if not
produce, other things that interplay in/with naming-things.[2] Furthermore,
while the bodied naming-thing is vital in this process, the things created and

arranged by these naming-things have fundamental importance. One might think of this in a rough sense as entailing the making of absurd circumstances familiar—or our "metaphysical servant" (*famulus*).

## The Situation

The bodied naming-thing is not fully known, but that is of limited consequence in that it remains historically felt, and the consequences of its movement inform and influence what we have come to call identity, community, society, and so on. In a certain way, one might consider this sense of the bodied naming-thing to constitute a "living media . . . by processing, revising, and transmitting images."[3] Along these lines, traditional theories of religion that point to a fixed "something," to a sense of the religious as sui generis (and to the body as closed off) might be categorized as those holding to the praxis of the image. Hence, they posit a "something" represented by the image, while this "something" seeks to point beyond itself.[4] Again, as noted earlier, my concern is not with the economic value or the tradability of things. I am concerned with things as things "constructed" and arranged by other things. Naming-things so understood do something; they forge, they make, they produce and reconstitute things. And they are affected and influenced by thing-things.

My goal here is not a discussion or study of material as such. But when viewed by means of religion as a technology, what are these things forged by these bodied naming-things (as well as things encountered but not made by naming-things)? What does the "creation" and placement in time and space of things tell us about embodied naming-things as represented by their relationship to other things?

Humans are naming-things, and we interact with other things, place them in time and space, and have them "speak" to, for, and through naming-things. Connection and distance mark the naming-thing's relationship to other things, and this mirroring urges a range of deep questions we cannot answer but that in asking afford greater awareness and lucidity of our circumstances without curing our existential-ontological ills. One might extend what Belting says regarding images and the body: "It is through the vast array of images to which humanity accords meaning that the human being proves himself a cultural being, a being that cannot be described solely in biological terms."[5] Of importance here are not the image-picture processes related to meaning making noted by Belting, but rather in a more general sense I call attention to the bodied naming-things and other things (objects turned things)

chapter two

shadowing his remark. There is "substantial" (as in substance) overlap here in that the bodied naming-thing can be conceived of as a thing and also as a container holding some*thing*.[6] The naming-thing stores other things—for example, organs and blood—as well as a range of cultural and social codes. Furthermore, the naming-thing as thing is connected to other things through the process of creation, movement, and attachment (physical as in artificial limbs, psychological as in security blankets, or emotional as in pictures). In another way, the bodied naming-thing uses other things to extend itself further into the world, and in the process both thing-things and naming-things are affected and influenced.[7] This is because the bodied naming-thing can be physically and culturally penetrated, altered, shifted in time and space; and interaction with thing-things serves as cartography of this characteristic.

According to Bill Brown, "The body is a thing among things."[8] For Brown this remark pushes toward a critical discussion on the nature and meaning of things—those objects we have tended to "look through" in order to discover a deeper meaning and purpose. Their "thingliness," he remarks, is present to us best when things no longer offer an opportunity to discover more, to unpack meaningful meaning. All this, from his perspective, says something about the human relationship to things.[9] Naming-things are always and already in the presence of other things. Mindful of this, and prompted by the previous chapter's argument, I end this section with a question: What does the arrangement and impact of things suggest? As will become clear, artistic production provides a useful way of mapping and exploring this question. I begin with the visual arts in order to mark out a particular way of framing artistic production's highlighting of naming-thing and thing-thing interplay. This is not to suggest an interest in only the visual arts; rather, the framework suggested throughout this discussion carries over to other modalities of the arts addressed later in the volume.

## Art

I am concerned with art developed from the twentieth century to the present, and I am most intrigued in this regard with art not of a Modernist mindset. That is to say, I am not concerned with art that seeks to devoutly represent or duplicate images of the world. Privileged in this volume is work (from a variety of genres) that calls into question that duplicity and instead seeks to challenge clean perception. As Arthur Danto notes, "Today art can be made of anything, put together with anything, in the service of presenting any ideas whatsoever."[10] Yet he tries to center on the concept of embodied meaning—the "thought of the work," which is expressed "nonverbally"—as a characteristic, a definition of art that captures its nature across genres and forms.[11] For Danto, this meaning provides particular and intimate information connected to each viewer, and in this way the work of art "tells them what, really, they already know."[12] While I disagree with the element of representation and instead think in terms of art as posing a challenge, I find significant Danto's recognition of art as drawing from anything and being constructed of anything. Still, I have to offer a shift in perspective in that art as a grammar (or one might call it a strategy) does not give information but rather is significant precisely because it offers no answer in the form of "truths" or even right feeling. Instead, art prompts awareness of our circumstances and our place within those circumstances without resolution.

Danto has argued that the nature and meaning—or definition—of art changed during the twentieth century when it could no longer be assumed to imitate reality or to promote beauty and taste. Particular art movements of the twentieth century—such as Dada and Pop Art—push beyond a framing of art and art history guided by those assumptions in ways that trouble what we can be and what should be categorized as art. Still, there is for Danto something compelling about art, something that distinguishes it. Hence, "there is really nothing like it when it comes to stirring the spirit."[13] It is this perception, this take on art that is of particular interest to me here. This thick relationship motivates questions and pushes forward concerns. The referencing of Dadaism and the highlighting of Pop Art point to a tragic perspective, a measured realism that signifies specialness as a quality of thought and being is significant for me in that it suggests the need for an alternate vocabulary and grammar for exploring the significance of cultural production.

Danto is interested in the manner in which Pop Art blurs the line between art and reality, as he puts it, and the questions promoted by that dissonance. I find that intriguing, and initially it is why I turned to Danto and continue to read him. However, my interest in artistic production has more to do with the thingliness of things and what that troubling of perception does to human experience. That is to say, I turn to art because art provides insight into incompleteness. Put differently, the placement of things in time and space constituted by art urges viewers to see something they might otherwise ignore, but this is a temporary situation. It is a condition that tells us equally about our limitation and our promise. It points to bodied naming-things' struggle against the world while being deeply enmeshed in the world and using resources from the world (cultural and "natural") to interrogate the world. More to the point, artistic production provides an invaluable means

chapter two

by which to isolate and interrogate the interplay between things—that is to the extent it recognizes rather than hides the thingliness of things.[14] Put differently, "perhaps, after all, it takes art to bring out the thing-li-ness of things."[15] Materials are combined to make things, and the artist then further manipulates these materials to create things that will urge us to think about, but more importantly, think within what is represented to what they offer as a prod toward awareness of the world and our circumstances. In saying this I remain human-centered over against what some call for as a thing-centered perspective.[16] Still, I appreciate in this work the manner in which things speak beyond fixed status and, in doing that, inform and influence a range of relations. Hence, I am not concerned with a guiding logic of beauty or a politics of aesthetic respectability; rather, I am concerned with exploring art that is attuned to circumstantial arrangements of life and their various sociocultural codes. If nothing else, they urge the naming-thing to speak questions and existential considerations.

Art both requires something and surrenders something. It shows the complexity of things—the multidirectional nature of their influence and impact—and the thick nature of the naming-thing's connection to other things. As Danto argues and I have noted numerous times in earlier work, if Warhol's *Brillo Box* could not be distinguished physically from the Brillo boxes at the grocery store, what then?[17] "Warhol had brought art and reality to such a point," writes Danto, "that it's only a matter of ingenuity to try and think of circumstances under which any masterpiece and something identical to it could have come into existence, under conditions in which one would and the other wouldn't have been a work of art."[18] The difference has something to do with thingliness—with the ability of the former to prompt certain considerations that are not achieved through the latter. And this must be in relationship to conscious placement in time and space that pulls things beyond status as objects and thereby exposes their porous nature. In a word, Pop Art and other contemporary art movements speak to the ability of this modality of expression, of placement of things (which is similar to the importance Danto gives to the exhibition as conveyer of meaning) to foster the types of questioning and insight religion as a technology exposes. For instance, take Danto's question—"Why do things look the way they look?"[19] This is not a question of aesthetics as beauty in that there is no assumption regarding the centrality of issues of wholeness embedded in this work. While there might be something resembling animosity toward beauty in Dada (which rejects the certainties and assumptions that made world war possible), there is in Pop Art something more akin to disinterestedness in beauty as a marker of "art." No, such questions encourage depth of exploration, including existential considerations but also epistemological and ontological considerations all related to fundamental concerns. Pop Art pushed for integration of what is "real," and in so doing it urged an interrogation of those realities that shape the manner in which the naming-thing touches and is touched by the world; such interrogation claws at our metaphysical frameworks. The blending of art and the "ordinary" became an invitation to explore. Naming-things and thing-things anchor both art and the "ordinary."

Keeping in place the theme of the *Brillo Box* produced by Warhol that is so very similar to the Brillo boxes designed by artist James Harvey and used in stores to transport Brillo pads, I suggest that the importance of art for my project, over against art for Danto, involves the tragicomic quality inherent in this re/presentation. Harvey, who provided the initial material and inspiration for Warhol's work, is practically forgotten for this connection to both things—*Brillo Box* and Brillo boxes.[20] It is the tragicomic quality to relationship with things that points in the direction of what I intend to suggest through *awareness* rather than *meaning* vis-à-vis the placement of things.

The naming-thing selecting and displacing other things is important not so much because of the things themselves but for that to which the interaction points.[21] As Dada artist Marcel Duchamp exemplifies with his "readymades," discussed at various points in this volume, it is not simply the thing that is of vital importance, but rather it is the selection and placement of the thing that is meant to motivate deeper thinking.[22] Things point beyond themselves—pushing toward their thingification and away from objectification. For instance, as Danto notes, Warhol's boxes meant to "subtract the perceptual differences between art and reality."[23] I would phrase it a bit differently in light of the intent of this book and say that Warhol's boxes, like Duchamp's readymades, push viewers to encounter.

What can be said about the things that play this role? And what is to be made of the bodied naming-things that construct these things? Meaning found, produced, or assumed is not the correct response to such questions. Meaning is too firm; it renders static or fixed what is pliable, flexible, and mutable. It is to view circumstances from only one vantage point.

Art prompts through an intentional manipulation of time and space, and secondly (but not secondarily) through the intentional positioning of things so as to urge viewers toward their thingliness.[24] On this score the worst an artist can do is demand her intent, as if it is a signifier that must be carried forward. And the curator's note highlighted typically in writing on the wall introducing the "meaning" of the work is not much better in that it, like the artist's statement, works to restrict the openness of the work once moved from the artist's mind to a selected time and space. Perhaps this is why Andy Warhol often gave limited insight into what his art was meant to achieve. To do so would have been to end his art.

The prompt proposed by artistic work is the only thing transhistorical about art, for which that language remains vital. Still, it is more accurate to say that art points us toward ourselves, that it holds us at that station and urges us to examine a naming-thing's condition and its relationship to other things' conditions. There are no restrictions to what this art can prompt in the viewer, and there is no one dimension of our openness—such as senses—through which it demands we process these offerings. Beauty—one way of thinking about aesthetics—is not the focus of art so conceived, at least not more traditional framings of aesthetics and art. However, this is not to say that beauty or wholeness is rendered unimportant. Aesthetics is transformed from being a way to measure art, and instead aesthetics becomes another way of describing things in their thingliness. Art exposes a human's effort to, on some level, in the words of Albert Camus, be other than she is. So presented, art then is an utterance of human interaction with other things staged in a particular time and space.[25] Art has been referenced as something of a question without firm resolution. Or as Camus remarks, "Art is the activity that exalts and denies simultaneously."[26] Still, I depart a bit from Camus, privileging a different moment in art history without mimetics in that I argue that what is left with art is the essence of characterization as interplay made possible. All this entails what I see as art's motivation toward openness maintained.

Danto raises a question: "How to distinguish between art and real things that are not art but that could very well have been used as works of art?"[27] At one point he decides to think of art as "wakeful dreams" that can be shared and discussed and that can be effective beyond the private world of the "dreamer."[28] He noted in 2013 that at a point he had thought of the intersection of art and reality as the end of art, the inability to discern a difference. Yet he had changed to posit that the difference might be invisible but substantive and might have to do with different modalities of embodiment.[29] In a word, there is something that gives art its difference from the "things" it interrogates, or symbolizes, or explores. There are ways in which this issue shades what interests me about religion as a technology: it marks out the difference not as essential or necessary but rather as a matter of consideration and presentation. And this technology of religion isolates particular arrangements of "things" and thereby stimulates.

I would say art prompts a tackling of experience, a repositioning of some of its pieces and forms, so as to urge difference of thought that encourages nothing more than lucidity—greater awareness of our circumstances and our desperate place within those circumstances.[30] Works of art symbolize a desire, the configuration of this desire, but they provide no answers. If anything, it is this moralistic awareness—of our circumstances and our place in these circumstances—that constitutes the gain made.

Art, then, becomes a particular geography in which and by means of which religion as a technology does its work.

### Why and Where Art?

Other arrangements of things seek to accomplish this same work; that is the nature of cultural production. Yet I suggest the multiple codes and strategies of communication represented by the arts as a general category of expression provide perhaps one of the most compelling of such strategies. This is not to suggest, as did figures such as W. E. B. Du Bois, that art is political and must serve the purpose of advancement on sociopolitical lines. Such a framing of art's function is too preoccupied with outcomes, with easily marked out transformation. There is some of that in my earlier theorizing of religion, but here I prioritize the process of engagement, the putting in play of particular techniques of interrogation and arrangement of experience as opposed to the existential and ontological outcomes of that process.

Art, in connection to religion as a technology, poses a question/comment: "Look through and think . . ." And though this yearning to examine experience (i.e., the interplay of things) is a part of our human nature, to do so through the mechanics of religion is to select a particular theoretical-methodological tool for this "natural" cross-examination of sorts. Mindful of this framing, and thinking with moralist Camus, what we have here is the dreadful invitation to contemplation—not resolution, not answers, nor meaning found or held, but simply contemplation, which in fact keeps alive those things that concern us.[31] And along the way we place markers, or things in relationship to things, that urge more contemplation, more struggle, and at our best a bit of moralistic awareness and lucidity of circumstance.

There is no hope embedded in this process, but rather the location—the gallery, for instance—does not provide final containment or a type of fixity of possibility beyond impingement. That is to say, it prompts a particular time and space for contemplation through things that are not just things. This pull-and-push dynamic I am describing is similar in effect to the "resonance" and "wonder" phenomenon described by Stephen Greenblatt. He argues that exhibits can be arranged along two possible effects. The first, resonance, allows the displayed object to pull viewers beyond that particular object and into a larger context. And wonder points the viewer in the direction of what is unique about that particular object.[32] For Greenblatt this seems to entail a relationship between distinct materials—the human viewer and the object viewed. A dimension of this involves an economic consideration of ownership, which, he suggests, is both encouraged by but prohibited by the museum's displaying of the goods.[33] The economics of presentation is not my concern. Still, although the flexibility of things in Greenblatt's formulation implies something of their thingliness, the relationship he describes is really about the bodied naming-thing observing things in ways that speak to other things. I suggest in my depiction the possibility of something more taking place, something that entails an interaction between naming-things and thing-things on a more fundamental level.[34]

I want to say more concerning the gallery as confinement but also as things—for example, building materials, light, sound, and art—in movement, in flux before moving on. Danto says the gallery is the new church, and for Duncan Cameron it is a temple (when it is not a forum). In addition, Carol Duncan notes the manner in which the museum is premised on earlier models such as "classical temples, medieval cathedrals, Renaissances palaces," and in this way represents a multilayered experience revolving around the architecture of the space meant to accommodate the interaction of various items as "secular ritual."[35] I find such thinking intriguing in that it blurs the line between notions of the sacred and secular, and the line between the placement and presentation of things (bodied naming-things and thing-things). Still, this alone does not capture enough. What if we were to think about the gallery space, the exhibit hall, any location consciously arranged in terms of art the way we think about other things? What if we refused a rigid distinction between the gallery as thing and other things—such as the naming-things and thing-things with which it interacts—and instead saw them as interacting and thereby shifting and changing each other? There is something organic about the gallery space (or any space of artistic production or performance—which by function could be said to constitute an intended gallery space) in that it holds connections in terms of substance and cultural codes with the things (e.g., works of art) connected to it and growing in and out of it.

One gets a sense of the interactive quality of things in time and space (and in relationship to the gallery) through a Pope.L exhibit at the Museum of Modern Art (NYC)—*member: Pope.L, 1978-2001*. Meant to highlight the manner in which multidimensional artist Pope.L uses his body and other mundane things to present and wrestle with a range of sociopolitical and economic questions, the exhibit included some of his more well-known pieces of body art–performance art. However, in addition to *Eating the Wall Street Journal*, for example, the gallery space includes cut-out sections of wall, a play on Pope.L's "Hole Theory" (as curator comments suggest), exposing the inner workings of space and disrupting a "superficial" gaze by calling attention to multiple dimensions of space and contact—internal and external. With one particular cut-out, next to the hole, is the Sheetrock turned inside out and attached to the wall. On that surface Pope.L has drawn a ghostlike figure (present but not known fully, present but without bodily detail—with one large black eye and another eye, black but smaller), with a thought bubble above it, a bit smudged but asking, "What do art works talk about when you leave the room?" Next to it is another ghostlike figure with similar eyes, and above its head is a thought bubble holding the answer to the question: "Us." This sentiment—the notion that things "speak," interact, impact other things—is written elsewhere in the exhibit, also through a ghostlike presence drawn with a thought bubble: "Exhibition." Above this word and to its right is this saying: "I was standing next to this and it began to speak to me."[36] Art demands something; as Pope.L notes, it resists objectification and instead draws us beyond viewer status. Art observes and queries naming-things; art entails graphic agency. Time and space fail to reify, to fix, content. Things amplify themselves in relationship to other things. As Daniel Miller remarks, "Before we can make things, we are ourselves grown up and matured in the light of things [understood as a collective rather than in terms of individual items]. . . . These unconsciously direct our footsteps and are the landscapes of our imagination, as well as the cultural environment to which we adapt."[37]

The gallery enables and restricts. This has to do with content (naming-things and thing-things) but also context as the latter relates to the manner in which the sociopolitical and cultural sensibility of curators and others shape exhibits.[38] Limiting focus to what is present while also encouraging thinking and engagement beyond the thinglinesses of the gallery as such, I argue, is what the gallery does. And this is not determined by factors such as the location or the economic resources of the gallery. I am describing the general nature of gallery space when it is space set aside and apart for the work done by art. Seeing naming-things and/or thing-things outside the gallery may spark particular reactions that pull toward or seek to push away from body-thingliness. However, the process of placing these same things—such as a chair, a cut-up magazine image, or the body of a body-thing—in the spatially conceived particularity of the gallery fosters a different view and an altered connection. Svetlana Alpers's comments regarding Renaissance altarpieces are appropriate in the context of my argument: "When objects like these are severed from the ritual site [or initial space associated with use], the invitation to look attentively remains and in certain respects may even be enhanced."[39]

Artistic expression—whether paintings, performance, dance, or song—consciously causes attention to the visible and invisible content of time and space in ways that urge introspection. And something about this introspection vis-à-vis art brings to the fore questions of significance.

There is a string of connection or concern between bodied naming-things that produce and arrange, and other things. Both bodied naming-things and things-things push against static and truncated perceptions of circumstances and prompt a sense of space as fluid and boundaries as porous. Forms of art at the "end" of this rethinking of things point out which assumptions concerning the nature and meaning of art are disbanded. Forms of art also spark recognition of the relationship between things with/in naming-things as well as the perception of this porousness. And in the process, they demand a new vocabulary and grammar for such engagement with things. In short, recognition of the thingliness of things points to the manner in which art articulates openness.

# interplay
## part ii

# artistic expression of transience

3

How does our outside reality reinvent itself?
—ANGELBERT METOYER, in conversation with the author

Humans and things are symmetrically involved.
—IAN HODDER, *Entangled: An Archaeology of the Relationships between Humans and Things*

With the claim that art articulates openness established and discussed in chapter 2, I want to now give some attention to the arrangement of things associated with this openness. And I want to do so by turning attention to the work of an artist, Angelbert Metoyer, for whom things are not always what they seem. That is to say, thing-things defy static categorization. They shift between locations and alter existential assurances as they challenge any sense of a closed system, or of stability and clear boundaries regarding content and form.

## Artistic Context

Drawing from family history and the larger history of peoples of African descent, Metoyer presents what I have called rituals of reference (i.e., practices and symbols meant to restrict racialized bodies), but he tames them by exposing their illogical and truncating intent.[1] In various ways, his art pieces speak to and about his wide-ranging experiences in moving between various points in the United States, experiencing China for two years, and living and working between Rotterdam and Houston. His paintings and installations draw personality and posture from family members, friends, and neighborhood figures associated with his years growing up in Houston. His aesthetic—by which I mean a certain "touch," a rhythm of expression and a particular process for selecting and placing things in time and space—has shifted and changed from his start as an artist in 1994, with work done in two rooms given him by Project Row House, to the present.[2] Early work led to exhibits and to interest among collectors as he, a bodied naming-thing, encountered other bodied naming-things and thing-things in various cultural contexts.[3]

There are reflections of his various artistic influences and his formal training (Savannah College of Art and Design in Atlanta), but all bends to his concern with rethinking what we can learn about and from things that shift awareness of our circumstances (i.e., world) and our place within those circumstances.[4] He is sensitive to the manner in which the brutality of racial difference has marked "epistemologically and ontologically blackened" naming-things, seeking to render them inert objects by means of which whiteness is reinforced as metaphysical truth. By naming them, bodied naming-things, he seeks to focus their significance as open, and in so doing he creates a space for rethinking embodied life and its inner workings that shadows and informs us. All this takes place within the context of the gallery space, but it is not limited to that arena in that the viewer is invited to continue that probing in other times and spaces.

ABP     What is the role of the artist in society?

AM     It depends on what's needed. I feel as if the artist should be an insider and an outsider. The studio practice involves understanding reality, an in-between space, articulated in between worlds.[5]

Pieces selected speak of travel, of relocation; they hold a vocabulary and grammar of what he references as the "sacred" and point to dynamics of embodied life as already and always complex, layered, and in search of and toward "More." This search is not simply more material goods, more status, but rather a deeper and robust sense of relationship to other "things." All this is marked by a vibrant yearning both internally and externally manifested as well as represented in and by the colors, signs, symbols, shapes, and configurations that code the exhibit and shape its spatial language. It is a language to which naming-things respond—and this is a type of thingified language to the extent it encompasses and is encompassed by things. This language is read on and through things; this is certainly part of what Metoyer portrays through self-portraits and mirrored surfaces that populate many of his installations and exhibits. Self-described as an abstract expressionist—also having what might be referenced as "Afrofuturistic" tendencies to explore past, present, and future in ways that challenge assumptions concerning the nature and meaning of bodied naming-things—he wrestles with issues of ontological development and integrity over against modes of technological advancement.[6] He pulls from history and thereby brings together fragments and "scraps" of remembered selves, and in this way he explores strategies for self-understanding in relationship to the signs and symbols that mark up and amplify collective life. Space has significance in this regard because it becomes (or perhaps has always been) the arena for movement, for transitions, and for overlap—the scope of confinement as intentional and floating locales occupied by various things. Metoyer draws from his personal encounters with the world to shape a general sense of what it means to travel across time and space—to effect both and be affected by both. This process, as he explores and explains through particular pieces and their arrangement, is always embodied.

The temple, and the self-reflection it affords, is meant to challenge this construction, to offer opportunity and ritualized processes by means of which to dis/cover, or to rename, by finally seeing ourselves and ourselves in relationship to other things. This is the intent, but not a necessary outcome to be sure. Yet it is a potentiality Metoyer means to highlight through the talismanic qualities of his work waiting to be probed and perhaps employed. Art, then, as Metoyer means to develop it, fosters a framework or moment of Camusian lucidity. It is an embodied awareness, a pulling, and an urging reconsideration of what we think we know about ourselves, about each other, and about the world in which we live. In short, it is awareness regarding the interplay of naming-things and other things. For Metoyer, the key to this process of mutuality involves the construction and presentation of passageways—openings that suggest shifts and changes made possible through cartographies of time marked out by complexities and uncertainties associated with the presence together of things.

**Wrestling History**

There is much about things moving through time and space that defies the ability of words to capture, control, and tame. It is consideration of an alternate vocabulary and grammar for envisioning existence as interplay that is so compellingly presented in the work of Metoyer, such as the exhibit titled *Wrestling History: Points along a Journey of Dis/covery Hidden in the Temple.*[7] As curator for this exhibit, I provided the following description. While there is a grammar of spirituality in the description, I call attention to the practice of things to which it also refers:

> Metoyer turns to life meaning(s) that surge up and out of encounters with the self, others, and world. All this is played out in shapes, colors, and forms of artistic expression. Paint isn't simply composition that covers a surface, and objects aren't simply "things." In the space of the gallery as temple they are used to present and decode knowledge and being. Here one enters a space framed, arranged, and outfitted with works meant to foster transformation. Bringing into contact images, signs, and symbols from an African past and contemporary markers of cultural meaning, objects become the equivalent of a "Vévé"—markings that point to confluence of powers, locations where worlds merge. One might alternately think of "crossroads," where worlds open, collide, and where opportunities and challenges present themselves. Here, at the point of convergence, one finds spheres of activity and cultural me(*an*)ing.
>
> Each piece contributes to vocabulary and grammar of the sacred shaping spatial language. Together they speak *discovery* of the world as the artist encounters, interprets and communicates it. Still this is only one dimension of that ritualized encounter presented in that it also involves *cover*. This covering entails layering of experiences as the viewer reads herself through the artist's presentation of life domains. Altars, totems, mirrors, images, and idols all point to the questions that surround our existence—questions that have such profound significance that we isolate them and make them more than ordinary.
>
> From self-portraits to pieces urging introspection, this exhibit prompts a confrontation with history and offers tools for rethinking the embodied and "spiritual" nature of human existence. In such a space the rituals of life are noted, expressed, and interrogated for what they say about the embodied and more ephemeral dimensions of our existence—occupation of and movement through time and space.[8]

Metoyer's approach involves a turn to the workings of bodied naming-things that surge up and out of encounters with the self, others, and the world—and all this is played out in shapes, colors, and forms that emerge on canvas. In charting this process, and as I note above, for Metoyer there is something spiritual about this artistic process of representing interplay between naming-things and thing-things, but by that he does not have in mind traditional notions of material distinction and nonhistorically arranged modalities of operation. Rather, spirituality in his art involves aggressive coordination of material experience (i.e., the presence together of naming-things and thing-things) for which our language is inadequate to name and position. It is a system of material arrangements that push the boundaries of our perception and our experience of others, the world, and ourselves as present to us (naming-things in relationship to thing-things responding to world as circumstances). Spirituality, then, speaks to a type of synergistic layering of thing-things that push beyond easy identification as one dimensional and nonresponsive. In a word, spirituality is secular and marked by materiality.

## With Things

As has been the case throughout the presence of African peoples in the Americas, movement has defined something of their being. It has arranged them physically, populated their dreams and desires, and cast a shadow over their longings. Metoyer thinks about movement along historical lines. So for him, as is the case for many, the Middle Passage marks a graphic and violent form of transition, but the process continued long after ships reached various points along the eastern coast of North America. Bodied naming-things reduced to blackness (more on this in later chapters), while rendered somewhat docile through sociocultural codes and political pronouncement, still defied elements of this transition and exploited others: desired movement from south to north, movement from east to west, movement across more localized areas, and metaphysical movement from status as slave to that of free person with recognition as fully human. Shifting locations as time and space rub against each other is a theme of exploration for him.

Movement defines the age, the point in the "Modern Period" when worlds collide in a massive way—creating new populations and dismantling others—changing the nature, scope, coding, and meaning of our visual signs and symbols. But is all done once the space Metoyer has fostered is left—on to the next event, the next evening out, the next exhibit and dinner—with little impact on how those events and activities are encountered, processed, and stored away as another dimension of personal history?

What he offers is presentation through versions of familiar and comfortable things. But rather than a push toward discovery, it is a covering of history with selected memories of things as they have been and as they "should" be. It is in this way that art speaks to and is an expression of bodied naming-things' most ingrained codes as well as our most troubling circumstances and scenarios. Although memory is fragile and fractured, Metoyer refuses to allow this to negate any requirement to re-member both the benefits and problems that mark our personal development and our relationship to others. Art, then, is an articulation of the human condition to the extent that naming-things produce and thing-things represent (and the opposite is also true) the interior and external markings of our existence. In this regard, Hans Belting is correct in saying that "the body is a place in the world."[9] The bodied naming-thing is entangled. In this context, things are more than objects that speak nothing more than their appearance.

There is something in what emerges that speaks both to the promise and pitfalls of existence as interplay. It communicates encounter consistent with the trickster figure bringing humans in contact with themselves and those things shadowing the thoughts and actions of bodied naming-things. Pulling images, signs, and symbols from an African past and contemporary markers of cultural meaning, Metoyer arranges throughout the gallery a type of large-scale equivalent of the Vodou "Vévé"—markings that point to the confluence of powers, the location where worlds merge—or perhaps the more Americanized cultural symbol of the "crossroads," where worlds open, collide, and where opportunities and challenges present themselves.[10] It is at the crossroads where one has the opportunity for alteration—a spatial arrangement with implications for those who, as Du Bois might put it, are born with the veil—the ability to see between worlds of activity and cultural me(an)ing (i.e., the introspective and circumstantial nature or quality of knowing vis-à-vis modalities of presence together).[11] Still, what then is the meaning of things? Is there more than a function for things—and arrangements of things—of images? Metoyer answers this question with an emphatic but still somewhat reserved yes.

Paint is not simply pigment composition that covers a surface. Feathers, wood, and so on, thing-things in other words, are not captured simply through their first incarnation—their mode of utility speaking to initial use.[12] To the contrary, paint covering—or the layering of feathers or the repositioning of wood over against other things—actually exposes a visual heuristic for presenting and decoding our metaphysics as a matter of open things confronting, merging, and separating. The canvas is coated by paint and other media, but in the process, one is encouraged to uncover self in relationship to the work of art—to recognize that something about its representation of thing-things speaks to and about naming-things within time and space.

Metoyer wrestles with presentation of movement and the manner in which such "travel" connotes transformation or substantial change in how we perceive larger arrangements of life. The inconclusive nature of interplay with other things remains intact, unresolved by artistic expression. This is not to suggest that Metoyer is an absurdist artist, but rather that there is a shared recognition that the world offers us only small comfort and that our knowing is only incomplete and shaped by a learned "not-knowing."

Yet there is in Metoyer what I would describe as moralist recognition of the nature of our relationship to the world, or our circumstances, in that his art says something about the hypocrisy of our structuring of life as bonded and recognizes the inability of naming-things to find resolve through firm boundaries. Art hints at something it cannot fix, or as Camus notes concerning absurd art and the concrete, "It [the concrete] cannot be the end, the meaning, and the consolation of a life."[13] Still, this porous and penetrable world is the one that intrigues Metoyer—the one he believes artistic expression opens.[14] The need to continuously wrestle, to consistently pursue, I find in Metoyer's art and philosophy of art, shares something with Camus's realism regarding the outcome of artistic production: "Creating or not creating changes nothing."[15] But still we work—despite all, we work.[16] In certain ways, for Metoyer art marks out history, tells history, and pushes through the interior uncertainties of history. Or history, as Bill Brown reflects, "can unabashedly begin with things and with the sense of which we apprehend them."[17]

## Placing Things

There is a complexity, a layering that already and always points to a deeper quality and significance to circumstances of interplay in which we find ourselves. Ritual items as thing-things used within Metoyer's art operate consistent with Hodder's analysis: "Spiritual energies flow through icons and relics and awaken our devotion. Familiar things are absorbed into our sense of identity; they become recognized and owned. . . . Things stimulate our cognitive capacities, flowing through our neural processes, leading to reflection upon reflection, creating pathways that stay with us. There is a dependence of humans on things."[18] But this is only one dimension of the bodied naming-thing's interaction with other things, and it describes only one dimension of things in that things interact, shift, change, impact, and influence. Multidirectional-significance operating in numerous networks of contact is a way one might describe this understanding of things beyond their initial use.[19]

There is a depth that pushes beyond what first meets the eye. Thing-things, in this sense, yield no certainty, no clear boundaries. They are things with thingliness that take away clarity in the form of distinction. As Brown remarks, "The quest for things may be a quest for a certainty, but thing is a word that tends, especially at its most banal, to index a certain limit or liminality, to hover over the threshold between the nameable and the figurable and unfigurable, the identifiable and unidentifiable."[20] Items serve in this way, and the gallery becomes for Metoyer the housing, or temple, complete with ordinary items that when brought together and arranged, hold the capacity to transform and transpose so as to make us aware. This, of course, is not to say that simply entering the gallery means a huge life transformation, revelations that radically change life. However, does any temple guarantee such things? No, it simply provides time and space, reminders or visual tools, and the rest is left to those who encounter the exhibit. Art is a ritual apparatus of sorts, and the gallery serves as an architectural harness for time and space. Perhaps the gallery is a location for introspection and interrogation—to be alone to a certain degree while otherwise getting lost in the existential midst of others who are themselves alone in their own particular (but similar) ways. In a word, the gallery is a time-space set apart for a certain type of interaction between things.

This is a portion of the angst of life noted and aestheticized in Metoyer's artistic productions. He pulls from personal history and the collective history of the larger population of which he is a part to collect and de/code materials so as to make them available to others—to offer the talisman that opens new worlds of challenge and possibility. And in this process, viewers (or better yet, participants) are invited to pull from their own histories, to wrestle those histories as it were, in order to configure differently themselves and their interplay with the world of things. This, on a fundamental level, is a mode of dis/covery. Every work of art speaks *discovery* of the world as the artist encounters, interprets, and communicates it for public consideration. It is exposure—types of laying claim through greater focus and presence. Still, this is only one dimension of the ritualized encounter presented by the exhibit *Wrestling History* in that it also involves *cover*. This covering amounts to the layering of experience(s) as the viewer does the following: (1) reads the artist through the artist's encounter with the world, and (2) reads the viewer's self through the re/presented experience of the artist. Multiple perspectives are presented as a way of avoiding what is uncomfortable. Hence, the experience—the viewing—is multidimensional and multidirectional. It is arranged and guided by placement of the various pieces of art, but it is also an open space and time maneuvered as the viewer/participant sees fit. All this is conditioned by what the viewer brings into the temple and what the viewer desires to take away from that encounter with works of art. There is a hint of what I mean in the words of Marcel Duchamp. "All in all," he said, "the creative act is not performed by the artist alone; the spectator brings the work in contact with the external world by deciphering and interpreting its inner qualifications and thus adds his contribution to the creative act."[21] Thing-things have been placed in accordance with the wishes of the artist, but once situated they tell stories, urge questions, and so on. Within the context of artistic production, thing-things communicate on a variety of levels that entail the presence of things as well as the quality of their thingliness (e.g., what it communicates beyond its initial function or intent).[22]

"ARTFUL" THINGS

Art begins where other modalities of expression fall short. Artistic expression pushes against the boundaries established in an effort to compartmentalize existence and calls into question the integrity of the discrete categories we develop to marshal along our lives. Altars, totems, mirrors, moving images, and idols all point to the questions and fundamental concerns that surround existence.[23] These are items rendered symbolic and invested with such profound significance that we isolate them and make them more than mundane, more than ordinary. There is something about what emerges through exhibits that speaks to both the promise and pitfalls of interplay, as well as the challenges posed by (and in) the process of interrogating what we call life framed within the confines of our existential narratives as we know them. The messy nature of human life and human interactions is highlighted, framed, and signified. What is the role of the artist in this? What Danto notes regarding abstract expressionists might be said of Metoyer, for whom there is a self-understanding as guide or shaman urging movement into the un/familiar as a way of gauging and coming to know the dynamics of interplay.[24]

ABP     How do you determine the arrangement of items in your installations?

AM      Based on moments, and the language they hold . . . their imbued nature. . . . I think of it as a body.[25]

Shamans of all sorts shift through history marking out pathways and existential possibilities not otherwise present to us. In this way, the trickster figure is a type of Sankofa experience that points forward and backward at the same time.[26]

From self-portraits to pieces urging introspection, Metoyer's exhibits prompt confrontation with historical interplay between things and offer tools for rethinking the embodied and porous (or what Metoyer calls "spiritual") nature of human existence. In such a space the rituals and ritualization(s) of life are noted, visualized, expressed aesthetically, and interrogated for what they say about the embodied and more ephemeral dimensions of our existence—our occupation of time and space and our intentional manipulation of both as a way of wrestling with (or undertaking a process of) "exorcism" as fully as circumstances allow and as graphically as the geography of encounter can bring to bear on bodied naming-things and thing-things torn, fused, torn and left unfinished. These bodied naming-things in transition are also in transit within a limited occupation of that space called gallery. Within a finite amount of time they engage and are engaged by works of art. Such activity involves interaction with what Danto called the "Artworld"—as this "world" impinges upon and also pulls us away from the existential circumstances of our psyche-physical world(s).[27] This is the situation for bodied naming-things.

ABP     What do you want to achieve with your installations?

AM      A space, a feeling of something else. . . . Achievement is that space for "something other" to be recognized.[28]

It is as if the space of the gallery, when framed by Metoyer's work, takes on a different quality—something akin to what the African ancestors might note as a sacred space, or a space set apart. In this space, through the geographies of encounter presented on canvas, viewers are invited to discover something of themselves by discovering something of him (i.e., the artist). This is a presentation of the self, exposed, pulled apart, and reconfigured. And in this process the viewer is pulled in and exposed as well. The bodied naming-thing has history flexible and porous—marking the outline of developments that define the past, position the present, and suggest something of what might be called the future. But could it be any other way? Again, every work of art speaks both a *discovery* and *cover*. Cover here entails containment, a type of confinement that pushes into place the bodied naming-thing by limiting the grammar and vocabulary of expression available for signifying the dominant discourse and its theory of wholeness (aesthetics). This dis/covery also speaks to the material employed.

As Metoyer notes, "The materials I employ include 'excrements of industry,' such as coal, glass, oil, tar and gold dust. With these tools I explore themes of waste and destruction, and existential issues of life and death."[29] The covered materials—the coal, glass, and so on—allow Metoyer and by extension the viewers to discover something about themselves and the issues that concern them in this process of interplay. This in a sense is the function of mirrors within his exhibits. These mirrors often with an embedded image allow for a triadic encounter: the viewer with the thing-thing as art, the viewer with the embedded image as other, and the viewer with self. This interaction entails an exchange between naming-things and thing-things that affects and influences through interrogation and inspection. In this regard, Metoyer's use of mirrors as framework for dynamic images (or the picture being an "image with a medium") presents a mode of what Hans Belting claims in terms of images.[30] "The image," writes Belting, "is defined not by its mere visibility, but by it being invested, by the beholder, with a symbolic meaning and a kind of mental 'frame.'"[31] One gets a sense of this in Metoyer's *Babies Walk on Water: Present, Future and Time Travel* exhibit in which, according to Steven Psyllos, "the weight of Metoyer's work comes from the multitude of symbols brought together to *interact before the viewer*."[32]

ABP     Is there a relationship between artistic production and our social conditions?

AM      If there was, then it would begin as early as illustration propaganda. . . . I feel as if art made for people should be charged with power—something that inspires and something that has the power of refraction and reflection.[33]

The experience, the viewing, is multidimensional and multidirectional; it is arranged and guided by means of the placement of the various pieces of art, but it is also an open space and time maneuvered and decoded as the viewers/participants see fitting in light of what they bring to the temple and what they seek to take away. As Metoyer seeks to highlight, art speaks when, where, and how we cannot. Thinking in terms of the images populating Metoyer's exhibits, one can argue that images say something about the "cultural history of the human body."[34] Artistic expression pushes against the boundaries of our compartmentalized lives and calls into question the integrity of the discrete categories we develop to marshal along those lives. From whom or what were these signs and symbols taken? To what do these signs and symbols point? What is the frame of reference for these signs and symbols, and how can they be reimagined and reassessed? And what becomes of us by means of this work? To what extent should the artist and the viewer of the work concern themselves with such considerations? Are such concerns part of art's nature, or a distraction from art's motivation and intent? Such questions point to a dynamic interaction between naming-thing and thing-thing in ways that push toward further entanglement.[35]

Metoyer is not seeking a pure expression of consciousness devoid of contact with the mundane that nags at us; rather, he concerns himself with encounters that inform and impinge upon us and upon which we assert some influence. The point of departure, the area of concern, and the geography of engagement is the mundane—the content of human experience (direct, which means personal; and indirect, which means collective) rather than some type of transcendent encounter beyond the scope of communicative coding to address. "A work of art," John Dewey reflects, "no matter how old and classical is actually not just potentiality, a work of art only when it lives in some individualized experience."[36] Assumptions of use or utility are suspended. There is something about the thingliness of things that allows art to express both what is familiar and what is foreign, and in this way there is some*thing* shared within the experience cataloged and explored.

Related to this claim, take as an example Metoyer's *Self Portrait (1998)*. It is not simply one image of the artist as bodied naming-thing engaging the viewer (as naming-thing) straight on (see fig. 3.1). Rather, it is composed of a naked, cold figure with arms crossed looking at a blue figure that, holding the same body posture, returns the gaze. Between the two is a black "object" with an encircled cross at the top, the rest of the object bearing the marks and shape of an African ritual item (as thing-thing). The self is multiple, involving interrogation of location within and postures toward the world. The background shows movement, variously positioned prints of the author's feet, as if he has walked between his selves as part of the process of de/construction. In addition, there are blue shapes resembling African-derived signs and symbols, and pieces of paper having other signs and symbols, layered onto the canvas. Some of the symbols cover the genital area of the two figures, and in this way they speak to the cultural context of the self and perhaps the manner in which the gendered body is not the authentic body to the extent symbolic constructions cover the genitals and thereby provide meaning not fixed through sexual organs. Even deeper into the canvas, behind the two selves, is a marked white background that both challenges and connects the two figures. The background both merges and disassociates the two beings that anchor this painting. By so doing, the background presents itself as having what might be called psychic and visual significance, as opposed to an assumption that the background is simply cleared space for presentation of what "matters" to the artist and what will best help the viewer focus. When

chapter three

the viewer attempts to see all that is on and in the canvas, movement is highlighted—as if to say the development of identity is not a static and fixed determination but rather is a fluid process.

ABP    What is art's function or purpose?

AM    In the function there's purpose. The medium is the message. Push and pull . . . a space for creating awareness, exercise, based on being human.[37]

Some might consider work like his self-portrait an indication that Metoyer holds to Afrofuturistic sensibilities, to the extent that Afrofuturism constitutes a distinct interrogation of time and space.

*Untitled #** demonstrates a similar layering of signs and symbols that shift notions of time and space as they mediate and blur distinctions between an African past and an American present, and what this means for the plausibility of a future marked by a difference (see fig. 3.2). The figure in this piece, a pale figure looking down with genitals covered by hands clasped in front, has an intense appearance—something of a grimace on the face as signs and symbols swirl around. The stern look and the covering of genitals speak to targets of racial violence—destroying emotional and psychological well-being and attempting to render docile the bodied naming-thing. It is important to remember that the lynching of blacks often involved the removal of the genitals as a symbolic statement concerning the power to control. In addition, there are African images and spheres within spheres upon which the figure stands, combined with what appears to be a red branch of a tree pushing up and through the figure, who remains transfixed.

Within the inner portion of the background of *Untitled #**, there is a black spotted line coming out of the spheres and pushing behind the figure to the top of the canvas. Coming out of the figure from the elbow to the top of the head are lines that resemble the visual presentation of energy, an intensity that matches the facial expression, which speaks to the serious nature of the figure's situation—stuck, still, but marked by transition. These elements moving around and in the figure are not mere static things. They speak to a depth, a shifting sphere of influence and perspective that take the viewer from some undisclosed period of Africanness to the present moment in which the viewer engages the naked figure. The viewer is encouraged to think about the implications of the imagery, particularly the manner in which issues of being (as constituting a quality of "closed off from . . .") are arranged in terms of types of thingliness unpacked and explored. This is done using a variety of imaginaries to both code and decode concerns and conditionings that fuel

artistic expression of transience

3.1 *Self Portrait (1998)*. Used by permission of the Zi Koolhaas-Metoyer Trust and Angelbert Metoyer.

3.2 *Untitled #**. Used by permission of Angelbert Metoyer.

and inform thing interplay. The naming-thing in *Untitled #\** and the naming-thing in the self-portrait are not simply representations of the physical form of naming-things but are also the gelling of cultural signs and markers (as dimensions of interplay).

## SPECULATING ON THINGS

*I'm a cut out Life* is not a mirror display, but it has a reflective quality to it. Behind glass, the shadowlike figure seems deep in thought, with signs and symbols related to various metaphysical concerns swimming around it (see fig. 3.3). And all this requires attention and speculation as to what their presence and arrangement entails for the artist. The color red that outlines various geometric shapes is pronounced due to the rather subtle and faded colors of yellow, gray, and black that make up much of the background. On the left side is a quarter moon, and on the far right is a sphere. Letters and signs speak a symbolic language of meaning, one that is couched in embodiment and unfixed by the gaze. The viewer has to decipher, in a sense, things in that the marks are not without significance. They have a presence beyond their initial look; they have a depth that points to concerns and tensions. And Metoyer presents them in such a manner as to make the viewer probe and explore—pushing for impulses. His work is meant to question and ultimately challenge the fixity of things as things—as epistemologically one-dimensional "stuff." Instead, they become passageways exposing markers that prompt us to view and respond to what confronts us and challenges our desired being as closed and whole.

While not challenging the thingliness of the door in this piece, *Father* (2000) pushes against the aesthetics of two worlds held apart. The piece centers around a male dressed in a black suit, shoes, and with a somber look. The expression is a bit difficult to read in that the face is marked and shaded. Yet around the head is an aura usually associated with the glow of divinity, and above that glow and seated on the figure's head is a striped platform upon which rests a white bowl—somewhat resembling a christening container holding "blessed" water (see fig. 3.4). The arms are folded behind the back, with the item on the head held by the stoic posture of the figure. Cutting in front of the figure is a white "X" running halfway through the painting, and connected to this is an "X" that runs behind the figure. The "X," the unknown—graphically represented, for example, in the teachings of the Nation of Islam as replacement for the slave name, for slave mentality and culture—then cuts through the figure, marking the heart of the figure and cutting through

3.3 *I'm a cut out Life*. Used by permission of the Zi Koolhaas-Metoyer Trust and Angelbert Metoyer.

the back of the legs. The emotional and physical dimensions of the figure are marked by uncertainty. Symbols of an African divinity and other cultural codes are present and arranged around the figure—including a star (perhaps noting insight) and a ladder (marking progression) to the figure's right. African symbols, with faint figures of persons, are on the left. Words and numbers are present, but they do not demand the same attention as the African figures pasted onto the paper. They are recognizable but feed background concerns and considerations that do not figure so prominently in this work. Near the feet and behind the figure is a black arch with white strips painted on it. At the right end of the arch—from the figure's perspective—is a boat, with the sail and flag raised high, and above that sail is the star mentioned earlier. The star is often assumed to provide guidance, but in this instance, it is also connected to the bottom of the "X" that cuts across his chest—tying knowledge to lack of knowledge, and lucidity to a lack of awareness. The European aesthetic of the suit is countered by the aesthetic shaped by an African sensibility. A type of "fixity" counters motion and is exposed as unfixed.

There is a tension promoted by thing-things placed against each other. That is to say, thing-things noted for their thingliness point a way. They are in this sense complex and layered arrangements of signs and symbols—a conduit of sorts—that gathers some of their emphasis through contact within the gallery space and contact between artistic "things" and viewers who enter anticipating that the art will "speak" to them, or that it should speak to them and should be recognizable as art not for its own sake but for their sake.

ABP     How do you pick items for your installations?

AM      I'm really comparing what's there. My real exhibition exercise is in the studio. This taxation results in a group morphing that constructs something more than was initially present. . . . My practice propels me to be more like someone who tends to the work, like a gardener or farmer.[38]

Things are and are not what they seem to be: They have a different and much more complex significance in that they come to be and represent multiple planes that extend beyond the thing itself to what it signifies and what it transforms. As things, and from particular perspectives, "things" are opaque, or dense, but there is another dimension to their import that renders them transparent—an opening by means of which we view larger considerations. This is the kaleidoscope effect of artistic expression.

Consider again the Vévé—the design made with things but that is believed to speak to an opening to worlds beyond those things that cannot be accessed without the Vévé's aid. This opening urges a certain range of questions as the symbol system is encountered: What are those things? What do they achieve when arranged in particular ways? In that, as Ian Hodder notes, "things are not isolated," and "things are not inert."[39] These are the questions concerning the porous nature of things that prompt and guide much of Metoyer's work. There is not a value judgment attached to this looking into things as a matter of artistic expression; rather, such simply is the nature of things when they are arranged consciously in time and space and are available to be viewed deeply—that is, in the context of their openness. Or, as Heather Pesanti notes, "Angelbert Metoyer is another kind of storyteller, perhaps a

3.4 *Father (2000)*. Used by permission of Angelbert Metoyer.

cosmological nomad interpreting the past, present, and future through an artistic lens. Fact and fiction weave together in the story of his life and work,
hinting at existential theories and fragmented memories of personal experience through painting, installations, sculpture, video and music."[40] Art, the
conscious placement in time and space of thing-things that in turn reshape
that time and space by means of their thingliness, opens rather than closes
off, exposes rather than limits, because "a work of art shows me the world I
inhabit; it shows me what a world is."[41]

This is certainly one way to think about *Dear Sirius-A (2015)*. The top half
of the piece is a gold-framed mirror—offering the viewer an opportunity to
examine the naming-thing, to view it as centered against the other thing-
things reflected by the mirror. The bottom portion, painted blue, contains
the covered image of a European woman with head bent. Between the mirror and this image of the woman is an African symbol. The image of self
is viewed against the self, against a Eurocentric rendition of beauty and
importance—or perfected self—and this is connected to the symbolism of
Africa as artifact. The viewer also recognizes that these three images emerge
out of a door, which is a thing opening space to other space—and inner space
to outer space. The door is a passage between locations and in this way a
means by which the self is transported and transfigured in relationship to
other selves initially hidden from our gaze. This is a process that begins directly after birth when, as a baby, one interacts with and absorbs "material"
from others, while also reshaping those same people through contact.[42] It is
a mutual and existential shifting that takes place.[43] There is in this process a
foreboding, a tension captured so well by Camus: "The contradiction is this:
man rejects the world as it is, without accepting the necessity of escaping
it. In fact, men cling to the world and by far the majority do not want to
abandon it. Far from always wanting to forget it, they suffer, on the contrary,
from not being able to possess it completely enough, estranged citizens of
the world, exiled from their own country."[44] Such is a journey made possible
by the charged space of the temple. Yes, again, the gallery is a temple of sorts,
in which time and space have a particular charge that urges recognition
of connection to other naming-things and thing-things.[45] The temple, as
Metoyer demonstrates, is a space defined by ritual movement and the markers of that movement—all drawn from us while drawing us to (and into) it. It
highlights particular cartographies—entering different space marked by de/
construction of assumed cultural codes used to articulate and arrange the
accepted technologies for socially authorized living.[46] In other words, in a
vein of thought not completely dissimilar from that offered by John Dewey,

"The product of art . . . is not the work of art. The work takes pace when a human being cooperates with the product."[47] Hence, one might say that the thingliness of things has something to do with the transmutability of things, which is the ability to transition, reflect, and mark.

Altars, totems, mirrors, moving images, and idols all point to questions that surround our existence, questions that have such profound significance that we isolate them and make them more than mundane, more than ordinary—all in an effort to hide our porous/open nature by practices of distinction. However, as Metoyer's work is meant to highlight, altars, totems, and so forth actually provide a passage to new dimensions by offering items that tug at bodied naming-things. Metoyer invites entrance in space framed, arranged, and outfitted with what is meant to foster a deeper view. Art and artistic display become prompts for exposure using vocabulary and grammar that privilege crafting of openness over against the descriptive properties of words to close off. *Jade Buddha* and *I-AOI (Room Full of Mirrors)* speak to the fluidity of identification as bodied naming-things and perception as the viewer confronts a mirror by means of which the viewer is also confronted by another image—a presentation that is both foreign and familiar. It is this awkward position of knowing something about what the mirror offers while also having not experienced that "something" that enhances the dissonance framing alternate modalities of possibility. It is a confrontation with the world as it impinges upon the "me" and "us" it has formed incompletely. There is in this gaze and the movement it prompts space for interrogation, for challenge, for desire. It is in this space that Metoyer wrestles with the dynamics of being a bodied naming-thing—a thing at the intersection of time and memory; the overlap of personal and collective histories; technologies of self-understanding in relationship to larger, more "objective" considerations of meaning; and all this in relationship to notions of knowledge and wisdom.[48] There, according to Metoyer's work, is no necessary or full distinction between the self, others, and the world. The barrier is a matter of awareness, of lucidity, rather than necessary ontological distinction. This involves a searching for ontological cover in a situation of epistemological exposure.

The viewer might expect to see herself and see herself reflected back—presenting a dimension of the self not normally realized and inspected. This would be the typical and comfortable experience, yet in *Jade Buddha* the mirror exposes the faint image of the Buddha—and reflects back a disregard for the materiality of existence (see fig. 3.5). It positions the viewer over against a subtle quest for awareness that means a certain type of dismissiveness. The

3.5 *Jade Buddha*. Used by permission of the Zi Koolhaas-Metoyer Trust and Angelbert Metoyer.

3.6 *I-AOI (Room Full of Mirrors)*. Used by permission of Angelbert Metoyer.

viewer engages a mechanism of self-awareness and sees in that moment the reflected presence of one who taught rejection of desire as a certain mode of self-regard. Something of a reprimand is evident in the eyes, and the look of the Buddha is both gentle and piercing. Something about that expression calls attention to the viewer's position and offers a soft call for introspection that goes deeper than the physical outline of one's existence evident in the reflected self. *The I-AOI (Room Full of Mirrors)* does not contain the same type of stoic look back at the viewer, but rather the viewer is confronted by the stare of the artist. An intense and displeased gaze confronts the viewer, whose natural inclination might be to wonder what occasioned this facial expression (see fig. 3.6). It probes subjectivity in relation to others by urging particular questions: What has occasioned that look? Why does that look impact me? How long must I entertain that look? Do I ever have such a look, and if so, in relation to whom? What are the consequences of this look for those to whom or at whom it is directed? How might they respond to this look, and what might that response mean to or do to me? The gaze sparks inspection and introspection, and the hope for Metoyer is that this process produces greater clarity regarding oneself and one's surroundings.

From self-portraits to pieces urging introspection, Metoyer's work taken together prompts confrontation with (personal and collective) history and offers tools for rethinking the embodied and "spiritual" nature of existence beyond what the word can carry. And it thereby pushes into what the fluidity of boundaries between things (form and function) might entail. In such space the rituals of life are noted, expressed, and interrogated for what they say about the embodied and more ephemeral dimensions of our existence— our occupation of time and space as bodied naming-things in relationship to thing-things. In the next chapter, attention is turned away from the presentation of thing-things, to the manipulation of the naming-thing as a way to speak openness—the fluidity of boundaries.

# the "stuff" of performance        4

I think twenty-first century should be art without objects.
—MARINA ABRAMOVIC, TV interview

Oh my body, make of me always a man who questions!
—FRANTZ FANON, *Black Skin, White Masks*

The following scene is from *The New Disciples*, a novel I wrote a few years ago:

> [Marina] Abramovic and [Kira] O'Reilly explore the ways in which pain
> and manipulation of the body allow interrogation of the limits of the body.
> These artists we saw that afternoon did that through cutting themselves
> with a series of knives and having it recorded. One of the artists was on a
> stage surrounded by the audience and the other was below the floorboards
> with a similar set of knives, and he mirrored the artist on stage by cut-
> ting himself on the opposite arm for example, or leg. According to the
> posted information, the purpose was to demonstrate the links between
> the visible body and the unconscious represented by the artist below the
> stage. The idea . . . is to test the limits of the body, to unpack and expose
> the way the manipulation of the body is felt and perceived. The fact that
> both artists were standing in what seemed awkward and perhaps pain-
> ful positions was meant to increase the viewer's awareness of the ways in

which pain is communicated and how it informs our thought and behavior. The body becomes both the means for understanding sensation and also the product of sensation. The body becomes fully aware of itself and known by others.[1]

In this section of the story a professor provides context for questionable activity: She had used the manipulation (i.e., cutting) of bodies to fuel the creativity necessary to finish the book that would gain her tenure. In the quotation above, she is discussing with a priest, Father Ford, what first triggered her turn to the physical penetration of the bodied naming-thing. She comes to realize a deep connection between herself as a naming-thing and her circumstances. In her case, the cutting of other naming-things, and eventually herself, produced states of mind and being that entailed a reimaging of relationships: naming-thing—thing-thing—naming-thing—thing-thing, and so on. The knife (thing-thing) and the body (naming-thing) cut by the knife gave her sensations that made possible the production of her manuscript (thing-thing).

## Performance

My limited encounter with Marina Abramovic inspired for me possibilities concerning the ways in which manipulation of bodied naming-things vis-à-vis exchange with other naming-things in relationship to thing-things might add perspective to my presentation of religion as a technology.[2] The vibrant encounter between time, space, naming-things, and other things all entwined captures, reads, and thinks that mapping of interplay. Performance art, then, is always and already a matter of interconnections to and between various cultural codes and social programs.[3] By extension, there is, I argue, a symbiotic relationship between art—in this case performance art—and religion as a technology in that they enact the same consideration on what Amelia Jones in another context calls "a different register."[4] I would add that this alternate "register" includes a grammar and vocabulary that capture what religion as a technology exposes, and articulates it mindful of its inherent fluidity. While still entailing a mediated modality of expression, its permissive and provocative nature gives performance art a receptive quality that makes it ideal for exposing and naming openness and interplay.[5] Performance art, as it is, implodes traditional arrangements of religious practices and teachings in the form of traditions such as Roman Catholicism and Protestant Pentecostalism, but it is just the type of structuring of experience that can enliven religion as I have sought to define and present it—a theorization of religion that assumes no intentional forms, privileges no particular intent, and challenges the very nature of religion as a "something" as opposed to a method of seeing.[6] This mode of artistic activity "embodies" the inclinations advanced by this technology regarding the openness of things in that it "has been a medium that challenges and violates borders between disciplines and genders, between private and public, and between everyday life and art, and that follows no rules."[7] The resulting and central questions are as follows: What are the limits of the naming-thing, and what are the limits of the naming-thing's ability to "speak" through the manipulation of itself as thing-thing? What are the necessary (if any distinctions) between bodied naming-thing and thing-thing?

What I intend to portray in the following pages will become clear. But for now, I simply point to an observation made by Allan Kaprow regarding the nature and function of art. He refuses to make a distinction between life and art, instead referencing "lifelike art" over against "artlike art."[8] The latter assumes art is a distinct modality of expression that is disconnected from mundane experience in any significant way. However, the former reflects art as already and always connected to life. It is, in his words, "art in the service of life."[9] It is this posture or function of "service" that is significant here. But rather than life in more general terms, I posit the benefit of understanding (and interrogating) art as the presentation of the openness of things. This is more than religious art, and more fundamentally lodged in the structuring of thing-things and naming-things than that. Or, as Kaprow notes regarding "lifelike art," "It is not a 'thing' like a piece of music or a sculpture that is put into a special art container or setting. It is inseparable from real life."[10]

## On the Art of Performance

The development of performance art is tied to sociopolitical shifts and changes in cultural sensibilities (toward collective life) during tumultuous years of the mid-twentieth century. Old artistic postures and assumptions failed to capture the times. Hence, "work," writes Lynn MacRitchie, "which came to be called live or performance art emerged most powerfully in Europe and the United States at moments of artistic or social crisis, when formal aesthetic or social structures were perceived to be inadequate or had actually collapsed."[11] Marked by World War II and followed by the Vietnam War, the trauma of violence on an international level, in all its existential madness, could not be soothed or even explored using artistic practices that maintained as stable the naming-things that were in fact the fuel for world conditions. Performance art entailed confrontation so as to urge reconsideration of naming-things by, in a deep and significant way, linking what they do to what they are.

Hence, using performance art, I make a turn and consider how one might think about bodied naming-things manipulating themselves as thing-things and thereby blurring if not destroying distinction.[12] This turn further shifts dynamics and creates awareness that neither naming-things nor thing-things have fixed meaning or function. Both are defined in a significant manner through their "li-ness": naming-thingliness and thing-thingliness. Here "li-ness" is meant to suggest a particular vibrancy that calls attention to the "qualities" of the naming-thing and thing-thing and in the process draws viewers and artists into circumstances otherwise invisible.[13] The conflation of naming-thing and thing-thing fosters this move because, again, it rejects the assumption of sustainable distinction.[14] A clear example of this is Jim Dine's *The Smiling Workman* (1960) in which, "dressed in a red smock, with hands and head painted red, and a large black mouth, he drank from jars of paint while painting 'I love what I'm . . .' on a large canvas, before pouring the remaining paint over his head and leaping through the canvas."[15]

To the extent it concerns itself with the portrayal of life in its ordinary arrangements and activities, performance art often requires a "space" of exchange beyond the restrictions of the formal gallery. Artistic movements such as Pop Art, Neo-Expressionism, and so on raised questions concerning the proper form and content of art, yet the questions raised by performance art push through a refusal to allow firm boundaries between artist and viewer. It raises issues regarding the nature of art but pushes the boundary by not simply challenging the nature of a thing-thing as art (i.e., Pop Art) or the naming-thing as the proper story and source of art, but instead it blurs the line between naming-thing and thing-thing.[16] I say this mindful of the manner in which performance art's "in the moment" quality supports my assertions but also poses a challenge noted by numerous scholars and artists: few are able to experience this mode of art "in real time" but rather come to know it through books, films, photographs, and so forth that reify it somewhat and move it at least a degree or two away from the initial expression of interplay. This work is of a limited duration. "Live" performance destabilizes by removing the opportunity to fix and reflect. The "work" of art takes place in "real" time and demands attention without the ability to hold and process at a later moment. It's gone, done, and there are memory and representations to provide a cartography of engagement and response. As Laurie

Anderson says when reflecting on developments during the late twentieth century, "Live art is especially ephemeral. Once performed, it tends to become myth and a few photos and tapes." It is, in a word, "an art form that resists documentation."[17] Still, this qualification notwithstanding, it offers a useful framework. There is support for my argument regarding the limited impact of this qualification in a thought offered by Laurie Carlos: "It is the element of duration, of time, that is at the heart of a performance. But there is a time of experiencing and a time of memory, of reliving in the imagination, and there is no essential contradiction between the two."[18] Nonetheless, the "live" quality also demands the involvement of other naming-things; demands can be made of the viewer that cannot be made when the viewer leaves the space and enters back into familiar restraint. To directly encounter performance art in the moment is to be pulled and pushed, to have naming-things engaged and challenged.[19] There are more pointed examples of this, such as "do-it-yourself artworks" in connection to which the viewer might be given a series of instructions or invitations that involve her doing the art by following the prompts provided.[20]

The ability to buy performance art would entail a falling back into distinction between naming-things and thing-things that this modality of art intends to disrupt. It is not knowledge for purchase; instead, it is to be experienced. Nonetheless, this statement is accurate only if "ownership" is understood in particular ways. When performance artists such as Yves Klein "sold" art, the transaction was simply symbolic and pointed to the inability to actually own the art with which he concerned himself. In other words,

> Klein sought a way to evaluate his "immaterial pictorial sensitivity" and decided that pure gold would be a fair exchange. He offered to sell it to any person willing to purchase such an extraordinary, if intangible, commodity, in exchange for gold leaf. . . . Gold leaf and a receipt changed hands between the artist and the purchaser. But since "immaterial sensitivity" could be nothing but a spiritual quality, Klein insisted that all remains of the transaction be destroyed: he threw the gold leaf into the river [Seine, February 10, 1962] and requested that the purchaser burn the receipt.[21]

Still, one should measure this act of commercialism against reflection on performance art by others like Clifford Owens, who says the following when thinking about more recent developments: "After all, dealers don't profit from performance art unless they inflate the value of documentary photographs of performances; hustle performance-based videos on DVD a practice I find criminal and exploitative; or sell dumb performance objects as sculpture. And museums and institutions generally don't fund performance art events because they are not willing to jeopardize federal funding or take curatorial risk."[22] The questionable ability to directly buy performance art as noted here does not mean it is beyond containment, cannot be captured so to speak, or that it cannot be made a moment in the historical record. Books, catalogues, interviews, articles, and so forth capture not the moment of performance—its quality of movement—but rather they allow an "artist's print" or a shadow or still shot of the event. I say this merely to provide a bit of balance by acknowledging the temporality of performance art—its resistance to confinement—while also noting the manner in which it is unable to fully and finally escape re-presentation or repetition.[23] On this point, keep in mind the words of Clifford Owens: "Copyrighting has never really been about art. Copyrighting is about commerce, commodities. One reason I've always been interested in performance art is that it isn't easily commodifiable. Some people are making a living at it. I've been fortunate enough to sell some work, but this practice was never intended as a moneymaker. In fact, it's costing a fortune (laughter)."[24]

Drawing inspiration directly or indirectly from figures such as Dada artist Duchamp and housed most firmly in Northern California and New York City, some body artists or performance artists, as they were called as of the 1970s, understood the naming-thing as a material by means of and through which art was produced. That is to say, through Duchamp's ready-mades or manipulations of the physical body, an artistic move developed that refused to distinguish the body over against other materials. Distinction between the naming-thing and thing-things—found or created—had little significance because product no longer was an important dimension of art. To the extent the clothed naming-thing was often viewed at least aesthetically as a distinct thing, particular modalities of performance art often involved the naming-thing without such covering, but instead the naked body became similar to any other uncovered thing present and open to manipulation and use—but also holding a certain integrity of form.[25]

Dada (and the early twentieth-century German school of "total" art called Bauhaus, for that matter) manipulated the body and called for more attention to process, as opposed to a finished and fixed "piece" that could be called art, but performance art—particularly in its more aggressive forms—interrogates the very distinction between naming-things and thing-things. Furthermore, it involves viewers in this questioning in new and at times disturbing ways.[26] The 1959 *18 Happenings in 6 Parts* by Allan Kaprow at the Reuben Gallery in New York City—with its slides, music, readings, and so forth, all conducted in three rooms—"changed the game," so to speak, and marked a major shift in performance art toward the practices with which we are most familiar.[27] Still, the meaning of performance art—that is, what is captured (and excluded) by that concept—remained somewhat illusive. "Performance is dead! Long live performance! This [so it goes] declaration reflects the paradoxical situation in which we find ourselves when we consider a contemporary understanding of performance within the sphere of visual art."[28] Despite tensions between differing ideas of performance art's content and meaning, there seems at least one common factor: naming-thing, as fixed, stable, and distinct, is troubled often in graphic and aggressive ways.[29] "Performance art," writes Dominic Johnson, "emerges as a means of testing how to live—to live more fully, more atypically, more perversely or more effectively than one might do without the sustaining practice of performance."[30] Any effort to sanitize art, to render it devoid of material consequence, to give it a purpose beyond the connotations of material life, was rejected as naming-things were pushed to the point of breaking and were exposed to pain and suffering. Thing-things and naming-things were brought into a felt interrelationality.

The naming-thing is put on display in certain instances, and in this process it is connected to thing-things in such a way as to reconfigure both—thereby becoming a way of filtering historical experience by absorbing particular dimensions of it and dismissing others. Lynn MacRitchie, in reflecting on the function of performance art in the late twentieth century, says, "The real and terrible destruction wrought by two world wars had made a mockery of any idealization of violent social change, however, and the development of live work post 1945 followed a dual path. While continuing to expand and explore its original premise of the critique of the position and purpose of the art object and the academic institutions, artists' own bodies, their physical being, came to be considered as a site of knowledge and a vehicle for affecting healing and transformation."[31] Conscious occupation of time and space took on a new significance with performance art.

### Performing Art

In some performance art the porous nature of the bodied naming-thing is highlighted through manipulation—exposing it naked and hypervisible. With regard to violence inflicted, performance art chronicles the manner in which penetration speaks to levels of clarity and lucidity that are valueless otherwise.[32] A process of mutilation and ritualized pain renders the naming-thing somehow more than itself. Outside such ritualized infliction known within traditional modalities of religious systems, performance art in general and body art or live art in particular seek to make felt (through the testing of strength and endurance of interplay) the manner in which thingliness is vibrant. Going back to Camus's analysis of Sisyphus, this heightened awareness, one would think, has something to do with the stress and strain—physicality as ritualized discomfort:[33]

> As for the myth, one sees merely the whole effort of a body straining to raise the huge stone, to roll it and push it up a slope a hundred times over; one sees A face screwed up, the cheek tight against the stone, the shoulder bracing the Clay-covered mass, the foot wedging it, the fresh start with arms outstretched, the wholly human security of two earth-clotted hands. . . . It is during that return, that pause, that Sisyphus interests me. . . . That hour like a breathing-space which Returns as surely as his suffering, that is the hour of consciousness.[34]

Think of Camus's depiction of Sisyphus's pain. This is not a theodical description in that it flies in the face of the gods as opposed to marking out an effort to justify them. Instead, it speaks to Sisyphus's performance (art) as a means of framing a process of exploration that urges a rethinking. Now compare Camus's depiction of Sisyphus and his stone to the description of the self-mutilation or living art of Ron Athey. There are clear distinctions, but a shared perception of naming-thing in pain as source of lucidity—without a theodical twist. "In Athey's work," remarks Dominic Johnson, "the triumphant conversion of disaster into a type of agency perhaps relies on his appropriation of body modification, as a troubled yet potent means of claiming agency over one's own body."[35] Sisyphus and his stone pushed, and Athey and his body pierced, point to the working of the naming-thing as/with thing-things. Sisyphus, monitored by the will of the gods, and Athey, always aware of the types of confinement that sociocultural codes of conduct mean within the West, offer body performance as response to authoritative demands for unity. In both instances, movement as performance of ritualized pain entails an artistic tackling of experience without much regard for traditional entertainment quality.[36] In a belligerent twist, both Sisyphus and Athey defy notions of the divine as distinct—Sisyphus through his defiance and Athey through his re-presentation of Christian mythology (e.g., martyrdom of saints reenacted). Performance art emphasizes the manner in which the naming-thing and thing-thing do not simply connect but instead become indistinguishable over against traditional markers of difference or relationship; the affective language of this is "pain" and "ecstasy."

Performance art amplifies activity over against the consequences of that activity (e.g., static work of art that exists after the "happening"). By so doing, it undercuts the ability to single out the naming-thing as that which produces thing-things—with the distinction lodged in the reified form of the thing-thing over against the active naming-thing. Still, the consequence remains somewhat consistent: performance art urges interrogation of things for what they tell us about circumstances and relationships to those circumstances. In its most graphic forms, performance art uses extreme manipulations of the naming-thing to bring to the fore a fluidity of form that in turn opens to increased awareness. For example, Metoyer's exhibits bring viewers into play as they move around the works and are drawn into the conversations urged by the configuration of new and found thing-things, and in this way they are brought into a framework of questioning themselves as naming-things. Yet this is not the same as the manner in which performance art brings the viewer into the project as part of the process of artistic expression. What is Abramovic's *Marina Abramovic: The Artist Is Present* without viewers sitting across from her, looking back into her as she sits motionless looking into them?[37]

Time and space remain the location, so to speak, for art, but neither is confined or cataloged in the same manner as when the traditional matrix of presence is used. That is to say, what "gallery" means alters through use.[38] Performance art—with its emphasis on process rather than product—configures time and space without concern with traditional thinking on artistic locations (in that the naming-thing and thing-things are the mobile location), but it is not ahistorical—for example, Ron Athey's work reflects on church history and does so as theater. Referencing the shift to performance art, Henry Sayre says the following: "Art is no longer that thing in which full-fledged aesthetic experience is held perpetually present; art no longer transcends history; instead, it admits its historicity, its implication in time."[39] The activity or process is hidden within other modalities of expression discussed in this volume. Only documentaries about the artists or their films, in the case of Metoyer, offer a glimpse into process, but this is an aside easily distinguished from the product, which is the primary focus for the artist. With performance art, the name—although its descriptive quality will ebb and flow—says so much about its focus: performance/process. Perhaps there is something about this arrangement, this commitment to process over against old standards of product, that lingers in the words of Abramovic. "The hardest thing," she reflects, "is to do something which is close to nothing."[40]

Thing-things used by a naming-thing are typically covered or transformed in such a way as to hide their initial design and utility. For example, pieces of paper no longer serve to present a complete image put in place by a naming-thing, and a refrigerator is no longer used to store foodstuffs. With performance art, thing-things and their initial function (e.g., knives are made to cut things) are not hidden but highlighted, and what is changed or made less visible are assumptions regarding the anthropology of the bodied naming-thing and its defined integrity. This is not the context of the surgery room, where naming-things use thing-things to maintain the distinct integrity of the naming-thing over against the tool used in the process. Still, even a medical space can serve as the location for body art, or performance art. One need only keep in mind the performance of body pain used to speak the porous and troubling nature of the naming-thing as represented by French artist Orlan, who used plastic surgery as a method of "bio-art" by means of which public surgeries serve to, in the words of Amelia Jones, test "the integrity of the embodied self by literally slicing through its boundaries."[41] It is true that technological advances through artificial limbs and so on become means by which thing-things alter naming-things, but not in ways that speak to the same public display of a porous or penetrable quality that remains visible rather than hidden. That is to say, the artificial limb is intended to be hidden; bio-art, as done by Orlan, is meant to keep visible and in tension foreignness and sameness. With technological change, the idea is to hide the penetration of the thing-thing so as to enhance the naming-thing as unified.[42] But this is not so with performance art.

### Bringing Something to Things

While the social coding layered on naming-things is discussed more fully in the final section of the book, it is important to say at this point that some performance art—for example, as produced by women and racial minorities—constantly reminds viewers that the sign of cultural penetrations marks these naming-things even before the artist "marks" them. Issues related to the cultural constructions of race, gender, and sexuality were often explored using performance art, and there is much to think about in such attacks on the confinements of cultural constructions.[43] As Valerie Cassel Oliver reflects,

> For black artists, the emphasis on "body as material" does not come without its own historical tethers. The black body carries within it signifiers and markers that are deeply rooted in historical narratives. They embody

the evolution, transcendence, and complexities of that same body long ago unshackled, affirmed, self-determined, and now immersed in myriad discourses that encompass multiethnic heritages, gender, and queer and transgender identity, as well as uncharted otherness. The performing self is at times the embodiment of the collective, and at other times it is simply the liberated individual exploring the conundrum of his or her own multifaceted being.[44]

A graphic example that binds together race, gender, and sexuality is *Sally's Rape* by Robbie McCauley and Jeannie Hutchins. It involves McCauley, an African American, on an auction block with members of the audience being directed by Hutchins, a white woman, to bid on McCauley.[45] One can add Spider Woman Theater, Bill T. Jones, and Arnie Zane Company, who explore issues of cultural configurations of race and gender.[46] Or there is something of what I am suggesting in the words of Lea Vergine when reflecting on body art turns in the 1990s:

> The use of the body as a language has returned to the scene of the world around us in new and different forms, and it speaks through altered declinations. The body as triumphant, immolated, diffused, propagated, dramatic, and tragic. The political, social, and mystic body. The body as the site of the extreme. . . . By way of tattoos, piercings, and citations of tribalism. Through manipulations of its organs. The instrument that speaks and communicates without the word, or sounds, or drawing. The body as a vehicle, once again, for declaring opposition to the dominant culture, but also of desperate conformism.[47]

Performance art by African Americans, like its counterparts (i.e., performance art by non–African Americans), pushes the naming-thing/thing-thing dynamic and does so within the context of a public. The encounter happens in a way that is reminiscent of what takes place within the context of white artists. The bodied naming-thing in both contexts—white artists and black artists—is supple, flexible, porous, penetrated, shifted, marked, and changed as it flows between what we have typically regarded as fixed categories of meaning: subject and object. Yet there is another dimension to performance art by African Americans that is inherent. In a word, there are other cultural codes (e.g., blackness, blackness and gender, blackness and gender and class) assigned to those naming-things, other ways in which the blending of naming-thing/thing-thing is challenged, but in this case not for the benefit of African Americans. The challenges of being and doing that have shaped the racial, sexual, and class (and, for black women, gender) dynamics defining the discourse on bodies in the United States is not bracketed off by performance art. Yes, performance art provides a way of interrogating, but it does so from within epistemological frameworks and strategies that speak to and about naming-things even as artists challenge these frameworks. This amplifies questions of what these naming-things are doing and what distinguishes them from other things—both having been understood historically as valuable for their utility—"blackened" naming-things as tools of labor and gratification and as references for white privilege. Perhaps this is one reason discussion of performance art from the 1970s to the present has privileged culturally white bodies in performance. Yet this discursive shadowing, if not silencing in certain ways, does not speak an unquestionable truth. To the contrary, African American performance artists have used this genre of artistic expression to raise and wrestle with questions of fundamental importance. As Cassel Oliver remarks, black performance art "occupies the liminal space between black eccentricity and bodacious behavior, between political protest and social criticism."[48] With a particular focus on black women performance artists, Uri McMillan speaks of "performing objecthood" as a way of expressing the manner in which black women manipulate their bodies to constitute thing-things. Or for McMillan, "avatars" challenge common perceptions and assumptions concerning black women as bodied naming-things and how they rightly occupy time and space. The development of alternate personalities and performing these personalities opened for artists such as Lorraine O'Grady ways to both represent and critique sociocultural codes.

In part, the impact of this method of expression involves the manner in which it challenges both traditional and more "progressive" depictions of the dichotomy of naming-thing/thing-thing by denying any totalizing properties for either. The legacy of slavery and ongoing discrimination notwithstanding, the latter half of that metaphysical equation can be presented—rather, performed—without having it reify a particular understanding.[49] This, for McMillan, has been the art of body performance utilized by black women for centuries. In a word, naming-thing/thing-thing relationships can in fact interrogate and expose restrictive and reifying sociocultural codes; it is not a necessary consequence that such performance can only reinforce the political status quo by means of art. Take, for example, Adrian Piper as discussed by McMillan as a key and deeply influential conceptual and performance artist. The manipulation of her body (in *Mythic Being: Cruising White Women* from 1973) involves shifting markers of identity and hence of social meaning, as she dons a new "uniform"—an Afro wig, clothing, glasses, and other markers of the 1970s—and performs a version of masculinity that signifies cultural codes of gender and consequently of agency.[50] Thing-things in this case— glasses, a wig, facial hair, and so forth—gain the type of agency noted by Bill Brown and other advocates of thing theory. Thing-things penetrate cultural identity, and shift and change it like the power of a talisman. Yet in this case they promote the transformation of gender, blurring thereby lines between the coding of masculinity and femininity. In addition, the Afro wig with its ties to black culture during the 1970s speaks a word regarding the embodiment of racial categorizations and discourse that have something to do with the metaphysical quality of cultural engagement. Still, this time, the tone and texture of that discourse and those categorizations are signified through performance: female to male and thing-thing to naming-thing. Is this artist the black male as threat that one fears, or an exaggerated being that one mocks? Or might it be the exotic beauty one desires? Is "it" the despised mixed race being betwixt and between cultural worlds? In what ways can the difference be discerned if it is not fixed? Upon what bases is authenticity determined and judged within a context of shifting things? The transformed naming-thing glares at the passersby and in that gaze turns them (through recognition) into naming-things. In an essay related to *Mythic Being*, Piper says the following, which speaks in significant ways to what we typically understand as totalizing properties and positionality of naming-things and thing-things: "I was trying to develop my arena by becoming an object in it. I now want to become the arena itself; I want to be, for a while, a consciousness within which I view myself and other objects. I'm thinking of the ghostly spectator, eternally viewing, taking in everything, recording and reflecting on everything, but not being an object of refraction him-herself because invisible."[51]

For Piper, the sociopolitical and cultural upheaval that marked the late twentieth century could not be ignored, and artistic production, particularly that which encompassed the primacy of the naming-thing, was a strong instrument for making statements regarding the racial, gender, and militarized destruction of personhood and agency. For her, like Metoyer to some extent, this meant emphasizing the transient nature of the naming-thing as well as the ability of the artist who emphasizes the bodied naming-thing to think of artistic space beyond the confines established by the formal and formalistic art world. She, in a literal sense, would take her art to the streets and perform it in front of nontraditional audiences, but it was not simply the wearing of a different identity. No, something about the performance also entailed her recognizing and tapping into the complexity of her own identity—the maleness of herself.[52] This "mythic being" points to a meta-symbol of cultural and social anxiety projected onto certain naming-things through discursive pronouncements housed within a process of interrogation and spectacle. Something "unifying" about this perception of the raced naming-thing gives it a type of narrative strength and reach that could not be captured by simply calling it the "black" being, or the "cultural" being, or even the "raced" being.[53] This conceptual strength allows the identity of the mythic being to penetrate, to impinge upon the artist in such a way as to blur lines of authority and agency. Put differently, as John Bowles recognizes, "Piper alienates herself from her self-image and from her artwork. In the first case, she renders herself available for self-reflection. In the second, the *Mythic Being* embodies a stereotype drawn from the popular imagination. Piper's earliest statements about the Mythic Being present him as someone whom she imagines is performing her."[54] Naming-things, when performed, blend into each other, fostering in the process new structuring(s) of cultural linkage with the capacity to short circuit social codes. Naming-things and thing-things are rendered fluid, and the social codes (e.g., masculinity and femininity) supporting structures of time and space are exposed and, through performance, questioned.

Such art, as represented by Piper and Clifford Owens among many others, arranges and confronts bodied naming-things/thing-things in such a way as to problematize social assumptions and predictable patterns of cultural engagement. It is real-time encounter that, unlike with "flat" works of art such as paintings, cannot be held off and processed later in the safety and comfort of one's inherited epistemology of life devoid of confrontation and conflict. Performance art, one might say, removes the cushion of distance and makes the encounter with naming-things/thing-things sustained, somewhat unpredictable, and marked by an arrangement of time outside the control of the audience. Inherent in performance art, for both the artist and the viewer-participant, is vulnerability. Unlike looking at a painting hung meticulously on a wall, performance art's shaping and running of time is more unfixed and warped. Perhaps this is one reason Piper's thought-provoking and transformative work has been called such things as "off-putting" and marked by an artist with a "morally bullying tone"—which is precisely the point.[55] Confrontation with bias and symbols of racial-gender injustice cannot be comfortable and simply insinuated with cultural decorum if it is to have even the hope of being useful. Piper produces an altered presentation of naming-things, complete with them covered in a variety of cultural signifiers. In a word, she assumes "different personae (she's a skilled and witty performer) and changing her looks as if she were herself a kind of malleable conceptual object."[56] And in this way, she forces viewers to recognize the characterizations of race, gender, sexuality, and class that promote their legacy. By playing these significations out, she offers an opportunity to dismantle them.

Discomfort is a tool used to disrupt thinking and the "doings" of naming-things. Piper disrupts social and cultural codes regarding gender play—for example, expression of desire—by shifting the appearance of her naming-thing through costume and custom (i.e., who gets to actively observe and perhaps pursue partners). The fluidity of identity that marks the naming-thing in relationship to thing-things grants opportunity to manipulate gender symbols and practices so as to short-circuit their internal logic and status. In that the costume is clearly a costume, observers on the street are unsettled epistemologically by the individual performance that mocks social performance.

It is interesting to note that Clifford Owens intends a similar type of work. Both Piper and Owens indicate social awareness and commitment through performance.[57] The script, so to speak, can be generated internally—coming from the artist and projected out. This is how Owens typically works. "I make art in my head," he reflects, "from my heart, and *through my body*." This is all to note the manner in which the naming-thing/thing-thing engagement and interplay for such artists moves from the naming-thing as artist to thing-things and naming-things as viewers and/or participants.[58] However, for his 2011 *Anthology* work for MoMA, Owens moved in another direction through an alternate highlighting of the naming-thing/thing-thing dynamic. He invited other artists to provide a total of twenty-six scripts—arranged activities and performances—that he would then undertake as his work of art. For instance, artist Kara Walker provided the following: "French kiss an audience member. Force them against a wall and demand sex. The audience/viewer should be an adult. If they are willing to participate in the forced sex act abruptly turn the tables and you assume the role of victim. Accuse your attacker. Seek help from others describe your ordeal. Repeat."[59] Using photographs and other thing-things (e.g., food and urine), along with particular arrangements of time and space, with *Anthology* Owens performed instructed movements in ways that reflect past activities by various artists (a process akin to what he has called "response" to "artists practices" over against reperforming).[60] He interpreted their work in line with his own sensibilities by having his naming-thing manipulated per the instructions given—such as kissing an audience member and so on. In this way, his naming-thing/thing-thing dynamic was highlighted by the shadow of other naming-things arranging and determining the flow of presence and practice.

The experience tugged at this naming-thing and in the process used other naming-things as "tools" impacting and penetrating him. The sensations and discomfort produced said something about sociocultural codes of conduct as well as the markers of time and space framed by relationship between naming-thing and thing-thing. A full range of emotional and psychological processes was enacted as part of this performance: Owens as naming-thing encountered the agency of other naming-things. Notions of community, of relationship, of the integrity and agency of the human as a matter of theological and cultural anthropology were tested. In his words, "Audience members kissed me, kicked me, slapped me, embraced me, dragged me, hoisted me, humiliated me, humbled me, befriended me, loved me, hated me, harmed me, hurt me, moved me, touched me, abandoned me, rescued me, stalked me, harassed me, intimidated me, frightened me, abused me, used me, exploited me, repulsed me, and some would later fuck me."[61]

The collaborative quality of performance art is made graphic vis-à-vis this process, but also exposed is risk entailed through an ethics of mutuality that leaves participants exposed (often literally) and open to what the human mind can imagine as the business of naming-things/thing-things/naming-things colliding both literally and figuratively. Within the space of the MoMA and expressed as interactive performance, Owens mapped out the movements and encounters that have shaped the sociocultural context of life in the United States for centuries. And he did so in a way that highlighted what we have already known on some level to be central. More to the point, for Owens, blackened naming-things matter, and through their work black performance artists enact the merit of this statement. There is in this multi-layered movement (that depends on numerous naming-things in coordinated flow) a blurring effect in that the end product holds only hints of this orchestration. The thing-things' bare codes are transformed into ritualized actions.

One can interpret the work of Piper and Owens through explicit attention to traditional religious-theological vocabulary and symbol systems. For instance, Piper's turn to costume might suggest something of the effort of religious figures such as Joan of Arc to morph identity through gender identification as a soldier. Or consider some devotees of Krishna who dress as women in order to portray Radha, who is significant for Krishna, or devotees of African-based traditions such as Candomblé who, when possessed, are changed into attire consistent with that particular divinity, which can involve men dressing as women and performing (dancing) in ways that reflect social codes of femininity. While Piper's morphing highlights shifts in active sexual desire performed, for Joan of Arc this shift of the naming-thing highlights the rituals of aggression typically associated with males. Although different in significant ways, what both entail, or can be read as suggesting, is the manner in which signifying presentation of the naming-thing has significant connotations that impact relationality to social ideals. Furthermore, at least one commentator has noted the manner in which the movement of Owens as bodied naming-thing by audience members around the performance space resembles the manipulation and transportation of the body of Christ in so many religious paintings.[62]

Such observations are intriguing, yet they map performance art on traditionally understood framings of the religious, while I want to point to a different perception of the religious. Mindful of this, I note that without words but through presentation and play, Piper and Owens raise fundamental challenges to assumptions of closed and fixed "things." True, the performance is focused on disruption of particular codes of conduct; still, the dissonance created allows for much more expansive consideration. Owens reinforces social codes and body practices, but even in this he causes disruption to the extent that the naming-thing is marked "black" and hence is already out of place and beyond the scope of its social freedoms. For instance, the script given him by Walker plays off centuries-old cultural assumptions regarding black men as sexual predators, but the performance seeks to disrupt agency and in the process points out the complex nature of American sexual terrorism: "You," as Walker instructs, "assume the role of victim." Hence, the naming-thing both penetrates other naming-things and is penetrated by them, and through this complexity performed in alternate space and as public act, the coding of sexual relations in the United States is exposed and highlighted. The interrelated nature of naming-thing to naming-thing is highlighted through the interactive quality of the series of performances while also pointing out the manner in which some influences, some actors so to speak, are not visible yet are still present (i.e., those providing the scripts). Put simply, writes Christopher Lew, "audience members are invited to talk back, to step to the fore and interact with the artist or each other; food and objects are thrown about; articles of clothing are removed or exchanged; physical violence is implied; rape and autocastration threatened."[63] Attentiveness to naming-things in action poses important questions concerning care, empathy, sympathy, agency, identity, freedom, and other qualities of engagement and positioning that matter. Piper and Owen offer what was at an earlier point in this chapter a particular "register" of human engagement with circumstances.

This work, performance art by African Americans as well as other so-called racial minorities, is important in that it says something about the sociocultural coding that informs what we say and "know" about naming-things. However, while it is important, here I am not concerned with the psychological work of performance art; my focus is not on the nature and meaning of subjectivity as articulated through performance art. Instead, my interest rests in this genre of art's ability to speak what the naming-thing is (and is not) in light of deep connection to thing-things—and it does so without full restriction of the spoken or written language. "Live work by artists," Laurie Carlos makes clear, "unites the psychological with the perceptual, the conceptual with the practical, thought with action."[64] So conceived, one can easily recognize the manner in which persistent attention to naming-things within performance art presents the bodied naming-thing, at least in part, as an alternate and dynamic language employable for the articulation of a particular range of considerations.

## Are They Beautiful or Ugly Things?

As stated earlier, my concern is not aesthetics—certainly not as understood prior to the shift in artistic thinking and production marked by the mid-twentieth century. Yet I am intrigued: Does performance art as discussed throughout this chapter further damage the reifying effects of beauty or theories of wholeness by entangling naming-things/thing-things in a web of what is typically referenced as ugly? Ugly behavior? Ugly appearance? Ugly surroundings?[65] And finally, are there ways in which discussion of race, gender, sexuality, and class are interrogated in performance art not always as they relate to sociopolitical justice, as is typically the approach, but rather through play with naming-thing/thing-thing in the domain of beauty/ugliness and pain/pleasure assumptions that undergird and to some degree guide the more commonly addressed structures of sociopolitical justice?

I offer just a few thoughts related to these questions before moving back into the general discussion of naming-thing/thing-thing implosion. And I begin with this statement from RoseLee Goldberg concerning troubling behavior as art:

> Public display of sex and death and other private concerns was a statement of artistic solidarity against the conservative backlash of the 1990s. The material was unquestionably shocking to even the most emancipated of audience. Bob Flanagan, suffering from cystic fibrosis, endured hours of excruciating physical therapy in a hospital bed in *Visiting Hours*, an installation at the Santa Monica Museum of Art in California (1992).

Male strippers, drag queens and drug-abusers participated in Ron Athey's *Martyrs and Saints* (1993), an hour-long work which included self-inflicted wounds so gruesome that several members of the audience passed out.[66]

As the naming of his performances more than suggests, an intriguing element of Athey's work involves the interrogation of traditional religious rituals and practices that are meant to discipline and control bodied naming-things.[67] However, mindful of his early years in a deeply religious household that claimed ministry as part of his future, he amplifies the discipline and punishment of the body, tying it to pleasure and in this way exploding categories of religious repentance and purification. The fact that ritualization of naming-things in/as pain is conducted by a white male (at times over against a black naming-thing assistant) raises questions concerning the relationship between whiteness and the exercise of control vis-à-vis pain and discipline of naming-things as well as modalities of "confession" of whiteness that both makes visible and renders undetected the pleasure of white privilege performed. These are important considerations, but they are beyond the purpose of this chapter in particular and this book in general.[68] Instead, I want to resist my intellectual-political inclination to more fully interrogate race dynamics and the cultural power being performed, and instead consider implications in a general sense as they relate to what has been a traditional religiously motivated activity on/with naming-things.

What the graphic depiction of ritualized aggression, the blood, and the penetration and marking of the bodied naming-thing points out is the degree to which traditional modalities of religiously understood practices within spaces perceived "sacred" really avoid the intended target—that is, the naming-thing. They symbolize attention to the body, but Athey creates a disturbing ritual space in which there is unflinching attention to the naming-thing marked out by thing-things and other naming-things. In so doing, with all the discomfort and anxiety produced, ritualized aggression raises questions: What happens (and how does it happen) when the naming-thing is actually disciplined and penetrated as ritual practice? What is the *look* and *texture* of a naming-thing postritual, in the company of other things? And what does such practice communicate to other naming-things?[69]

There are ways performance artists—white artists—push against false categories of importance, but this is never done and cannot be done in a way that fully negates their whiteness. The privileges associated with whiteness, in certain ways, make possible and important their manipulations of the naming-thing. But these naming-things challenged, twisted, and altered remain whitened with all whiteness entails. Such naming-things—even against the desire of these artists—resist ugliness as a permanent, sociocultural condition in that ugliness remains trumped by the salve of whiteness always applied to the ritualized wounds. Maleness has a similar effect as it is layered on the naming-thing performed and performing.

Performance art challenges but does not escape cultural codes that guide the structuring and speaking of life. This art is not the solution to issues of social justice, although through its history it has often been used as an alternate language and performance of political issues. What it does is destabilize socially desired conditioning of the naming-thing, while also challenging the assumed distinction of the naming-thing and its relationship to thing-things premised on their utility. And all this has something to do with the embodied grammar of ugliness. In a general sense, there is something about ugliness that "speaks" to unintended interaction—features as running contrary to the preferred symmetry—or the use of bodied naming-things that runs contrary to desired perfection, and so on. Ugliness may not be the opposite of beautifulness in that they are both dimensions of the same intention—the same attachment to manipulated naming-things. Artists force encounter with the naming-thing, and the takeaway from that encounter is contextual and therefore not fixed.

*Sally's Rape* depicts extreme circumstances that highlight and exaggerate. To be clear, I *do not* mean to overplay the tragic but rather to force a longer look into the tragic picking apart of naming-things. Compare *Sally's Rape* to Orlan's public plastic surgery that is meant to bring her visually in line with beauty as outlined in various works of art. Both elicit strong reactions that mark encounter with the unintended.[70] One, the former, does so through depiction of the ugly nature of the United States' relationship to black women as the "other" and the surgeries mark a radical transformation meant to shift the naming-thing toward aesthetic "perfection." Still, both entail violent encounter, both call for a strong response that blurs the line between beauty and ugliness, and in this way both point out the conflation of the two made possible through certain genres of performance art. Both push against symmetry of form or static appeal to comfort by shifting the dynamics of the naming-things and rendering their relationship to markers of meaning unstable. Both, in distinct ways, aim to destroy beauty/ugliness as representative of anything substantive in relationship to naming-things/thing-things.

Graphically presented by Orlan and Athey, performance art blurs beauty/ugliness as it plays out manipulations of the bodied naming-thing that stretch its form and content and, in the process, render naming-thing/thing-thing

chapter four

exposed and laid out. Kristine Stiles describes the situation with Orlan as such: "Among the most dramatic and troubling performances in the 1990s were Orlan's numerous cosmetic surgeries. These operations, which increasingly threatened the artist's health and well-being, initially were attempts to reconstruct and transform her face and body into a composite of the ideal Western art-historical notions of beauty, and later became pure physical disfigurations."[71] Not beautiful, nor ugly—instead unsettling, an attack on Christian theological assumptions of wholeness and perfection. The distinction between the frames of beauty and ugliness, to put it another way, is insignificant because both point to the function of performance art to conflate naming-things/thing-things in such a way as to nudge us in the direction of greater awareness of the "constructed" nature of meaning frameworks as fixed and bounded standards. One gets a sense of what I intend to highlight when considering Guillermo Gómez-Peña's description of the work of the performance artist. "Our job," he says, "may be to open up a temporary utopian/dystopian space, a de-militarised zone in which meaningful 'radical' behaviour and progressive thought are hopefully allowed to take place, even if only for the duration of the piece. . . . In this border zone, the distance between 'us' and 'them,' self and other, art and life, becomes blurry and non-specific." And here is the most telling statement: "We do not look for answers; we merely raise impertinent questions."[72] Continuing this idea, one might say with Athey that there is a conceptual shift away from beauty or ugliness to "realness" and "atrocity," for instance. "In my performance material," Athey reflects, "I am guilty of enhancing my history, situation and surroundings into a perfectly depicted apocalypse, or at least a more visual atrocity."[73] He cuts; he penetrates. Blood flows covering him and other things, pointing out as it oozes on stage the reality of naming-things as exposed, open, or—as Bakhtin notes—degraded.

What Athey offers is far more graphic and penetrating than what, for instance, video artist Bill Viola provides in *Inverted Birth*—a large video screen within an otherwise empty, dark room.[74] There is no furniture, nothing upon which to sit other than the floor. Those who enter hear the sound of liquid flowing. It is a dark liquid—which could be blood. Viola, the large image of the artist in only a pair of pants, stands staring at those present. He is covered with this liquid; it hits him, affecting his breathing, altering his posture as it pounds him, and limiting his vision as it enters his eyes. The vulnerability of the naming-thing—the manner in which this dark liquid impinges and alters the position, breathing, seeing, and so forth, of the naming-thing—is profound. Yet it is inverted birth in that the final stage is not the naming-thing emerging into the world covered with a substance both associated with and foreign to the new naming-thing. With time, for viewers who are patient enough to wait, the dark liquid is replaced by a white liquid that does not obscure to the same extent. It moves from darkness to light, and in this way from death to birth. In other words, "the fluids represent the essence of human life: earth, blood, milk, water, air, and the life cycle from birth to death, here inverted into a transformation from darkness to light."[75] After the shift from dark to light, the liquid flows up and away from Viola, eventually leaving him clean—shirtless, light paints unstained, and more closed off than at the beginning. Offered here is the naming-thing affected and influenced by other things (in this case liquids) that impinge and modify positioning in the world. There is an affective component as the figure's composure and comportment alter as the liquid changes from dark to light. This thing—liquid—modifies the naming-thing by altering its perception of itself in relationship to other things—as well as its ability to maintain its posture and stamina as the liquid pounds him. While done within the context of an individual thing encountering another thing, Viola's *The Raft* (2004), extends the model of interplay by bringing multiple naming-things together. The piece involves the coming together of a diverse range of bodied naming-things. They arrange themselves—suggesting a particular type of interaction. And after finding their places, they are bombarded by water at a high pressure. It penetrates their grouping—pushing against and into them, moving them and rearranging them as they brace themselves with and against each other in order to withstand the water pounding them.[76] The porous, somewhat unbounded nature of the bodied naming-thing is further explored by Viola in his Royal Academy of Arts exhibit titled *Life, Death, Rebirth*. In it, Viola's work is juxtaposed to that of Michelangelo, and in this way, it wrestles with the spiritual dimensions of mortality and transcendence across time—all marked out through the presentation and exploration of the body. One piece, *The Messenger* (1996), in particular demands recognition of the open nature of the body, as the body of a man is viewed over time and over against water (representing for Viola both life and death) in which he is submerged. As one stands in front and waits, the viewer sees the body as it seems to blend into the water, becoming little more than the colored wave and movement of the liquid without boundaries secure and certain. This says something about the nature of the human in relationship to other "things"—a relationship that dismisses the utility of rigid distinction and thereby forces a rethinking of what we name with language and what that language falsely establishes as certitude of expression.[77]

From the flow of liquid over the naming-thing and water pounding naming-things, we move to the amplification of the bodied naming-thing as thing-thing in relationship to the work of Yves Klein, who abandoned the traditional tools of the painter. Klein's practice, extending beyond that of Jackson Pollock, removes the brush from the canvas, rethinks what constitutes the brush, and allows the body to hover above the canvas as something more akin to the unconscious guiding the work.[78] Klein took the naming-thing as tool as he had naked bodies roll on canvas and in that way spread the blue paint. "They became living brushes," he remarked. "At my direction the flesh itself applied the colour to the surface and with perfect exactness."[79]

In addition, some performance artists use their work as a way to explore and critique dominant social sensibilities meant to close off naming-things, and they do so by highlighting segments of the population and their behaviors typically critiqued and hidden from public view. Stuart Brisley, for instance, brought into performance art stigmatized addictions such as alcoholism and mental illness. In this way, he challenged societal assumptions concerning normativity of appearance, behavior, and conduct in ways that play off and challenge the grammar of ugliness and beauty. This time it was done through the performance of despised or feared personalities akin to becoming that which is despised in the manner of Orlan and Athey: What is this I am seeing, participating in? This becomes a central question that prompts interrogations both internal and in relationship to other things.

## Discomfort with Things

Artists discussed thus far work with a level of anger, disappointment, and perhaps angst, and they express these affective dimensions in their work. In more graphic and aggressive modes of performance art, bodied naming-things are violently encountered as thing-things open to manipulation and penetration (literally). Anger, disappointment, and angst are presented in a three-dimensional and vibrant manner. The audience, then, is pulled in as both a part of and a party to the emotional twists and turns of the performed naming-thing. One gets a sense of this interplay with the audience when considering performance artist Chris Burden, whose art has included crucifixion not on a cross but on the hood of a car and crawling through broken glass—naked.[80] His work is illuminating as it sheds further light (think in terms of Owens) on the false distinction between the active naming-thing of the artist and the assumed passively observing naming-things of the viewers. While to some extent the interplay depicted by others in this chapter points in the direction of active engagement, I find something particularly compelling about Burden. As Cynthia Carr writes, "He denies any interest in either pain or transcendence. As he explained in 1975, 'when I use pain or fear in a work, it seems to energize the situation.' That 'situation' was the relationship between him and the audience. It was their fear and distress as much as his that 'energized the situation.' Burden's work examines physical phenomena in their natural context, the land of human error."[81] There is interaction, a merging of sorts involving various naming-things connected in tense ways and without full knowledge of this encounter. Turning to Burden again, Carr said the following concerning his 1972 piece titled *Jaizu*:

> Burden sat facing a gallery door, wearing sunglasses painted black on the inside, so he couldn't see. Spectators were unaware of this. They assumed, then, that he was watching, as they entered one at a time and faced him alone. Just inside the door were two cushions and some marijuana cigarettes. As Burden described it, "many people tried to talk to me, one assaulted me, and one left sobbing hysterically." The artist remained passive, immobile and speechless—the blank slate to whom each visitor gave an identity: judge? shaman? entertainer?[82]

The action was not always so physically intense and challenging. For instance, Piero Manzoni's *Living Sculpture* in Rome in 1961 involved naming-things he signed—in this way blurring the distinction between the naming-thing as producer of art and naming-thing as artistic thing-thing.[83] "Manzoni's Sculpture Viventi," it was noted, "was completed by a declaration of authenticity. A red stamp certified that the subject was a whole work of art for life. A yellow stamp limited the artistic status to a body part, while a green one meant that the individual signed was a work of art under certain circumstances (i.e. only while sleeping or running). Finally, a purple stamp stuck on the receipt of authenticity meant that the service was paid for."[84] In either Manzoni's *Sculpture Viventi* or Kaprow's *18 Happenings in 6 Parts*, performance as an art movement marked a new pulling at the naming-thing so as to highlight its instability as a distinct "something" in relationship with thing-things, but still the slightest bit distinct. The audience did not simply observe this statement. "Kaprow," observes RoseLee Goldberg, "issued invitations that included the statement 'you will become a part of the happenings; you will simultaneously experience them.' Shortly after this first announcement, some of the same people who had been invited received mysterious plastic envelopes containing bits of paper, photographs, wood, painted fragments and cut-out figures. They were also given a vague idea of what to expect:

chapter four

'there are three rooms for this work, each different in size and feeling. . . . Some guests will also act.'"[85] Something about the very contested nature of the concept "performance" supports the effort of art to trouble the familiar and the distant—to demand attention to what is assumed regarding boundaries between naming-things and thing-things.[86] This is an alternate way of communicating a concern with awareness of circumstances and the impingement of circumstances. Its bodied language is coded by a particular sense of muscle memory, so to speak.

Performance art as discussed here is understood as seeking a blurring of difference between the naming-thing and the thing-thing, between the naming-thing doing and the thing-thing to which it is done: Thing-things shift and change naming-things. The ability to distinguish between the two is challenged, if not removed altogether. This is more than to say, "Humans and things are stuck to each other," and dependency does not capture sufficiently the nature of togetherness that marks the naming-thing/thing-thing in certain practices of performance art.[87] The assumed integrity of the naming-thing is challenged as soon as the viewer is forced to wrestle with an emotive question: Who does that to the bodied naming-thing, and why would anyone do that?

By becoming much more visible, the bodied naming-thing is blurred, and its porous condition is "named." This mode of art pushes for a different relationship between viewer and artist, one that places the question of art in the reaction of the viewer in that "the reception is as crucial as the creation of art."[88] Even when one thinks about thing-things as not inert but active within a range of circumstances (i.e., world), there is still a relationship between naming-things and thing-things marked by even the smallest distinction between types. But there are modalities of performance art that seek to challenge even this slight difference by making art what the bodied naming-thing is and what it does. Naming-things and thing-things and their relationship are given a particular charge through graphic, public acting. The porous nature of their borders is highlighted, and it is the blurred space in between to which performance art pushes viewers-participants.

# the art of elimination 5

We dare not speak about shit. But, since the beginning of time, no other subject—not even sex—has caused us to speak so much.
—DOMINIQUE LAPORTE, *History of Shit*

For all our lofty philosophies and religious visions, we still have to shit.
—DAVID WALTNER-TOEWS, *The Origin of Feces*

Experiencing body art as performance of openness, like that discussed in the previous chapter in relationship to Athey, Owen, and Piper, is only one method of encountering a "work" of art. Some other methods involve a type of participation requiring a wait.

I have spent my share of minutes queued up for everything from the fine arts to my turn to relieve myself in a public restroom. During a trip to New York City, these two moments of waiting were brought together in an intriguing manner. I went to the Guggenheim to experience *America* by Maurizio Cattelan.[1] This exhibit—a not-so-subtle comedic critique/signification of consumerism, materialism, and the pretense of democratic ideals—is a functioning toilet.[2] There is nothing unique, in a practical sense, about this toilet. And everything else in the restroom is typical—a presentation of alter-functional "readymade" items of sorts. Yet this toilet is no readymade; it is a precious metal—gold—and therefore not purchased from an average plumbing shop. One could think of this Guggenheim exhibit as reflecting the application of what Hal Poster called the "shit movement"[3]—or in more conversational language, artistic expression using one of the most common and despised of substances—human waste.[4]

## A Particular Encounter

I was prepared to wait my turn in line for as long as it took, although I was uncertain what I would actually do when I finally entered. There is something psychologically distasteful in following too closely on the heels of another who has left the seat warm, the paper disrupted, and unused toilet seat covers thrown about. But this was even more unsettling: it was a golden toilet with a long line of people who might relieve themselves but who were also assuming something artistic about this "crapper." All this thinking was guided by social rules of decorum regarding human waste—what it is, and where it is deposited as well as what we are to assume regarding that process of disposal.[5] Undergirding this situation is recognition of the bodied naming-thing as yet another thing that produces . . . things.[6] Or as Michael Thompson phrases it, "Bodily excretions serve as daily reminders of how our bodies are getting on with things."[7]

*America* is more than a container for "refuse" displayed, unlike what one gets with the artist Justin Gignac, who collects New York City trash and packages it for sale.[8] Gignac offers "one offs"—items that have been used or otherwise associated with bodied naming-things. The arrangements in clear containers are safe—at some distance from the bodied naming-thing and therefore without the capacity to impinge upon it. What has been said concerning trash collection and/as art elsewhere is applicable in the context of Gignac in New York City: "The 'dark and unsanitary is transmogrified into the sublime and the beautiful.'"[9] Growing out of the assemblage movement in the mid-twentieth century, art such as what Gignac presents signifies—whether intentionally stated or not—the modern world by exposing what it wants hidden away. In short, collecting garbage exposes habits and desires. And this collecting of the hidden promotes a push against the art world and the larger social arrangements supporting that world.[10] Such art says something about the need to inspect "stuff" for what it says to and about life.[11] Still, Gignac's work produces no discomfort and does not entail a source of anxiety or uncertainty. It is garbage of a certain form—captured and made manageable.

What I have in mind in this chapter, based on application of the technology of religion, is a more intimate connection between naming-things and thing-things. It is a connection that names openness in a more graphic and socioculturally troubling manner.

My time at the Guggenheim was in search of speculation regarding waste not so easily tamed and separated from the naming-thing. What could take place in/on *America* could not be so easily managed away—not even within the white walls of one of the United States' widely regarded museums. More than urine—another matter of human waste associated with the golden toilet—fecal matter troubles. And so, writes Gillian Whiteley, "we work constantly to remove dirt and human waste from our everyday lives. The fear and disorder unleashed when it seeps out is palpable."[12] But for a period of time at the Guggenheim, feces was not only anticipated—it was part of an installation.[13] Producing it, then, had something of an artistic quality.

The golden toilet "malfunctioned" and needed repair. The amount of time necessary for the properly trained staff to assess and address the issue was uncertain. As I waited, a series of questions came to mind: Are they plumbers or curators—or some unique combination of the two? Is the plunger used for the golden toilet the equivalent of a paintbrush, for instance? Is the waste that caused the malfunction not artistic?

Due to vagueness regarding the stated repair time, many left the line, and my projected wait of an hour was reduced (see fig. 5.1). The person ahead of me entered, and I thought of what was taking place in there. Just looking? Taking pictures? Using it? Using it *and* taking pictures? I tried to guess based on my time calculations: how long to urinate over against the amount of time to . . . do more than that. The door opened, and based on the time frame, I was confident I could move right in. I entered the small room and closed the door. It was all too familiar—a typical sink, soap, and a cloth for drying hands. Over to the left was the golden toilet—the artist's representation of American-ness. And I, within reason, could do with it as I like—but even before making that determination, I had to throw toilet paper in it. I needed to produce a contrast to its shine and the luxuriousness it had no choice but to represent. The common paper served to regularize it. Only then could I be comfortable having my turn with *America*.

In that small room, occupants are urged to encounter themselves as naming-things producing what they must surrender and hide. Of course, as noted above, there is a critique of the art industry and U.S. consumerism, but there is also reflection—whether intended does not matter—on the openness of the bodied naming-thing: the value, so to speak, of what it produces and its relationship to that waste. Simply put, here I am interested in the lucid naming-thing's interaction with material, a nonlucid item—shit.[14]

chapter five

5.1 Sign announcing the wait time for *America*. Photo by the author.

Questions, such as those raised by Susan Signe Morrison, abound: "Why is the excremental body so threatening? Why don't we want to be near the person covered in shit? Why don't we want to be the person covered in shit? If society is a body, what is the role of excrement? Who or what is the 'excrement' in a social context?"[15]

### Waste . . . No, Shit

There is some discomfort in using this word—*shit*—in print, and many show a preference for *excrement*. Yet as some scholars argue, this is too general a term in that it can mean anything expelled.[16] I have something more focused in mind; hence, *shit* is appropriate for making my point in that it, as David Waltner-Toews reflects, "storms successfully through all the artificial barricades we have erected to block the streets and alleys between the deodorized proletariat and the sanitized ruling class, between popular and academic culture, between science and every day."[17] This is not a reference to the metaphorical mess of "Shit happens" or "Cut the shit"; rather, I mean the physical human waste.

To know something of the bodied naming-thing requires attention to what marks it as alive and moving, what gives it something of its physicality and presence. It is to say something about its shit. Literally . . . **shit**—the physical substance and its cultural connotations are captured in the dictionary as archive of language:[18]

### Shit

Vulgar slang

*Noun* 1. Feces 2. An act of defecation[19]

Polite conversation does not often include this terminology—not directly stated but often implied—but still it is widely recognized and utilized during our more commonly impolite exchanges.[20] I use this descriptive term, *shit*, not to provoke discomfort, nor to be crude without cause, but because it speaks in significant ways to the natural and yet uncomfortable character of this product that is both intimate and foreign to the bodied naming-thing. Shit connects us in ways that, like the other things discussed in this volume, reveal something about the openness of things and the interaction between things.[21]

More to the point, the challenge with the porous bodied naming-thing is the perpetual threat of spillage: the bodied naming-thing, to maintain function, must consume calories; and food waste and other items must be omitted (see fig. 5.2). The bodied naming-thing lives, and the residue—the dead substance omitted—points to that continued living. Such residue—with its smell, look, texture, and location outside the bodied naming-thing—points to the thingliness of the naming-thing.

Shit forces confrontation with openness in that there is wide-ranging applicability of shit as a mode of exchange, of shock, of spoiling normative sensibility, of denying and defying the beautiful through the imposition of the assumed impure: human waste—dead bacteria, food remains, cells, and so on—evacuated. Or as Waltner-Toews defines it, "Excrement is whatever your body doesn't use of the food it takes in, plus millions of bacteria that grow in your gut, plus quite a few of the cells from your gut lining. More specifically, excrement is defined in terms of an anal sphincter; it is defined by the animal it is leaving behind. Hence, we speak of cow dung and baby poop, otter spraints and dog turds."[22] Again, turning to Waltner-Toews, one is forced to recognize that before life there was no shit.[23] To physically "be" is to shit. That is to say, as a substance, shit is a type of rough cartography of the material art of porous being. Its ongoing use speaks to its chemical and nutritional value as waste used to fuel (fertilizer and art, for instance) production and creativity. In a variety of forms, shit symbolizes the naming-thing producing things it needs and despises—and the naming-thing's reincorporation of this thing (shit) into its constructions.[24]

Shit, in discussion ("language makes excrement manifest"), as well as through physical presence, promotes a particular type of discord and discomfort—a graphic effort to contain, place, and arrange it so as to make a significant and verifiable distinction between it and the things emitting it.[25] More than the familiar-foreign such as vomit, urine, and tears, or the familiar such as blood, shit has use but is believed—despite the obvious—to have "no place" in relationship to bodied naming-things. This is also the case with vomit, urine, and tears, but traditionally there is a more-graphic response to the presence of shit. Desire for these things is limited—but the reaction to shit is perhaps stronger than it is to the other materials that naming-things eliminate from time to time. Yet despite all, the value—the importance—of shit to life is undeniable and too true. Notwithstanding its undeniable utility, it is a troubling substance—one that motivates a variety of questions, as noted by Waltner-Toews: "How and why has excrement—which is absolutely necessary for the resilient functioning of our planet, and which has, in fact, been a solution to a myriad of biological problems thrown up by the long haul of evolution—become, in the past mere few thousands of years, a problem to be solved?"[26]

There is shit—the physical substance that speaks to the life of things—its relationship to itself and other things, and there are the ways in which we are in a tangled network of relations named through a variety of technologies and mechanisms of collective cooperation related to shit. In a word, the process of shitting is multidimensional and layered in that it addresses our perception of naming-things in addition to our practices as well as the larger frameworks through which we are placed in time and space. Desirable and undesirable terms of being are tied together through shit: it connects us to the world and also pulls us away from the "naturalness" of that world. It renders us material but also aware of our materiality through our effort to control and counter materiality through the strategic hiding away of certain substances associated with our materiality. The open naming-thing is a "body" of gaps, of inconsistences, of tangibility, and of certain "fungibility."[27]

Shit produces reaction through visceral challenges to boundaries of being that reflect life and death at the same moment: the blending of both into one foul substance posing a threat to the open bodied naming-thing. It can compromise other naming-things when they are put in contact with it, and it points out the uncomfortable activities of the naming-things producing it. Shit is substantive death—dependent on texture, color, and so forth—or what others call "dead life of the body" that can be a nonverbal articulation of normalcy and well-being.[28] As St. Augustine is believed to have said so sarcastically, we are born *inter far em et urinam*, that is, "between feces and urine." One might add that aging involves changing control over both, and then we die within the boundaries of a similar arrangement. All the while, we fight this reality.

### Significant Shit

Historically, shit shaped public behavior and infrastructure. And as a consequence, it troubles desire—encouraged through numerous ideological platforms such as traditional theological doctrine—for a fixed, closed, and "clean" spirit corresponding to a comparably closed body.[29] To broaden this out in terms of a generic sense of "filth," the despised substance and what it constitutes troubles perception to the extent that "filth challenges the very dichotomy between subject and object." Hence, filth is "object-making and subject-unsettling."[30] Corresponding to this, Mary Douglas speaks of the nature of dirt as "disorder" marked by a troubling discontinuity between location and utility understood broadly.[31] Unlike Douglas, I am not interested in distinctions between the sacred and secular, or pure and impure; such boundaries, whether false or true, are not my primary concern. And while one might question the assumption Douglas imposes regarding a universal sense of disgust related to wrong location, there is something to be said concerning the dissonance fostered by placement or proximity associated with what has been called filth. The naming of filth has something to do with a desire for things to be where they belong.

Bodied naming-things want to believe and to act as if they are self-contained "vessels" promoting separation and a prophylactic quality of distinction. Through a narrative of two statuses—insider and outsider—emerges a wish for integrity tied to boundaries between the naming-thing and the things in the world encountered.[32] Yet the narrative is disrupted as human waste, and the naming-thing's relationship to it forces confrontation.[33] The categories of "pure" and "impure" speak a type of social delusion broken through rituals of elimination. The management and in/visibility of waste has sociopolitical and cultural ramifications. For example, rumors of human waste thrown during protests or the smearing of bodies and walls with human waste to amplify the degrading conditions of life within certain prison contexts speaks to the social role of human waste as a mechanism of confrontation.[34] This, however, is not to say human waste has a materiality that is undeniably political or social.

While not wanting to linger on the psychological dimensions of shit and naming-things' relationship to shit, another way of getting at this situation is through Julia Kristeva's sense of the abject. Kristeva discusses the abject in a way that notes at least a hope for purity over against filth or contamination of some sort. One finds this, I would argue, in the response to the object loathed. "Loathing an item of good, a piece of filth waste, or dung," writes Kristeva, "the spasms and vomiting that project me. The repugnance, the retching that thrusts me to the side and turns me away from defilement, sewage, muck."[35] In this act, the "retching," the naming-thing seeks to address the "presence" of a thing-thing—to separate itself from that which it finds problematic. This movement of the bodied naming-thing tied to "repugnance" suggests a response to openness that amplifies openness as traumatic. Shit, in this case, represents what exists on "the other side of the border," and signifies "what life withstands."[36] Shit, and Kristeva uses this categorical term, sets out a distinction or what she references as marking "the place where I am not and which permits me to be." Shit points to what the naming-thing must void in order to remain alive to or be in a particular way.[37] Yet this is not a clean distinction in that the "I" who expels shit, in the act expels something of the "I"—that is, the naming-thing expels something that is constituted by and entails a "piece" of that bodied naming-thing. And to the extent that shit does not respect distinction but demands to speak the openness of the naming-thing, it produces abjection—entailing a sense that this openness is perpetual, and in its ongoing nature it has consequences in that it corrupts or taints.[38] My interest here, however, is not with abjection per se, which I would label a psycho-ethical response. (I say more on this in the last section of the book.) Rather, I am intrigued by the manner in which shit provides a context by means of which we are better enabled to "name" the moment/process of interplay between naming-things and thing-things. Such a concern is more limited in scope than how that interplay is "felt" and responded to through practice. Still, to acknowledge the naming-thing is to acknowledge the necessity of shit.

The bodied naming-thing is "bounded" only in a slight sense; more to the point, it is vulnerable and penetrated.[39] As Kristeva points out, the openness of the body and what shit says about this openness need not constitute a source of worry or marginality to be avoided—a sign of compromise as if boundaries are more than an idea. And fecal matter, as Douglas notes, is one of the things that points out the vulnerability of the naming-thing—the

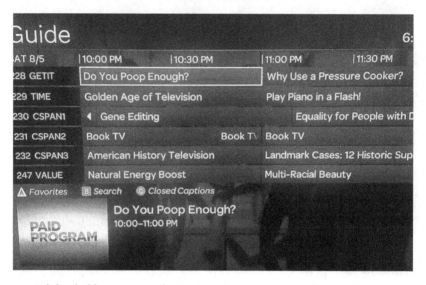

Guide                                                                    6:

| AT 8/5 | 10:00 PM | 10:30 PM | 11:00 PM | 11:30 PM |
|---|---|---|---|---|
| 228 GETIT | Do You Poop Enough? | | Why Use a Pressure Cooker? | |
| 229 TIME | Golden Age of Television | | Play Piano in a Flash! | |
| 230 CSPAN1 | ◀ Gene Editing | | Equality for People with [ | |
| 231 CSPAN2 | Book TV | Book T\ | Book TV | |
| 232 CSPAN3 | American History Television | | Landmark Cases: 12 Historic Sup | |
| 247 VALUE | Natural Energy Boost | | Multi-Racial Beauty | |

△ Favorites    B Search    © Closed Captions

PAID
PROGRAM

Do You Poop Enough?
10:00–11:00 PM

5.2 While a hidden practice, elimination of waste is a topic of public discussion. This image is a screen shot of a television guide. Photo by the author.

manner in which it is exposed. But this situation need not be a negative arrangement to overcome.[40] Rather, this naming-thing exposed through the shit it produces is not to be condemned. Fecal matter is a story, a narrative of life and death—of bodied naming-thing and other things interacting. Shit tells us something of what it means to be human, and the limited nature of that meaning. For instance, its content tells us of diet and well-being, and its location, scholars argue, says something about the nature of sociocultural codes as well as economic and political developments. What is more, the production of waste raises questions regarding the ability to keep at a distance or bracket things as it were. What does "right place" or "wrong place" mean when the body produces the shit that challenges the fixed nature of margins and boundaries? Naming-things and thing-things are entwined—necessary partners continuously reproducing this dependency.[41] This is a relationship that keeps the bodied naming-thing exposed—penetrated by things while also voiding things. "We have remarkably intimate ties to waste and trash," reflects Elizabeth Spelman. "They not only bear the stamp of our creation but figure prominently in accounts of the kinds of beings we are and in the crafting of our relations to each other."[42] Shit is a violation of sorts, a betrayal to a certain degree. It breaks the myth of boundary between naming-things and the things it manufactures and, in the process, exposes tension between relief/pleasure and filth/guilt. It is a throwaway but also a source of importance with its own wide-ranging utility.

## A Shitty Story

Despite (or perhaps because of) the stigma, shit has received a significant amount of popular and scholarly attention. From children's books—for example, Taro Gomi's *Everybody Poops*—to theoretically rich work, shit is despised but is also a widespread topic of conversation.[43] Dominique Laporte, for example, in his text *History of Shit*, presents a keen relationship between the individual and the management of human waste.[44] Using the Paris Edict of 1539 as a launching point for discussion and speculation, he notes the connection between waste recognition (e.g., disgust) and management and ties both to the physical structuring of communal space. The sight and smell of shit removed to a space of confinement, according to Laporte, speaks to the development of the "bourgeois" family—one with the capacity for and sensibility to find its waste disgusting and to manage it away. However, he points to the physical maneuvering of human waste as a secondary and civilizing step, the first being the removal of waste from acceptable speech.[45] The cultural implication of shit—particularly as it relates to smell and odor—is significant. Smells are not naturally determined; rather, they are socially and cultural coded. They tell us more about our values and views than they do the substance of that which by smell we believe offends or delights.[46]

> I know you like to think your shit don't stank;
> But lean a little bit closer;
> See that roses really smell like poo-poo-oo.
> —OUTKAST, "Roses"

Both in language and physicality, shit is handled in such a way as to separate the naming-thing from natural attachment. It is a matter of intent to remove a burden of words or waste, of separating out that which has no added value but is simply useless bulk. That is, "in both policing of language and the politics of shit," Laporte writes, "it is a matter of uprooting oneself from the clinging 'remnant of earth,'" and in this process to reflect particular practices of civilized life.[47] That is to say, the sociology of shitting tells us something about the cultural arrangement of individual and collective life—something with significant implications.[48] Some have argued that the normalized arrangements for shit speak about evolutionary and ecological changes but also our public life as citizens (see fig. 5.3). Laporte takes this further to connect shit

5.3 The toilet-supply aisle at Home Depot. Photo by the author.

with the dynamic life of capitalism—constituting a departure from the realm of nature to the constructed conditions of societal organization and its trappings.[49] In an ironic twist, this connection is artistically presented through the Denmark-based group Ingen Frygt that consumed money for fourteen days then eliminated it—literally turning currency into shit.[50]

Over the course of history (and I reference here the West), the ability of the state to mandate a relationship to shit and to arrange its collection and disposal/use suggest its ability to control the bodied naming-thing—to highlight but also give the impression of closure to the open naming-thing. Mechanisms of the state such as religious and secular rituals give the illusion of concealment to these bodied naming-things if by no other way than by determining how and where the most troubling moments of openness take place. Exclusion is a consequence of this recognition; anything, if not everything, associated with disgust (read difference) takes on something of a shitty quality and thereby merits confinement if not disregard.[51] Yet shit poses a challenge. It is composed of things in relationship to things in relationship to naming-things. According to Rose George, "A gram of feces

chapter five

can contain 10 million viruses, 1 million bacteria, 1,000 parasite cysts, and 100 worm eggs. Bacteria can be beneficial: the human body needs bacteria to function and only 10 percent of cells in our body are actually human."[52] In certain ways, then, growth into citizenship, like the infant's maturation as a "self," involves willingness to acquiesce to the rules for shitting—including aversion to its presence and smell.[53]

This, as Laporte demonstrates, involves how one speaks about waste as well as how one relates physically to one's waste. In both cases—discourse and practice—one cannot escape a concern with shit for what it says about the bodied naming-thing and its interplay with other things. It is not simply that the body has openings, places that eliminate substances and from which locations the naming-thing can be penetrated. It is the manner in which openness challenges assumptions concerning completeness, independence, and full integrity—that is, the illusions of closed subjectivity. This openness in terms of defecation reminds us that bodied naming-things are alive and as a consequence are always already in the process of dying, and this is despite the manner in which the toilet has enhanced life spans.[54] Shit and shitting open a range of interplay and interaction—as well as an overlap between things. Both visible and hidden qualities of naming-thing-ness can be measured in relationship to defilement, and this includes the degree to which the normal elimination of waste is evident on one's embodied person: Does one smell of shit? Is it visibly splattered on one's person or lodged under one's fingernails? Are one's living conditions marred by the presence of shit?[55] This is not to suggest the elimination of waste and all the evidence of this waste can be complete; to the contrary—waste remains present and vital (fig. 5.4). Naming-thing waste entails both attraction and revolution—the enjoyment of producing shit and the desire for socially recognizable "goods." Waste pulls at both of these desires.

Theologically considered, this pull of competing desires speaks to the religious depiction of the human as torn—both of an evil disposition and capable of potential good. In some traditions, evil beings and spirits are associated with shit and the places used for defecation. Furthermore, in some religious traditions, places of defecation are associated with defilement and impurity.[56] More literal Christians, for instance, might frame this in terms of original sin—the soiled nature of human life based on a fundamental departure from divine will.[57] That which is associated with the lower portion of the body, with its dank point of exit, is associated with what is undesirable and symbolically with a place of darkness, odor, and defilement—hell.[58]

5.4 Outside an apartment building in New York City. Photo by the author.

Religion expands this dismissal by rendering not just distinguishable waste a sociocultural and political problem but by equating all ethical outreach of the body as waste—as excrement.

To carry forward this theological reasoning, to be removed from shit, is to be moved symbolically from contamination in a more general sense. And while both men and women produce and are marked by shit, scholars have pointed out the manner in which gender figures into this to the extent, for instance, that menstrual blood occupies a similar place of disregard tied to a sexual nature; and this, combined with shit production, provides an additional physical and spiritual weight for women. The open-bodied naming-thing, oozing with physical defilement, was translated religiously into the body prone to lasting immorality and distance from the divine.[59] In such a case, "dung stinks less than moral stench."[60] Bodied naming-things that can produce such physical defilement must also be marked by a deeper, spiritual defilement. The defecating naming-thing is transformed theologically and redeemed *only* by a God that does not shit.

The waste produced speaks metaphorically to this spiritual stain. "It would seem," writes Laporte, "that human excrement, like the soul, carries the

chapter five

'noxious' trace of the body it departs. There is a wickedness in shit that must be given time to dissipate or it will turn on man."[61] Yet, he continues, the places of deposit have a shrine quality to them in many instances, places "where civilized man deposited offerings and prayers to ward off the very awareness of his primordial organs."[62] In a word, as the removal of waste in London suggested, "the master of waste and the warden of souls are one and the same."[63] For Laporte this is a theological read of a biochemical process of allowing human waste to remain unused as fertilizer for a good period of time to allow the smell and harmful components to dissipate in power.[64] There is a lingering truth: We remain tied to the waste we produce, and this truth both frightens and inspires.[65] Knowledge of this sort lends itself to a negative theologizing of embodiment, as Morrison describes: "By analogizing sin—particularly sexually related sins—with filth, the Church fathers attempted to control and shame the individual into socially constructive behavior. Our bodies are cause enough for us to be disgusted with ourselves. Excrement became a means to control the body and to punish the soul."[66] The very substance and its symbolic channeling align shit and other naming-thing waste with damning theological pronouncements. Against this negativity, some have pointed out the theologically positive creativity Martin Luther enjoyed while on the toilet but, as William James highlights, shit language becomes a means by which to communicate the trauma that constitutes life.[67] Such a view may not ground a posture toward the world marked by an unwillingness to bracket pain and misery (i.e., the sick soul), but it does say something about those viewing the world from a perspective that seeks escape—such as James's "healthy minded" who convert to the attitude that the world cannot be defined by misery. They want to hide shit, so to speak. But the "sick souls," those whom James actually favors, are content with shit and shittiness as dimensions of life. Shit exposes the dynamics of existence and our relationship to those dynamics. "Nothing in Catholic theology, I imagine," James reflects, "has ever spoken to sick souls [those individuals who are deeply aware of the pain and suffering in the world] as straight as this message from Luther's personal experience. As Protestants are not all sick souls, of course reliance on what Luther exults in calling the dung of one's merits, the filthy puddle of one's own righteousness, has come to the front again in their religion."[68]

Responses within religious communities and within discourses assuming a theological normativity are not of concern here. Hence, notions of defilement or cleanliness, or dirt and purity, within such contexts are not the best geography upon which to map out my particular sense of the naming-thing's relationship to shit. In certain contexts, it is vital for proper occupation of spiritual space when it, as some have argued regarding the Grand Lama of Tibet, is dried, "packaged in little boxes or in small bags suitable for being carried around one's neck. Some were also used as condiments or snuff."[69]

Mary Douglas speaks of cleaning, of reordering; however, none of this addresses the openness constituted by shitting. Shit is targeted, removed from view, but in a limited sense, in that it is also consumed as the food for our food. That which is removed from private life can be used to sustain, literally, the agricultural arrangements of life. One way of thinking this situation through is to see the connection between waste and production (e.g., agriculture). In this regard, waste makes life possible; it rewards us with continuation and wealth conceived in a variety of ways. Yet this connection between shit and gold requires restriction on the locations for producing, placing, and using waste.[70] In a crude sense, shitting—both symbolically and physically—tells us something about well-being, about the nature of porous embodiment; something about private space, about communal relationships and dynamics; as well as something about economic-political developments and concerns. To continue with this argument, whoever smells shit says something about the boundaries of intimate connection. Shit—its producing, placement, "reception"—tells us something about an individual naming-thing's connection to larger structures of relationship; and while it points to connections, it also speaks to the boundaries of concern: one's shit is one's business. Still, shit matters beyond the individual to the extent that its removal from its initial point of production, to its use as fertilizer, and to the collection of the food item nurtured by it involves others. Beyond ingestion of what shit makes possible, the long-held use of shit as a beauty aid when applied to the skin and the hair ties it yet again to the individual naming-thing.[71]

What is more, shit can be used to express outrage, to suggest intimacy, to promote recognition of the place and functions of naming-things, and so on. In the nineteenth century, John G. Bourke chronicled this dynamic in a ritualized form when describing the "feast of fools," during which religious authority was mocked as the ordinary donned the robes of clergy, and others dressed as clowns riding in dung carts throwing shit on those standing about.[72] The tables are turned in this instance; authority is questioned and turned upside down, and the substance to be hidden from view is highlighted and used to publicly mark the private functions of the naming-thing. Eventually challenged by church hierarchy, the ritualized and symbolic value of shit as a sociocultural and political device of recalibration is exaggerated. In a word, filth is multidimensional. In William Cohen's description, "filth

chapter five

represents a cultural location at which the human body, social hierarchy, psychological subjectivity, and material objects converge."[73]


## The Art of Shit

Shit matters, and its mattering influences and informs overlapping dimensions of individual and collective engagement. As Dave Praeger remarks, "It affects us psychologically, manifests social relations and hierarchy, influences childrearing, and makes an impact on the environment, art, media, culture, and commerce. Few aspects of human life escape the influence of its ubiquitous and inevitably urgent presence."[74] I want to pull out of this statement one category: art.

In using shit, an artist urges viewers to reassess a particular boundary and thereby interrogate relationship between the naming-thing and the thing produced. Turning again to Kristeva's notion of the abject/abjection, one gains another way of situating the relationship between shit and art. Abjection, Kristeva argues, is tied to "religious structurings," and in this way "exclusion" is tied to the "sacred." The goal of religious engagement related to abject/abjection involves a mode of catharsis with a purifying function. And while this is the goal of religion, according to Kristeva, the most compelling modality of catharsis is art or aesthetic (as a component of religion), by means of which openness is tested and explored, named and explained through what might be called, to borrow from Kristeva, "abject art."[75] And this, as some commentary on shit in art would suggest, is more than plausible.[76] Yet my concern is circumscribed to one dimension of art's work—exposure through shit of the moment/process of interplay.[77]

The idea that shit is not devoid of a certain artistic necessity is not a new notion. For example, Erhard Schon's *Peasant Wedding Celebration* wood carving shows a scene from a peasant festival complete with shitting.[78] Yet my concern is not whether shitting was being cautioned against or celebrated within this image; rather, the mere depiction of the act points to an intersection between art and shit.[79] So it is not that attention to shit in the context of artistic rendering is novel: Schon did it, as did Rembrandt, and one could add to the list *Alimentation Doctrinaire (1889)* by James Ensor, in which various persons of leadership—such as a military figure and a religious figure—are depicted shitting.[80] Rather, it is merely the number of artists working along these lines of openness displayed that increases in the modern period through the present.[81]

There are, at times, economic-political and social intent behind the art. For instance, work by Gilbert and George in 1982's *Shit* and *Shit Faith* entails shit "coming out of four buttocks facing each other and of a man receiving shit in his mouth." And in the 1990s, they continued this attention to the interplay of waste and bodied naming-things—disturbing the function of shit—through an exhibit titled *The Naked Shit Pictures*. This exhibit, according to Gilbert, is meant to disrupt moral assumptions by bringing into view a realm of interaction or exchange that is typically despised and hidden, and in this way they seek to "make a history of two thousand years of civilization and morals look like shit, because it tried to inculcate into us that nakedness and faeces are bad."[82] This is an important dimension of what shit in public can entail, as writers such as Jojada Verrips have stated. Yet while acknowledging these circumstances, I want to better understand the manner in which art corresponds to a naming of the interplay between bodied naming-things and thing-things as a more fundamental dimension of the work.[83] Although it amplifies the effect, one need not see shit for it to have this impact. It is present—at least potentially—nonetheless. But whether physically present or not, it remains visible in our language; art exposes both through interplay and presents the porous margins of naming-things and thing-things through interaction.

My concerns, unlike Kristeva's, do not entail psychoanalytical understandings of the abject as it relates to separation from the mother and the workings of gendered disregard. Rather, I am concerned with what shit and proximity to it might help us name. Yet there is something of note in Kristeva's comment concerning the character of defecation and the fragile self. "It is as if the skin, a fragile container," she writes, "no longer guaranteed the integrity of one's 'own and clean self' but, scraped or transparent, invisible or taught, gave way before the dejection of its contents."[84] Shit points to the already tainted self, in this case the open naming-thing portrayed through the open-and-closed nature of the anus. The anus as a point of betrayal practices the interplay of naming-thing and thing-thing as it releases into the world—as a marker of living and of demise—pieces of the bodied naming-thing (i.e., the food, bacteria, etc., contained in it). "What goes out of the body," according to Kristeva, "out of its pores and openings, points to the infinitude of the body proper and gives rise to abjection" to the extent that shit troubles the nature and meaning of "I." She continues: "Fecal matter signifies, as it were, what never ceases to separate from a body in a state of permanent loss in order to become autonomous, distinct from the mixtures, alterations, and decay that run through it."[85] Shit is from the bodied naming-thing's border, but more than this—it is from the naming-thing but is also foreign to that thing, and this situating of shit points also to a rationale for its troubling effect on the illusion of fixity. Attention to shit is a type of recuperation.[86]

What Kristeva says concerning literature's ability "through the crisis of the word" to expose the abject, I would extend to art more generally. That is to say, art entails an "unveiling" of the naming-thing's openness—a presentation, in this case, of the manner in which shit speaks to and also occasions reflection on this openness and its implications.[87] Art provides a way of exploring this interplay between naming-things and thing-things, and particularly the manner in which the presence of a detested substance exposes (even signifies) and encourages a different take on this interplay. "The body," writes Jan Koenot, "is indeed omnipresent in the art of the 20th century whether figured or not, in all cases it is required; it collaborates and the work assigns a place to it even when bringing about a displacement, a letting go, a passage, an opening."[88] Even, for instance, Jackson Pollock's effort to detangle the body and object so as to free the subconscious to expression does not obliterate the naming-thing/thing-thing biomancy at the heart of expression.

To step away from shit for a moment, the porous or exposed nature of the naming-thing is highlighted through body fluids such as blood flowing from this nonfixed and sealed thing.[89] Blood, a red substance of life, speaks to the vitality of the body—or the loss of that vitality when its confinement to the formal body is disrupted or spilled. Ron Athey's performances—his body art— draw from his Pentecostal background and contemplation of death. They present blood and the ways in which it exposes the naming-thing—marks it as open and penetrated. Blood speaks to the flow of life, the energy of the naming-thing; hence its ability to interplay with other naming-things and thing-things.[90] Blood (and I would argue shit as well) speaks to the persistent intersection of creation and destruction as at least a potentiality, which is to say at its most forceful impingement on the naming-thing and its relationship to other things. Some have bled for or in front of audiences as performance meant to tackle deep human inclinations, attitudes, and behaviors. Spilled outside bodies, blood points to the end of vitality, the end of flow and life. But as in certain ritualization, the flow of blood outside the confines of embodiment can also serve as an offering of sorts, a marker of potential restitution and gain.[91]

Artists have used other body fluids such as urine to make sociopolitical statements, often with a node in the direction of religious imagery. Examples include the 1986 photograph by Andres Serrano titled *Piss Christ*—the Christ on a cross, submerged in the artist's very own urine.[92] Some critics responded by noting the depth of presentation, the "beauty" of the image. Through application of religion as a technology, one might also express the manner in which it brings Christology to the body by degrading it, to use Bakhtin's concept; it highlights the embodied nature of the Christ event, the manner in which it points to the intimacies of the bodied naming-thing and seeks to present what is most metaphysically significant about our sense of ourselves as already connected to our presence and omission. In this case, there is in this degrading another way to reflect on life presented twice already: we are born (perhaps born again) between feces and urine.[93] We are located existentially and epistemological within the realm of that which we disregard. There is no escape from that which we despise. We are intimately connected to that which we, as naming-things, reject.

Prior to *Piss Christ*, the early twentieth century was marked by the denied presence of human waste. One need only think of Dada artist Duchamp's "readymade" of the urinal displayed—to the dismay of many. Brought into the art gallery, it was seen by those who challenged its presence as a mass-produced item, without scent or sight of waste yet still reminiscent of it.[94] More than half a century since its first presentation, I saw the *Fountain*—the urinal—on display at London's Royal Academy of Arts. It was set behind glass next to a variety of items from both Duchamp and Dali.[95] Beyond reach, it was carefully placed on a gray platform, and as a consequence it lost something of its quality of thingliness. It is sterile: one cannot imagine it painted with urine. It is a thing penetrated in only a limited sense, with potential for full openness unfulfilled. It is no longer *ready*made. It is shiny—glossy, really—with openings where I imagine in another context it would be connected to the pipe rendering piss invisible and to the water removing any visible evidence that bodies are open and project a stream of waste. Here it is just exposed without a use. There is a concern for the naming-thing, but its quality is only erotic—by which I mean it is concerned with the affective dimension of openness. Readymade—or already made? The transfer of the thing impacts perception and alters the manner of interplay. Furthermore, the inscription on the side—"R. Mutt"—suggests this alteration by a naming-thing onto a thing-thing. Perhaps this is what Duchamp meant in saying that bringing it into display and signing it "created a new thought for that object." This is both disgust and design.

This points to waste through a device meant to help us remove it, but what of machines made to bring waste into full view? Of course, shitting can be artificially depicted—mechanized—and rendered the work of machines. For instance, artist Wim Devoye's *Cloaca—New and Improved* involves an electronic device that simulates the production and elimination of waste.[96] The color, odor, and even the shape mimics that produced as the naming-thing purges itself from itself. That is, "electronic and mechanical systems play the part of the enteric nervous system, regulating food's passage through glass jars acting as Cloaca's stomach, small intestine, large intestine, and rectum. . . . Hours later, out the other end comes poop."[97] There is much that could be made of this within the context of transhuman or posthuman studies or even animal studies, pushing them to explore the nature of shitting as a challenge to distinctions of being.

Does this machine somehow sterilize shitting—remove from it the element of cleanliness or privatization regulation intended to instill? In removing from the biological naming-thing, the process of production and expulsion of shit, does this artwork tell us about the dynamics of embodiment and the degree to which we can decentralize and deprioritize certain functions? If we could have such devices shit for us, perhaps we could remove all disgust and a deeply troubling sign of openness? However intriguing, these questions are not my interest here. In a word, I intend to examine what this piece of art (and the $1,000 samples of its shit collectors purchased) tells us about the vacuous nature of shitting.

Shit matters, and its mattering is expressed artistically.

It is hard to think of shitting as a matter of cultural evolution, but artistic expression based on and showing shit makes this realization more aesthetically confrontational. Shit in a gallery is still shit, but it has a distinction from that deposited in the gas station restroom. The former one might buy for display, but the latter is a source of shame. In either case, shit exposes the naming-thing as having the capacity to produce what it would rather deny. In this regard, shit is a matter of insult but also celebration.

Take conceptual art, for example. This mode of art signifies dimensions of the aesthetic and removes a quality of artistic meaning and production. It ties art to the mundane in ways that challenge the very substance or meaning of art. As Dave Praeger writes, "Poop is the ultimate tool for conceptual art—because nothing is aesthetically less appealing than poop."[98] Furthermore, this statement, I believe, is akin to what Jojada Verrips had in mind when saying, "By painting (with) shit(ting bodies) and/or smearing what is inside their bodies on their outside, artists express a specific view of the very fragile nature of our capacity to always remain the civilized creatures we think we are."[99]

A prime example of this turn to shit, one documented and explored in numerous articles and books, is *Artist's Shit* (*Merda d'Artista*), produced in the early 1960s by Piero Manzoni. Photographs related to this "work" of art show the artist smiling and holding one of the cans containing a "piece" of him. Like Pop Art, which questions the difference between things natural and things intentional, Manzoni challenged the distinction between the ordinary and art. In fact, he took this to its biological extreme by positioning ninety small cans of his shit as art to be sold at the price of gold per ounce.[100] His shit is not seen in these cans—one of which I viewed at MoMA in New York. As art critics have noted, one must assume the artist's statement is matched by his defecation and storage of that waste, sealed, numbered, and presented.[101] In this regard, Manzoni highlights the ever-present nature of shit, while also noting the manner in which even when it is invisible it is still with us— marking us and forming a sense of what we are as bodied and open. Mindful of this, one could say that Manzoni takes the bodied naming-thing as pro- ducer of waste and turns that production into art. That is to say, it is, in this case, because the bodied naming-thing is open that it can produce art. Or as Martin Engler says, "What is provocatively radical in this sense are not the faeces he declares to be art, but the process of artistic-physical transforma- tion that turns the (artist's) body into a producer of works of art operating along the interface of biology and aesthetics."[102]

Manzoni was not alone in using shit to make metaphysical and existen- tial statements. The 1960s and 1970s in a more general artistic sense (in the Western world) is marked by the presentation of human shit.[103] This might have something to do with the cultural-political and social concerns that pen- etrated Western society during this time—concerns that were best noted and challenged through the exposing of what "should" be hidden and that by being out of place spoke a powerful word to the political-social-cultural and economic connotations of being in place.[104] By extension, and in a very important way, this work with shit deconstructs the naming of things as being "in" or "out of" place because interaction and mutuality, or connection, be- tween naming-things and thing-things means there is no predetermined lo- cation or "place."

Turning back to the exhibit with which I started, Cattelan is missing ex- cept for the golden toilet he leaves behind. He demonstrates the openness of all naming-things to the extent that all shit, and in this shitting all bodied naming-things exist in a state of interplay with internal/external things. The idea of the artist remains intact, but all else—the turning of a toilet into some- thing else—is left to other naming-things. Can what is said about Manzoni be applied to the patrons taking advantage of Cattelan's exhibition? "Here the body becomes a medium for the ingestion, production and excretion of art."[105] Hence, it is not shit that is for sale here at the Guggenheim; rather, patrons purchase an opportunity to contribute something of "substance" to the project. Cattelan privileges biological process, and Manzoni privileges product. Yet on some level, both artists are concerned with the ability to name and observe interplay outside its normal arrangements and constitution. There is hidden in the larger ethos of shit-based art another concern—one that troubles. By its very nature, it disrupts the ability to judge "quality" in terms of traditional markers of "good" or "bad" art.[106] The normative standards of reflection do not function in the realm of shit.

I disagree with those who argue for a secular theological platform for Manzoni's work and who do so by casting it in terms of Communion and other Christian ritualization. I suggest that it is more fruitful to think in terms of shit for sale, for example, outside the framework, say, of the Eucharist. Christian ritual entails a pull beyond human historical experience and involves attention to a different modality of knowledge. I argue that the more significant impact of Manzoni's work—and others like it—is the very deconstruction of such efforts to seal off the body through divine impingement and to maintain the realization of openness. Eucharist, for instance, maintains a rather narrow sense of defilement and purity, which I argue Manzoni and others, through the presentation of shit, seek to dismantle. To cast their work in terms of theological ritual in a strict sense is to downplay the value of its grotesque quality.[107]

For both Cattelan and Manzoni, art is a (fecal) matter of distinction denied by repositioning the naming-thing and what it produces. For Cattelan, *Americas* invites participants to acknowledge their shit by having it simultaneously celebrated and denounced. *Americas* is a toilet that hides waste, like all toilets, yet it is in a museum and thereby celebrates the "once was and still is" quality of the human connection to the thing called shit. Manzoni's attention to naming-thing and thing-thing is more mobile and requires more of the participant. It is one thing to pay to take a shit—as is the case with the cover charge for *Americas*. But is this the same as paying for another's shit? Buying one of Manzoni's cans is not simply an acknowledgment that shit matters and that we produce this matter, but that open naming-things are not hidden and cannot hide this substance. It also points to a certain type of utility of shit—not as fertilizer but as a reminder of mutuality. That is to say, Cattelan and Manzoni, among others, point out through the presentation of shit/shitting the manner in which engaged naming-things share agency as a matter of productive interactivity with other things.[108] The significance of this artwork is the manner in which it serves to highlight a common but undervisualized process of engagement based on intentional naming. Or as Kristina Wirtz notes in terms of Cuban popular religion, rubbish (I would specify shit) "acts on us as much as we act on it, but does so without drawing our conscious attention most of the time."[109] The difference is this: while Wirtz is thinking in terms of the transfer of spiritual emphasis through touch, I am concerned with a more standard process of mutuality vis-à-vis porous naming-things and thing-things. Wirtz, that is, gives consideration to the spiritual vitality of things, and I suggest that this is to see these things for what cannot be seen—for the manner in which their importance is genealogically beyond them. *Ritual* waste is not just waste in that the ritualization either exposes or invests it with a potentially dangerous quality of "more." Contrary to this position, I want to see the importance of waste, in this case shit, for itself as a porous thing whose materiality is and is not the naming-thing.[110]

Manzoni loses something in the process—the body surrenders a piece of itself, which another buys and in a sense makes his or her own.[111] The openings, the most porous locations of the body, connect us. In this case, the connection takes place through the passing and collecting of shit. The goal is not simply to shock, but rather to expose and to mediate that exposition, perhaps, by means of what Stella Santacatterina references as "the continual mutability of art" by means of which the patron participates in the "active realization of the artistic event."[112] In the case of Manzoni, buying his shit is more than buying art; in the case of Cattelan, the "active realization" involves evacuating the content of the open naming-thing into the artistic context provided by the Guggenheim. In either case, the intersection between viewer and artist is blurred in the same manner that naming-things and thing-things are open and involved in a process of interplay. Both modes of artistic shitting involve ritualization of a naming-thing function pointing to openness, but without standard theological connotations and theologicalized disregard.

chapter five

# restricting
## part iii

# pieces of things                                        6

Things are not inert.
—IAN HODDER, *Entangled: An Archaeology of the Relationships between Humans and Things*

Mikhail Bakhtin assumes that the grotesque body (or what I have labeled the bodied naming-thing) is coded in particular ways. And this raises a nagging question associated with an accompanying dilemma: What happens when the social coding imposed on the bodied naming-thing serves to hamper its openness?

Taking further the significance of shit discussed in chapter 5, in part 3 I explore the nature of this dilemma—one that might be phrased in a manner reminiscent of David Marriott's question: "What of those subjects whose rule of life is to endure life under the ownership of another and consequently are said to live as objects?"[1] Or, as Judith Butler announced, there are mechanisms, strategies, and practices by means of which some naming-things are collapsed or repressed into representing despised thing-things. Stated simply, there are ways in which, on the sociocultural and political level, some naming-things "become shit."[2] Marriott might call this situation "corpsing."[3] I would simply add that it involves not the interplay between naming-thing and thing-thing but rather the corruption of interplay through an effort to close off particular bodies coded as raced, gendered, and classed, for instance.

In other words, interplay between naming-thing and thing-thing is warped, as the former and the latter are misnamed through effort to constitute sociopolitical, cultural, and economic boundaries rehearsed as narratives of a biohistorical tenor. In these pages, I point out that naming-things and thing-things are named and positioned even prior to their involvement. That is to say, they are constructed and involved through a process of interpretation.

## Art as Protest, or What Does Art Do?

Art and life bleed into each other, and in certain intriguing ways the vehicle for this interplay is the naming-thing that does the work in the first instance. And for the artist explored in this chapter, there is also the naming-thing consumed in and by the art. The artist "thinks" this work but is also guided through it by the social realities that have shaped his relationship to other things. In this regard, art has a function that pushes beyond art for art's sake, to a sense of art as fostering experience (understood as moments of interplay) that is "political and instrumental."[4] This is another way of noting what many have referenced as the political function of art, and this function is sensitive to the details of the historical moment in which things and bodied naming-things interact.

For some time, thinkers and activists within African American communities have argued the importance of artistic expression for shifting sociopolitical perceptions of African American naming-things. In this regard, art is something of an aesthetically sophisticated "picket sign." What sermons, lectures, and political protest of a physical kind could not accomplish—it has been argued by many advocates of racial equality—could be captured through the symbols and poetics of art in all its forms. Earlier slave narratives such as those produced by Frederick Douglass intend to position African American naming-things for full rights in part through their presentation as open—for example, the pain experienced by them and their right to full participation. Writers tackled the angst of black life as racialized naming-things rendered truncated and closed through racial violence.[5] Poets such as Countee Collen spoke the stuff of life encountered by embodied people of African descent, but he did not leave it with this; instead, he spoke of the supple nature of the blackened naming-thing. Musicians such as Bessie Smith and Billie Holiday sang the depth of black life in ways that pushed against the presumption that black naming-things are one-dimensional, and they did this by celebrating the degrading, to appeal once again to Bakhtin (or bluesy quality), of black naming-things. In this way they repositioned racialized naming-things through a shift in how they occupy time and space as well as how they interact within that time and space.[6]

But in that the primary concern here is with the visual arts, I offer these examples simply as context before turning to the manner in which the blackened naming-thing projected outward, beyond itself, through visual art, speaks a depth denied within the flat and bounded circumstances of our race-biased social circumstances. The creative process captured by the arts and the involvement of racialized naming-things in the arts speak to a depth of relationship, one that signifies assumptions of inferiority through a poetic quality challenging the assumption of African Americans as naming-things constituted by a fixed, a reified, and an ontological limit. The key here is not necessarily the production of pleasure but rather the transformative potentiality of discomfort—the requirement to view and to reevaluate held assumptions concerning the meaning of certain naming-things. The key, the purpose, is multidimensional.

To what is art so conceived responding? What is the history, the cartography of sociopolitical, economic, and cultural markings of life for African American naming-things that informs how the visual arts are made and read? The answer is simple but does not entail a simplistic framing of collective life. Art, by racialized naming-things, speaks to the significance and value of a collective group whose history has been written to suggest something other than their value and relationality. Art is a rich rejection of dehumanization and other modalities of ontological violence. Furthermore, in a fundamental sense, it speaks to a collective identity, but one must exercise caution not to reify this shared history.

Reflecting on the definition of "black" in "black popular culture," Richard J. Powell notes that shared experience of "racial and cultural discrimination, segregation, recognition, and identification—should not be viewed as a litmus tests for blackness per se, since many peoples of African descent have experienced these to varying degrees."[7] Looking at this not from the perspective of art historian, philosopher of art, or art critic, I push a particular dimension of this discussion, one that notes the significance of artistic thinking and the presentation of openness.[8] The artistic production of African American naming-things frames existential considerations through a visual re-presentation of worth and interplay celebrated—and presented in exhibits such as *Soul of a Nation: Art in the Age of Black Power 1963–1983*.[9] Pulling together a variety of ontological and epistemological concerns is significant here. The "desire to visualize something racial and cultural," notes Powell, "yet also conceptual and metaphysical, found the ideal subject in black religion." It is only the case in these pages that religion is pushed beyond the typical terrain of doctrines and creeds and instead is understood as a technology.[10] As Powell, among others, cautions, this is not to assume a "black aesthetic." Such a singular or unified approach is not necessary in order to appreciate a shared range of concerns encountered due to blackness" and what it means within the grammar and vocabulary of life in the United States. The openness of blackened naming-things is not dependent on approval from white Americans. Hence, there is something about the artistic production of African Americans that suggests a stating of the known but denied—not a creation of ontological meaning, but rather a celebration of meaning as openness or Bakhtian degradation in such a way as to cause discomfort for those who have denied it.

Still, there is no intention here to assume through omission that only people of African descent must (or should) wrestle with the nature and meaning of interplay. No, this is a concern for "white" Americans as well, but the privilege of whiteness also entails a certain in/visibility that makes matters of thingliness curiosity as opposed to necessity. So here attention is given to the thingliness of "white" Americans. Yet this is done through attention to how whites relate to the visualization of blackened naming-things interacting and performing openness. This is not to reify the latter, to make the latter objects for speculation, but rather the opposite. This move is made to demonstrate the manner in which whiteness is dependent on blackness. In other words, the effort of whites to promote a narrative of distinction or difference based on clear boundaries requires the presence of blackness.

White bodied naming-things occupy time and space to a significant degree over against the manner in which blackened naming-things occupy time and space. In this regard, "right" occupation has significant socioeconomic, political, and cultural ramifications. In either case, subjectivity is pieced together. If naming-things, in fact, occupy numerous social spaces simultaneously, is not this to be expected? Perception of life, cartographies of what the experiences of life entail, would then need to be patched together from the stuff we can gather, from the elements of life we can arrange and hold long enough to note their significance. In a sense, then, artistic production— the visual arts in this instance—is a poetic rehearsal of the fact of ontological significance, which is colorful, vibrant, challenging, and compelling in its presentation. Done from within the very cultural worlds that question this ontological given, significance is much harder to hide and deny. Black naming-things once flattened are given depth through signifying their truncated presence.

## Changing Things

The presentation of self over against presentations by others marks the start of this ontological shift to the already and always openness of African Americans. Such a move was presented to the art world, in the case of Romare Bearden, through manipulation of scraps of things often used for another purpose. In this way, the purpose of "things" is recast, reshaped, and magnified. These things—scraps of paper, pieces of wood, letters, and so forth—have their thingliness transformed and used to mirror other and deeper realities.

What stories do things tell when arranged by this artist? And what is to be made of his stories when disconnected things are brought into relationship through application—through an intentional push to place them differently?

Things matter in multiple, overlapping ways in his art. There is the naming-thing manipulating things in order to tell stories. These naming-things doing work say something about the structuring of life in a society marked by suspicion concerning openness and interplay. Added to this is the manner in which such art depicts the performative and plastic nature of identification—the manner in which things can be pressured and manipulated and "worn" so as to produce something other than their first and most visible intent.[11] There is something significant about the shaping and massaging of "things," and Bearden speaks to this situation. His art is dimensionally visual, but this seeing does not render it fixed, rigid, or easily held. Through presentation of things, Bearden also points to absence, and through this fosters alternate possibilities of interplay. For some, this type of process points to a problem, but there is another perspective possible. What Powell notes when discussing "a homoerotic gaze on the black male body" through photography can be read for its larger relevance:

> The black body as a photographed object of desire, while unquestionably nuanced, elicited what author Alice Walker pronounced in her novel *Meridian* (1976) as the ultimate sin: turning of real, thinking and feeling people into Art. Yet one could also argue that, at this moment of an expanded black consciousness [the 1970s], it was precisely this sense that blacks could be both objects of artistic contemplation and actors in their own aesthetic discernment, that made these works provocative and central to a revised art history of transgressive, radical black images.[12]

The metaphysical and existential content of this work, by means of a variety of styles, was meant to dislodge racialized naming-things and their conceptual counterpoints from the confinement of white supremacy and aesthetic dominance spoken through it. Art, in this regard, was already and always engaged—either implicitly or explicitly—with the configuration of interplay marked up and/or out.

Designations and artistic styles changed to reflect the ebb and flow of perceived interaction within geographies of altered socioeconomic and political discourses and arrangements. In describing the presence of race, Michael Harris articulates an applicable sensibility. "Racial discourses, though they are discourses of power," he writes, "ultimately rely on the visual in the sense that the visible body must be used by those in power to represent nonvisual realities that differentiate insiders from outsiders."[13] By extension, Harris notes, "the individual physical body eventually symbolized in various ways one's membership in a particular social body or body politic."[14] If, as African American visual arts at least implies, visual representation can be used to reify and fix racialized naming-things, visual arts can be used to challenge and signify such constructions and thereby foster a new sense of openness. In a word, things are linked and manipulated through visual markers to alter cultural worlds, and such a shift is possible because rules of the social hierarchy are written, spoken, but also presented on and through things. The ways in which bodies occupy time and space says something about the merit and worth of particular things. The implicit and explicit manner in which this plays out can be captured in the language and moves of the visual arts. "Pictures and words," notes Arthur Danto, "may be grossly distinguished in terms of how they represent their subjects, and they exemplify, again grossly, the two chief systems by which we represent the world."[15]

What Danto argues in terms of Robert Irwin's sense of art's function as meant to "heighten awareness" is applicable in this context as well. "Not to heighten awareness of art as art," writes Danto, "but of the dimensions and features of life that art raises to the highest powers of enhancement while remaining invisible directing the viewer's sensibilities with a kind of aesthetic Hidden Hand."[16] Yet for many, this use of the visual arts became the normative and required intent of the artist: African American art was a political act of reenvisioning ontological and existential meaning through the proclamation of openness. And this visual proclamation worked to adjust the perception of a particular context in that—as Hans Belting argues regarding particular types of images and I extend to visual images more broadly developed—images have contextual significance in that they speak to and from a particular cultural world, and "it is in this place that they exert their effect."[17] Naming-things create art so as to speak to and about the world, and in so doing this art massages the manner in which viewers think of themselves, others, and worlds in light of the artist's visual monologue. The work of naming-things can change minds and encourage modalities of behavior and perceptions of what all this means to a sense of being.

Art involves something made, a transposition and transformation of place and function. As Elizabeth Grosz says with respect to Australian art, "Art is created, always made, never found, even if it is made from what is found. This is its transformative effect—as it is made, so it makes."[18] It is not simply that art intensifies and makes more vibrant "life." No, the work of African American artists brings into question the very content and form of life and the bodies that map out "life." The certainty of the past and the comfort of the present as structured through the dominant narrative of the meaning of "American" life is challenged and exposed for the warped take on the real it really is.

## Bearden's Collages

Romare Bearden (1911–1988) shifted the position, and hence meaning, of racialized naming-things by challenging dominant aesthetic standards and consideration that surround if not engulf them. He spoke a new "word" about the nature and meaning of black naming-things by shifting the presentation of discourse—new aesthetics, new stylistic consideration, and new ontological, epistemological, and existential insights. This was an artistic shift riddled with potential consequences that move against the intended reification of blackened naming-things. There is the racialized naming-thing of the artist that represents and presents the meanings of racialization and truncation signified. This complicates matters: Which body is signified, and does the embodied artist's presence say something that is not countered by the presence of the art? Is the artist an extension of the "sign" or the deconstruction of the "sign"?[19]

Abstract Expressionism ended in the 1960s, and Pop Art emerged as a means by which to blur the line between art and the ordinary. During that same period, Bearden began an alternate creative process by piecing together scraps to create collages portraying different dimensions of African American experience.[20] Bearden had spent a good number of years working in light of the premises of Abstract Expressionism, but this changed.[21] It was not simply the end of Abstract Expressionism as such, but rather his need to respond to issues of identity in a way that required forceful reconstruction of contextualized meaning. Having spent time employed as a social worker, Bearden had a sense of "real" life—its complexities, its thickness, and the way in which it informs, shapes, and presents naming-things. Hence, collages mark Bearden's wrestling with identity and interplay—the reenvisioning of meaning in light of the sociohistorical framing of experience encountered and known by African Americans.[22] Perhaps something of the layered nature of human life—the occupation of numerous social spaces simultaneously—is portrayed through the collage process informing work such as *Projections*, collage-styled presentations of moments of interaction called black life that were first exhibited in 1964.

The manner in which African Americans entail a blending of cultural worlds to foster identities that sustain and enliven is presented artistically through the layering process of the collage, whereby pieces of things are brought together to form frameworks of meaning and relationship.[23] For Bearden, the construction of identity had to involve attention to memory, but memory funneled through contemporary structures and frameworks of experience. Such was of concern to Bearden as he shifted away from his earlier stylistic commitments. He gave ample attention to the role of the artist in the construction of new ontological and existential possibilities for African Americans during and after the civil rights struggle.[24] History mattered to Bearden, and history—its tone and texture—had to be represented. Yet this history had to involve the layered nature of human experience, the intersections and connections between the individual's encounter with the world and the larger framing of life of which those more focused encounters are a significant part.

The pieces pulled together to produce an imperfect image of life lived contain in their roughness something of the "earthy" nature of life, the inconsistencies and "fits and starts" that constitute movement through the world. Bearden's social work, his time in the military, and his movement through the South and the North only fed this approach to understanding life. These personal experiences were something of a bridge to the macrorealities of African American life; they feed, in particular ways, lucidity and sensitivity to the moments that mark out existence. There is something chaotic about life so conceived, and then art might be said to involve, as Bearden notes, the artist attempting to "organize chaos."[25]

Bearden recognized the ability to define, name, and present the bodied naming-thing through the manipulation of things—flattened out in order to interrogate what pieces brought together tell us about the nature and meaning of life. I have in mind the collage series produced in the 1960s by means of which Bearden depicted personalities and religious-spiritual figures and scenes through the manipulation of images and words intended for another purpose. His collage work demonstrated the layers of meaning that constitute our perception of life and living. In both cases, the socially imposed structuring of blackness through the body is rethought, pushing against the assumption that such blackened bodies hold no great worth or value—and say nothing to and about life meaning in substantive ways. This restructuring away from restriction "paints" blackened naming-things as "signs" of great importance and worth. The complexities of life are forged in light of "things" and experiences arranged and rearranged—so as to be used to construct new possibilities.

American imagination involves a certain spin on the substance of African American cultural life, a type of simplification of African American experience so as to think it less significant than that of white Americans. However, Bearden builds African American cultural life anew, out of various pieces of experience, and in this retelling or remaking Bearden challenges poetically truncated depictions of African American life by showing the stuff of which it is made and by encouraging viewers to recognize the layered and complex nature of cultural systems constructed by African Americans.

*The Prevalence of Ritual: The Baptism,* part of the *Projections* series of 1964, takes the practice of Christian baptism so important to African American Christians and pushes beyond dull depictions by including pieces in the collage that speak to an African past (i.e., images resembling African ritual masks). In so doing, it ties this water ritual to a richness of cultural life that extends beyond the confinements of North American slavery. There is a church structure in the background, but it is of minor concern as it surrenders to the vitality, the energy, of bodies in the act of ritualization. The people, the bodied naming-things, involved in the ritual are highlighted and placed in the foreground so that the viewer is forced to see and recognize them. In this way, the tendency within the larger society for the invisibility of African Americans is controlled and negated through a layered presence that constitutes bodies demanding consideration. Pieces of images, pieces of life so to speak, might be said to represent the manner in which the violence of the United States pulled black lives apart and did violence to them that was meant to render them unrecognizable as fully formed, embodied bodies of merit. Through the collages, Bearden chronicles the manner in which African Americans have pulled these pieces together and constructed worlds of meaning. The cuts and tears necessary to produce these bodies are graphic, not hidden in the art, and something about these marks, these lines, speaks to the marking of black bodies during the period of slavery and ongoing structured discrimination—the markings of discrimination the civil rights movement sought to address. Think of these collage images, the sharp edges and rips pronounced in light of the scars on black bodies imprinted by means of a whip or other devices marking a trail of suffering, or the hardships imprinted on black bodies by the harsh realities of Jim and Jane Crow. The viewer has to focus, to train the eyes to seek the pieces and to see that the pieces constitute a greater (but imperfect) arrangement forming naming-things active and vibrant. As numerous scholars have noted, that these collages reflect the times is no accident when one considers the fact that civil rights leaders asked Bearden and others to give some thought to how artists might contribute to the struggle for justice. The conversations generated Spiral, a group of artists committed to art with public meaning, so to speak. The objective, as Gail Gelburd notes, was to "find a way to fulfill their social responsibility without turning their art into mere propaganda, to be a part of their times without relinquishing their commitment to aesthetics."[26] As Bearden shifted away from Abstract Expressionism, thing-things pushed their way forward; constructed of pieces of "things" each with its own stories that merge into a structure of grouped vibrancy, these composite and interacting things dominate and demand attention—requiring consideration. These were bodies unlike his earlier bodies painted and drawn.

Beginning during the turmoil of the civil rights efforts of the 1960s, the collage process would remain Bearden's mode of presentation. The piecing together would alter over time and not necessarily contain the same sharp edges and the jerking intensity, but the layering of realities remained vital.[27] Perhaps the softening had something to do with the sociopolitical shifts and cultural nuances of different decades—shifting performances of interplay? The presentation of the bodied thingliness of African American life had to be expressed, but with a different energy and emphasis. Bearden's collage work exposes the inner workings of bodies to the extent that these bodies, as he presents them, are composed of pieces pulled together. In this process there is the whole—the composite—but the viewer also sees the bits and pieces that compose this whole. All this suggests the nature of interplay—various things penetrating, layered, interacting.

Through the layering of substances that constitute the collage style there emerges a situation thick and vibrant with complex meaning. Parts are somewhat exaggerated, extended, and their distinctions pronounced, but all this adds to the visual depiction of embodiment that gives cultural-historical weight and importance, and that gives a certain degree of significance to naming-things as open. Full, layered, representation wins out for Bearden, and he uses it to discuss the nature and meaning of life for African Americans and by extension what it means for African Americans to be naming-things interacting with and through the world. Naming-things show their complexity; they are made visible, their "inners" exposed, so to speak. The complexities often hidden in other circumstances are highlighted and brought to the fore. This artistic move was not a full departure from earlier sensibilities; rather, Bearden came to understand that concern with universals required equal attention to the local and the specific. For him, this meant a solid, graphic, and vibrant turn to his experience—including the damaging effect of economic hardship and white supremacy fueled by structured discrimination that marked his North Carolina homeland, as well as the turmoil of world wars, the Great Depression, the Harlem Renaissance, and the organized struggle for civil rights—and that of the larger collective of African Americans.[28]

There is a visual "double-talk," so to speak, in that there are pieces within this series drawn from other projects, other artistic traditions, and they are put to a different work.[29] The energy of African American life—its sharp and ragged edges—speaks to the manner in which this despised but gifted community has had to rip away pieces of itself in order to construct signs of and spaces for identity. While Bearden at times used a photostat process to downplay the roughness of the cuts and layering (as in life people might try to decrease "difference" so as to highlight their sameness with social standards), the effect was never complete.[30] The edges, the roughness of the tears and cuts, were always present. These collage images were not produced on an easel as one might imagine paintings positioned; rather, they were made flat on a table.[31]

Each piece perhaps is unrecognizable alone, but together they shape and offer contour to the mechanics of African American being and meaning. *Conjur Woman*, also from *Projections*, speaks to the African American engagement with the rest of the environment—relationship to and manipulation of plant life so as to foster new possibilities of life. Animals, plants, and humans interact, expressing an overlap of engagement and relationship that transforms all involved. In this, Bearden highlights the thickness of African American experience, its layered connotations, and its ability to speak to the nature and meaning of life within the larger U.S. urban and rural contexts as well as life on the microlevel. The conjur woman depends on the plants and the animals present, and the animals and plants are impacted by the conjur woman's careful engagement.

What serves to hold these various geographies of meaning together is the configured naming-things occupying and manipulating time and space.

"Bearden and his peers," writes Leslie King-Hammond, "sought to create aesthetic voices that would give visual meaning and presence to ordinary people—living ordinary lives, in ordinary environments—in an extraordinary era of modernist invention."[32] Bearden presents the poetic quality of African American experience within various social realms, and in this way he exposes the vitality of embodied black life over against what are often truncated and reified assumptions concerning what it means to be black and alive—shifting through time and space.

Of course, there are the most readily apparent and easily recognized markers of this quest for meaning. Think in terms of conjure, baptism, and other elements of African-based traditional practices and Christianity that have for an extended period marked the landscape of African American metaphysical concern. Still there are more, less easily registered modalities of interplay presented through these collages. Bearden maps out the soul—or genius of African American engagement with the world. These collages make a statement concerning meaning that is important to note: meaning is not found whole but is constructed in an imperfect manner by consciously selecting bits and pieces of experience and pulling them together for what they can say about larger systems of concerns. What is more, this process of intentionally constructing involves also a process of destruction, a privileging of certain experiences (or moments of interplay) and the ignoring of others, as Bearden selects particular pieces of images from *Life* magazine and others for inclusion and dismisses others. And once selected, the images must be dismantled—their initial intended meaning ripped apart—in order for them to point to something beyond themselves. Or as Ralph Ellison notes when describing Bearden's *Projections* series, "The work of the arts is a matter of destroying moribund images of reality and creating the new." What is more, "it is of the true artist's nature and mode of action to dominate all the world and time through technique and vision." This is tied to a task, an objective which is "to bring a new visual order into the world, and through [the artist's] art he seeks to reset society's clock by imposing upon it his own method of defining the times."[33]

*Fish Fry* (1967) presents activity that is not spectacular or extraordinary but still speaks to the depth of human meaning expressed through embodied activities. Cooking together and sharing food and conversation or preparing for the day as the sun signals a new beginning, or sitting over coffee, when presented by Bearden, speak in different ways to a shared concern for connection, for relationship, and for a way to interrogate experience. Within the ordinary activities of communal existence, Bearden distills through his collages the depth of meaning of vibrant vision that marks embodied life.

*Interplay.*

The distinctions between these various forms of life are evident, while they also merge with and depend on both the presence and absence of "others." Presence and absence overlap and point in the direction of the other. The local points in the direction of larger commonalities, and shared markers of ritual life also push back to local activities and concerns. There is fluidity here that is epistemological and existential in nature. Or as Gail Gelburd notes when reflecting on Bearden's collages, "Our perception of space is then psychological as well as visual, and we are reminded that no perspective, myth, ritual, or memory is ever fixed."[34] It is not simply the explicit religious themes such as *Of the Blues: Carolina Shout* (1974) that speak to Bearden's layered depiction of interplay as embodied and vibrant. The scenes of mundane activities and celebration speak to the significance of embodied bodies encountering others as the outline of history, the content of experience, and the sign of identity formation.

Of concern in the 1960s, collage work is not blackness per se but rather the arena of ontology that gives shape and meaning to blackness as a cover for certain naming-things. There is complexity to Bearden's depictions of life within African American contexts, and in certain ways the collage process itself speaks to this complexity and depth of meaning. However, it is also expressed through the range of activities presented by Bearden that mark out the richness of relationship and the world not fully captured by opposition to whiteness—scope of experience, depth of meaning, lucidity—expressed with a fluidity of form and visualized movement within these captured moments.[35]

These cut and ripped pieces call to the viewer, but in such a way as to signal their presence—but their presence in relationship to other pieces that form something of a whole. Robert G. O'Meally captures this process using musical metaphor: Bearden constructs through a blues and jazz aesthetic—improvisation.[36] Another way to put this, one centered within a concern for religion, is that Bearden's collages point to the microexperiences that blend to form a more unified sense of meaning—but as a sense of complex meaning that is always part of the incomplete and fractured nature of life: Complexity. While scholars such as O'Meally see Bearden as a jazz or blues figure, one could just as easily perceive him as a conjurer—one who pulls from the familiar to produce a particular type of work. One might be familiar with the use of roots, herbs, and other plants by traditional conjurers, but doesn't Bearden use "things"—the scraps of paper from magazines—which, at their core, are drawn from those same woods and other environments? Using these captured and manipulated elements, he pushes viewers to confront the commonalities of human experience as they also observe the spaces of activity marking out African American experiences within time and space. The imperfection is itself transformative. Elements of the collages are proportionate, and each element demands a certain level of attention in part determined by size. Yet, isn't it the case with experiences that some are more graphic, "larger" so to speak, and therefore more prominent and more prone to demand attention?

Pieces are important here in that they point to the value of our images of life, while also pointing out that these images are incomplete. When layered, when joined, they tell us something more and point to the significance of presence. Bearden pulls and pushes history in an effort to expose its content, contours, depth, and aesthetic qualities—the interplay of various things that constitutes experience.[37] Bearden's collages in the *Projections* series visualize the process of exploration, interrogation, analysis, and mapping. In terms of identity, of being and meaning, the conjur woman, for instance, represents the blending of traditions, the harnessing of worlds—African, European, and North American—to stabilize African American being through a study of the construction of bodies. The collage structuring of things creates a type of epistemological dissonance that brings into question assumptions concerning what a blackened naming-thing constitutes and how it is constituted. The exaggerated features and limbs signify the stereotypical depiction of African Americans as having no aesthetic value in that their features, such as lips and noses, are too large, too broad—too unlike that of European Americans. In a word, stereotypically depicted black bodies do not survive the normative gaze, as Cornel West names European features understood as signifying totalizing standards of beauty, worth, and intelligence.[38] Ralph Ellison captures what is taking place through the layering of materials: "Bearden knows that the true complexity of the slum dweller and the Tenant farmer requires a release from the prison of our media-dulled perception and a reassembling in forms which would convey something of the depth and wonder of the Negro American's stubborn humanity."[39] All this metaphysical work is present in the collages produced.

The features of these bodies are extended, enlarged, often out of proportion. These bodies are active; they have depth manifest as they engage the story of the collage and the viewer. What Bearden offers, then, is a study in anthropology as ontological mosaic. This series, the collage series, was a work of memory, an effort to capture the tone and texture of life familiar to Bearden growing up, and that marked out the form and content of life for many African Americans in the North and the South. It humanized, so to speak, those who—like the conjur woman—protected the integrity of embodied life. Collages, like pictures with a poetic quality, forced a rethinking of embodied bodies through the reconstruction of bodies by means of other materials. These collages speak to how bodies occupy time and space in ways that manipulate the unseen and produce the unintended. In other words, contends Gelburd, "the metaphors and the myths that he visualized are not merely a description of the scene but a mirror of life's experiences."[40] So much of what constitutes these collages involves an experiment with what naming-things do by means of their porousness—how they occupy space and how they produce meaning through ritual, celebration, and everyday activities in the company of others.[41]

# "captured" things 7

If there is anything universal about human beings, it is that given a largely identical biology, they will represent the world differently from stage to stage of the histories in which they participate.
—ARTHUR DANTO, *The Body/Body Problem*

Moving from Romare Bearden's collage work as signifying the interplay of things over against efforts to foster racialized boundaries and modes of confinement, this chapter presents the second of three scenarios in which the racialization of certain naming-things is used to foster the illusion of culturally coded boundaries over against the openness exposed by religion as a technology. In this instance, these are boundaries resting on racial narratives of distinction; but it should not be forgotten that boundaries impact both those who seek to establish them and those against whom they are drawn. Hence, attention to racialization of boundaries does not assume one-directional activity, nor is this push toward (and against) confinement to be understood over against some pure and universal sense of the human.

### The Situation

How do the once despised and subjugated enter into (and interact within) places in ways that alter those spaces and give new depth and vitality to blackened naming-things? I explore the nature and significance of blackness as a categorization of certain naming-things in relationship to this question. In so doing, I am committed to sketching particular examples of blackened naming-things in a way that involves loose movement through periods and locations, ultimately coming to rest on the work of Jean-Michel Basquiat—explored in connection to the politics and production of art in response to race as a cultural sealant applied to naming-things.[1]

Basquiat's work and bodied history mark out the movement between Africa and the American hemisphere in ways that speak to elements of a shared experience of the world framed by a politics of whiteness. Put differently, I use Basquiat to mount a push for openness that does not respect national boundaries but instead cuts across cultural geographies and constructions of naming-things. That is to say, the diasporic, as so many scholars have remarked, has a quality of openness played out that can be just as vital as its political and economic markers.[2] In a sense, and I reference this phrase rather frequently, the art under consideration here involves a smashing of idols (as Alain Locke described the work of the Harlem Renaissance) in that it entails a working against staid depictions of the blackened naming-thing—its cultural shape and physical significance.[3]

## Connection One: African Aesthetics
## and the "Saving" of Western Art

The postcolonial environment involves a struggle over ontology as well as the meaning of aesthetics as once racially subjected naming-things seek to reconstitute themselves through an alternate cultural reading. Involved in this process is a signifying of the rules and assumptions of the art world, tied as they have been to dominant discourses of European superiority.[4] Without doubt, cultural discourses and related geographies of interaction were played out and housed for observation in so many galleries and museums. In the words of Rasheed Araeen, "Art institutions in the West . . . have not yet abandoned the concept of art history and its 'Grand Narrative' that was established as part of the colonial world view."[5] Markers of inferiority extended from the verbal to the visual because the art world served as a mechanism for bestowing aesthetic significance on philosophical and political notions of difference as negative. The need to fix black naming-things in comforting ways—to control, display, "own" them—had to involve more than verbal discourse and accompanying written regulations and justifications.

Cultural production—visual and expressive dynamics of creativity—also played a role in that through it, aesthetics became the handmaiden of political, economic, and social arrangements privileging whiteness. This, of course, did not require a complete erasure of the African–African American naming-thing, but could instead involve demonstration of power through the ability to manipulate cultural production of the "other" and put it into service for the validation of a certain Western aesthetic sense of the proper and properly positioned naming-thing (read white). Think, for example, of the manipulation of African aesthetics represented by the mask and co-opting of this style of artistic presentation by Picasso, or the accumulation of things from the "other" found within British museums: the colonial power artistically inspired by the colonized—"Modernist Primitivism." In this regard, the museum and/or gallery might be said to have replaced the colonial government agency as the symbol of control and power.[6] The racial-ized naming-thing had long been a subject of aesthetic concern—arranged, studied, displayed so as to investigate its nature and meaning. In this regard, the display of enslaved bodied naming-things, the march of South African workers, and the display of blackened naming-things within the work of contemporary artists all speak to this preoccupation with the materiality of existence. The intention of such display is to access the dynamics of this ma-teriality and trouble the openness of black naming-things—for example, the ability to relate to other things.

There are ways in which fascination with an African aesthetic marked an effort to address the angst of aggressive industrial and technological advances in the Western world.[7] I should provide a note of context here: While the use of African art shifted over the course of the twentieth century, I am less con-cerned with these various points of use as discrete markers—use of the for-mal art versus interest in the implications of the art vis-à-vis angst regarding Western culture—and more concerned with the manner in which African art is utilized within the larger framework of twentieth-century colonialism as a general conceptual paradigm.[8] And I am intrigued by the ways in which late twentieth-century artistic production by the "children of Africa" works over against this early manipulation of cultural forms. Whether through the me-dium of painting, sculpture, or photography, art became a means by which to explore both existential and ontological issues not disconnected from sociopo-litical developments—including both the strength and decline of colonial power and authority as the marker of collective, national identity as well as individual and communal identity formation within the context of a changing world in which the power of racial dynamics is growing less fixed and certain.[9] It was an aesthetic, an artistic, consumption of the "other"—that is, racialized naming-thing—in ways meant (whether conscious or not is of little consequence) to fix a certain type of superiority couched in the ability to create and name—and have that naming "matter." This was done through reconstruction (consumption) of the African continent along colonial lines as well as similar processes in the Americas, and through developments within the context of the gallery and museum matrix of expressed and displayed cultural (and political) coding.

Europeans and Americans sought to signify, if not enliven, Western modes of interplay through the energy of an African aesthetic unleashed within the imaginaries of Western artistic expression. In this way, this aesthetic was remade in the image of the colonizer to the extent the colonizer controlled the location and context for display—as well as the interpretation of the items displayed. The initial meaning or purpose of things—such as masks—was consumed by the exotic quality bestowed on them by their new arrangement and a "Western" gaze. And they were to be fixed, or tamed, by means of this gaze. Furthermore, capture of these items marked fascination with them, but the altered purpose and place assigned them also demonstrates a certain type of discomfort with them: they cannot be what their initial creation by racialized naming-things intends. An item is emptied of one code and given another through its circumscribed location. It can then be marked by display not interplay. But all of this takes place within the confines of certain language games, marked out by a set of signs and symbols drawing on, while also critiquing, the queue of modernity.

Artists involved in this process are not involved in a turn to postmodernism; they appreciate the subject too much for that. However, they want to strip the blackened naming-thing down to the most basic precepts and assumptions. It is a manipulation of time and space, one that hopes to draw new codes and boundaries for and placements in both so as to revitalize the European bodied (and cultural) naming-thing. This goal involves effort toward integration for certain (whitened) naming-things as opposed to isolation *for* others (blackened naming bodies) and *from* troubling dimensions of world. This is not a surrender to an "other"; an African aesthetic could not be given that type of importance without jeopardizing the inner workings of European superiority. One needs, however, to be able to touch the markers of this aesthetic without defilement: one had to use Africanness without being consumed by it. This was a seek-and-rescue mission, a concern with the preservation of the subject as aesthetic entity over against the mechanical nature of modern life. Coming as no surprise, this turn to African art was also meant to free European culture to a fuller embrace of a less "managed" (but still controllable) energy of life over against restrictive modalities of reason.[10]

By posing with African art, by using it as an artistic hermeneutic, they "went native."

These masks (thing-things), for instance, could be owned and presented in a manner consistent with the nature of power within the more explicit dimensions of twentieth-century colonialism. Efforts to hide this connection served only to reinforce it, to demonstrate the inevitable linkage between sociocultural politics and artistic production. Museums and other "containers" for artistic production displayed are not devoid of such considerations, and the works they hold are also charged in the same manner and with the same cultural-political dilemmas.[11] Are these pieces representations of art or artifact?[12] Whether they were in museums or less public spaces, the ability to move between these possibilities entailed some of the power to proscribe significance inherent in the claiming, displaying, and use of African art—that is, racialized things—and the sensibilities entailed by that art. In some ways, however, this co-optation of African aesthetics served to promote a less brutal stylized use of blackness and black naming-things marking the colonial enterprise. After all, it was the globalization marked by colonial endeavors and American empire that gave occasion for more contact with African art and its underlying stylistic qualities. Whereas missionary interest in Africa and similar efforts in the American context were meant to exercise the otherness of African-related approaches to thought and action, artists consumed this otherness as a way of enlivening their sense of meaning and purpose and as a way of revitalizing Western aesthetics. With the former, Africanness needed the service of a redeemer (i.e., embrace of Western Christianity), and with respect to the latter, Africanness in particular—and otherness in general—as an aesthetic served to "save" Western art from/to itself while also damaging its epistemological connection to its context of origin.[13]

Not only was aesthetics, the nature and meaning of creativity, "saved," but attention to blackness in the form of an African artistic aesthetic was also consumed by individuals and groups outside the confines of galleries and museums. Take, for example, Paris during the early twentieth century. Drawing from France's colonial contacts, "blackness," writes Archer-Straw, was a sign of a Parisian's "modernity, reflected in the African sculptures that scattered their rooms, in the look of natural furs that fringed their coats, and in the frenzy of their dancing that mimicked the black bottom." But, as should come as no surprise based on the logic of colonialism, "only rarely are black people depicted in this world. They and their mystique are the invisible presence."[14] The concern, rather, was the place of white bodied naming-things in time and space deeply damaged by war and marked by the penetrating signs of optimism gone wrong. The dangers associated with colonial and imperialistic impulses that eventually destroy are covered over by the materials of artistic production, and what remains is a type of hopefulness that does not deny the colonial processes but seeks to redeem the West (e.g., Western art). Africa is not the source of fear in this case, but rather a means by which to enliven the aesthetics of the West.[15]

There are two sides to modernism—content (economics/politics of colonialism) and form (Western versus African aesthetics). Regarding either side, there was a sense of superiority over Africanness and the accompanying racialized naming-things in various configurations and incarnations. For instance, it was uncommon in the "art world" for there to be surprise that this aesthetic comes from the "dark" continent—the implication being a "colonialized" take on the capacities of the colonized for intellectual greatness and artistic depth. Yet this very conversation was couched in manipulation of the achievements of the very peoples disparaged. For the colonizer, the benefits were many—including economic expansion and cultural voyeurism.[16] Western artists imagined and romanticized a certain simplicity of expression over against the suffocating environs of modern technology, economic expansion, and the delicate nature of twentieth-century political arrangements. Whether through photographs displayed, museums, galleries, private collections, and so on, this artistic consumption of African art (i.e., thing-things) as a source of a "fresh" aesthetic said something about the creativity of Africa (either as art or craft), but it said more concerning the reach of colonial intent and need. Yet in other ways, the art became something of a talisman for the Western viewer, housing a certain type of power—a power to rethink the Western world. But it was a confined and limited power in that it did little to change or significantly alter the discourse of belonging or sociopolitical and ontological coding of blackened naming-things. These things were rendered visible, although those creating them were invisible—rendered irrelevant in the same way colonialism as an economic and political project makes the labor of the colonized visible but denies their depth of meaning beyond this one dimension. "Museums," writes Svetlana Alpers, "turn cultural materials into art objects. The products of other cultures are made into something that we can look at. It is to ourselves, then that we are representing things in museums."[17] History—the events, meanings, and so on associated with things—is lost, and replacing it are signs of a "fantastic" cultural trans/figuration.

Those who embody this blackness (as racialized naming-things) are restricted to what one interpreter calls "a history of silent meaning," but even this realm of ontology was marked by a persistent sense of blackness as some-*thing* to be consumed or worn at will.[18] In short, the African masks, for instance, authorized a certain covering process whereby the benefactors of cultural colonialism (and racial-difference philosophies) could critique the arrangements of modernity from inside its structures without having to fully acknowledge the contradiction. Moving from African art to the blackness of naming-things, the exotic persisted as a creative alternative to the cultural death that is modernity. "The very sense of modernism's beginning in a Western primitivism, an alterity that also allowed modernism to declare itself an alternate to modernity," writes Will Rea, "is denied to the African modern artist, a denial entirely based upon Western appropriation of the notion of the primitive, which is simultaneously coupled to a total denial of the people and culture of Africa."[19]

### Desire to "Be" the Other: Bridge Ideas

Movement is the paradigm of significance in the above presentation of blackness coding certain naming-things. One would expect this to be the case in light of the nature and meaning of colonialism and conquest. In this regard, movement—the fluidity of epistemological and ontological geography—is not limited to the nature and function of art and aesthetics, but it also says something about the general identity of bodied blackness—black material bodied naming-things. African Americans signified depictions of African-ness in particular and blackness in general. According to some scholars, the Harlem Renaissance's push for a new aesthetic encapsulates one of the early and clear efforts of African Americans to recast the cultural world and production of the African continent as their own and as something other than the visual residue of colonial politics. This cultural matrix of movement is played out across various locations and has a significant role in the relationship of Africa, Europe, and the Americas. Segments of the art world during the twentieth century positioned blackness as a custom of sorts that could be adorned and displayed, and in this way, both express a certain type of ontology while denying another. Blackness became a critique of particular aspects of modernity in the West—the nastier elements of colonialism, for example.

My concern does not rest with the "negritude" debates, but rather with the manner in which artistic expression wrestles with existential and ontological issues raised by appropriation of an African aesthetic (aesthetic as wholeness and beauty). While there are a variety of ways to tackle my interest, I want to use this as an opportunity to interrogate this process from

chapter seven

within my own context—one indebted to Africa and Europe, fueled through a centuries-long blending of both within the Americas. My question is something along these lines: What is the look of artistic production that seeks to acknowledge, signify, and restructure interplay within the context of shifting, coded geographies?

At times, cultural surveyors also embodied this Western angst and African corrective—for example, the fixing of blackened naming-things so as to preserve the integrity of white naming-things through the illusion of boundaries. A clear example of this is found in the work and life of Dada artists—such as Man Ray, who played a major role in the presentation of blackness as corrective—in Paris during the early twentieth century. "They," writes Archer-Straw, "rejected civilized bourgeois values, and styled themselves instead as primitives." And what is more, "Dada's instinct for the regressive, and its open display of hostility, were the outward expressions of negative artistic sentiments that were already an undercurrent of modernist thought."[20] The self and "other" are altered, creating something along the lines of a new aesthetic ontology: the other self, blackened and different. Others also saw the benefits in this process in that the "African" represented the "other" for whites and many African Americans. Numerous figures, including Aaron Douglas, turned at some point to an African aesthetic as a way to reconfigure African American artistic production and the "rhythm" informing it. Yet they seem to have done so in ways that still reflect a somewhat respectful glimpse at modernity—and with "limited," so to speak, anger. And while I find the work of Douglas compelling—pieces that demand one linger—more to the point of this chapter is the short but intense period of naming offered by Jean-Michel Basquiat.

Basquiat draws on the mindset and posture toward the world promoted by the emergence of hip-hop culture and uses it as a conceptual paradigm and language. There has been attention given to a blues aesthetic and a jazz aesthetic—with the latter often used in reference to Basquiat—but I suggest a hip-hop aesthetic, one that draws from these others but invests them with a unique restlessness that was only possible for racialized naming-things in the nadir of civil rights rhetoric and the birth of crack cocaine.[21] For those seeking performance of life in this particular age, the construction is along the lines of a labyrinth. By pulling viewers through this existential maze and by forcing a confrontation with a thick and complex association of codes, Basquiat promotes a messy and alternate depiction of blackness—one not easily borrowed by whites to the extent it seeks to maintain a sense of openness over against racially formed boundaries. That is to say, Basquiat's arrangement of things involves a depiction of interaction, of overlap, and engagement chaotic and intense—words written and crossed out, figures drawn with jagged lines to depict intensity, vibrant colors spilling out beyond outlines. Embedded in and oozing out is a rebellious aesthetic through which an awareness of dominant social codes (e.g., beauty, agency, and meaning) is known but undone. While I have some difficulties with the terminology of primitivism, there is something in the following statement that speaks to my point:

> Primitivism as practiced by Pablo Picasso and other white artists early in this century, in the late-colonial heyday of Modernism, was a matter of white culture imitating the products of non-white culture. To white Europeans and Americans of the time, generally speaking, white culture was the norm and nonwhite cultures were aberrations. To borrow from them showed not the impoverishment of white culture, its need for vital input from outside, but its imperial generosity in recognizing the nonwhite. This was a kind of royal slumming, as it were, like the visits of downtown white esthetes to upper Manhattan during the Harlem Renaissance. Basquiat's practice of primitivism was an ironic inversion of all that.[22]

Thomas McEvilley, from whose analysis of Basquiat the above quotation is drawn, believes Basquiat's engagement with notions of the artistically "primitive" serves to do deep damage to the colonial holdovers in the art world. It does so by denying ontological distance between black and white. Basquiat's art, McEvilley argues, serves to foster exchange (i.e., interplay on a grand scale) between worlds, to signify both the nature and meaning of whiteness and blackness through a process of artistic double-talk based on a language marked by a grammar of fluidity.[23] He sees justification of his position in an image of Basquiat. And in unpacking this image, McEvilley suggests a poetic and noble quality, but he also betrays a misperception:

> His feet were bare. Yet he wore an expensive Giorgio Armani suit—which, however, was soiled with paint. The dirty Armani brought up the cliché of the primitive who comprehends use value but not exchange value, the bare feet similarly suggested a denizen of preurbanized culture. . . . Carelessly yet carefully enthroned, he evoked the mood of *spressatura*, the feigned or studied casualness cultivated by the Italian nobility of the Renaissance.[24]

He continues, and this makes the point:

> This ambiguous or double self—image-barefoot in Armani—embodies the paradox that W. E. B. DuBois described.[25]

I think McEvilley's stance is both existentially and ontologically naive in that it fails to grasp the troubled and troubling nature of what W. E. B. Du Bois understood of twoness or double consciousness. McEvilley assumes falsely that one can artistically toy with twoness without suffering long-term consequences; this assumes that the discourse of power and be*ing* is rearranged and modified artistically without effect for those promoting the effort. He seems to believe one can step outside this twoness and describe, revise, and play with it. However, the demons haunting Basquiat—struggles with identity and meaning as artist and as blackened naming-thing who names while also being named for the benefit of collectors—would suggest otherwise. His struggle with the notion and attainment of fame speak to the damaging consequence of twoness within the art world, a doubling that both exposes and seeks to hide the power of naming. Basquiat is aware, deeply lucid regarding this process but without the ability to break free, so to speak. He is no longer a tagger working outside the recognized art world; now he is captured by the gallery space as a type of confinement despite his wild life as an attempt to live beyond that space.

I argue a different read of Basquiat, one that is not as postmodern in that it does not reject the naming-thing as it names. Instead, it simply troubles the ability to know or hold the naming-thing even within the context of artistic production. Basquiat questions the West; on this point I agree with McEvilley. However, he does so from within the West—hopelessly tied to the West—loving and hating that binding together, and speaking this love/hate using the tools given him by the Western art world. As Michael Harris remarks, "Like the hip-hop expression he emerged from, Basquiat sampled fragments from a variety of sources, and his own identity suggested hybridity with its roots in Puerto Rico, Haiti, and lived middle-class experience in Brooklyn."[26] Perhaps there is something of negritude or Haiti's indigenist in Basquiat's work—an effort to reconstitute blackness and bodied blackness for racialized naming-things as a rejection of the tragedy of modernism's proclamation of the primitive filtered, of course, through the pulse and texture of hip-hop culture.[27] In this regard, hip-hop serves as a type of signification—an exposing and manipulation of social practices and codes through a poetic turn, and by poetic I mean the destruction of signs and symbols so as to free them to make alternate claims. This effort to tame if not dismantle racism-laced primitivism and its kin does not begin with Basquiat—such a qualification should not be necessary—but there are ways in which Basquiat's cultural ontology, combined with his hip-hop posture, provide a rather interesting dimension of this challenge to modernism. Is his alleged primitive aesthetic *their* primitive?

In some ways, it might be said that I am attempting to trace a particular line of coding through artistic production involving the African American artist signifying blackness, signifying the question above, and doing this through a re-presentation of the bodied naming-thing exposed. More to the point, with Basquiat one gets a graphic example of an effort to re/constitute the naming-thing as an act of art-based rebellion. But he does so not through an effort to jettison the discomforts of life that seek to reify the blackened naming-thing as idea. This effort is apparent in the work of figures such as Henry Ossawa Tanner with his *The Banjo Lesson*, through which he seeks to give visual representation to the affective quality of the narrative (written) tradition whereby black life is reconstituted as mimetic. Instead, with Basquiat, one gets a visual representation of subjectivity much more akin to the writing of the embodied black body offered by figures such as Lorraine Hansberry.[28] In Hansberry's writing, subjectivity does not involve fixity, by which I mean a sense of being associated with full distinction from other things; rather, a sense of self is determined through connections forged over against social forces seeking to pull things apart.

One has to be able to see and read in order to unpack Basquiat's work. By this I do not mean the ability to decipher letters and arrange them into words that signify certain actions or ideas. Instead, I mean having a sense of the sociohistorical, political, and economic interplay informing his struggles—to understand the implications of the age of crack on perceptions of life and death for racialized naming-things—as well as the power dynamics informing interaction. And I mean the ability to gather in the hidden, to decode the various signs and symbols embedded within signs and symbols; this requires a hip-hop sensibility to the extent coded and artistically arranged messages are the hallmark of graffiti. This style of expression is the effort of despised naming-things to maintain their ability to name despite circumstances. So from tagging through which names of naming-things are embedded in designs, to complex portraits that are layered with multiple stories and meanings, hip-hop culture's artistic language exposes as much as it hides. Mindful of this function, it is important to keep in mind that Basquiat's identity, his presence in the world of visual language, is first tied to graffiti:

| HENRY GELDZAHLER | Did you work in the streets and subways because you didn't have materials or because you wanted to communicate? |
| JEAN-MICHEL BASQUIAT | I wanted to build up a name for myself.[29] |

There are ways in which painting, the act of creating visual representations, speaks to the rhythm of his life—the performance of interplay as he understood it. He touches things, bringing them into his realm of expression, and in the process these things impact him and serve to shift his sensibilities so that the idea depicted in the work is dependent as much on thing-things as on Basquiat as the naming-thing. And to remove or reposition any of the thing-things produces consequential changes to the depiction and, by extension, response to the visual. Creativity, or creation, in this way is dynamic and multidirectional. Artistic expression chronicles or maps his movement through the world, not disconnected from his bodied experience of the world but rather as static moments within that larger arena of engagement.

| HENRY GELDZAHLER | Do you feel a hectic need to get a lot of work done? |
| JEAN-MICHEL BASQUIAT | No. I just don't know what else to do with myself.[30] |

Life is layered for him, and this is represented in the layered quality of his work. (More interested in sells than finished work, dealers often moved his canvases before he was done.)

In some instances, there is a minimal quality, a way in which Basquiat seeks to more directly capture the tone and "feeling" of bodied thought and movement—with less paint the more direct the idea expressed with fewer filters. In these cases, there is a type of starkness that amplifies the circumstances he addresses—less to distract the viewer, less to "cover" the fundamental interactions.

### Connection Two: Basquiat and the Signifying of Aesthetics

There is a picture of Basquiat in his New York City studio dated 1987.[31] Like images from an earlier period (e.g., pictures of artists taken by Man Ray), Basquiat is situated next to his art supplies—brushes, paints—as well as an African statue and African drums. Things are layered upon things, situated next to other things—all playing off each other and, in this way, offering a mosaic of motion and entanglement that casts these things as more than functional but also representational. In contrast to containers full of paintbrushes used to depict without themselves representing, as well as containers of paints with the same limitation (presenting without representing), there is an African carved figure and drums, which serve to both embody and communicate a range of meanings. Perhaps these last items speak to a sense of cultural code and historical origin, or inspiration, as they entail things that point beyond themselves both backward (e.g., the ancestors and the ability to call to them) and forward (e.g., ongoing generations of descendants within contemporary contexts). Both are of a firm substance—wood—carved so as to speak particular significance. But there is also fluidity to them in that their importance spills out through contact with other things—thoughts of eyes that have taken in these images, hands that have beaten the drum, and ears that have soaked in the sound. The naming-thing breaks free from it at points, but not fully. Basquiat, the naming-thing, is distinguishable from the thing-things around him, yet he cannot be fully understood apart from them and the work they do. There is Basquiat, who situates both things by positioning himself in relation to them, while also over against them. His flesh and the wood are physically different, yet they are things in relationship—speaking something of a common history and geography of engagement with the West. Both those wooden things and Basquiat (a naming-thing) are touched by gallery space, and in a certain way are defined by that encounter. The social meaning of the gallery as Western framing for containment is further represented by the sweater and tie worn. But the tie seems not fully tied, and the sweater is ripped around the shoulder, and Basquiat's hair defies Western standards of beauty. A stylistic limitation on the artist—in the form of a Western clothing aesthetic and grooming—cannot confine and cannot define the blackened naming-thing. Instead, this aesthetic as a boundary is exposed and negotiated. That is to say, while Basquiat's reshaping of clothing points to a type of fluidity, a form of boundary compromised, it does not wipe out boundaries and does not make openness complete and sustained. Both boundaries and openness are exposed for their limitations. The surroundings are chaotic, nothing seems arranged, and the points of contact appear random; but Basquiat's face is calm—his look fixed and without emotion. Nonetheless, what is telling is not so much these items or the look on Basquiat's face; rather, it is the wooden cut-out of a gun he holds to his head. This effort to fix him, to truncate interplay, threatens to end him by simplifying his occupation of time and space—to kill and render docile Basquiat as a naming-thing and by extension other racialized naming-things like him.[32]

One might argue that the presence of African things spoke for white artists and white patrons of the arts to a certain critique of modernism, an embrace of the exotic related to the nature and meaning of the embodied West. But for Basquiat, the image is more demanding and less romanticized. For the artist, the presence of these items reflects both creativity and an effort to confine the significance of the racialized other. On one hand, these things speak to an African aesthetic, an African framing of the world in ways meant to represent themselves in the world. Yet the ability to handle these items, to rearrange them, to transport them (as Africans were transported) suggests a certain reduction of meaning shaped by the pleasure of those manipulating the items. The pulling of this blackness out of him, placing it beside his body for visual consumption and artistic use, does damage.

This image of Basquiat offers a different take on blackness and an African aesthetic within artistic production. It affords another and less pacifying look at identity formation when race cannot be ignored and when it pushes the dilemma of existence to the forefront. There is something political about much of his work, both as an overt discourse on the history of human engagement and also as the mandatory rhythm of life as a blackened naming-thing within racialized society. Put differently, much of Basquiat's work defies easy engagement; it pushes the viewer to confront a type of creative chaos that envisions something both familiar and foreign. The presentation of familiar items such as pieces of wood, connected by common words drawn using standard things like paint and pencils, confirms a common sensibility; but then they are layered and overlapped, put in contact, in a manner that pulls them beyond what the viewer understood as first "use" and instead calls attention to new possibilities when things affect things. There is ruggedness to Basquiat's work (e.g., words written in what appears a haphazard manner, and colors spilling outside the drawn lines) by means of which he presents interaction between things as frenetic.

Particular forms of artistic production—and I would include this fascination with an African aesthetic or the artistic appeal of "blackness"—were meant to enliven, to maintain the meaning of embodied and thought life over against its draining away. In other words, it was intended to end porousness. But the late twentieth century removed some of the allure and prevented some of the optimism. Postmodernism did damage to assumptions of inevitable progress. This raises a question, one borrowed and placed in a different context, that I believe the work of Basquiat seeks to answer. "What," writes Peter Halley, "could fill the role once served by art as vanquisher of death, as beacon in the void?"[33] What is to be made of art as symbol of openness in a context marked by a push for closure—a commitment to exposure over against social-coding privileging boundaries?

In certain ways, the presentation of skeletal figures, innards exposed, speaks to life closer to the core and life as structures of interplay based on openness.[34] One might argue that it is a push to more fundamental circumstances based on the removal of easily recognized sociocultural codes and constructions. Henry David Thoreau, for instance, also recognized the significance of life close to its inner core, but for him this is where it is sweetest. For Basquiat, such comfort is not possible. There is no transcendentalism in Basquiat, just the existential angst of the rebel open to the world.[35]

| | |
|---|---|
| HENRY GELDZAHLER | Is there anger in your work now? |
| JEAN-MICHEL BASQUIAT | It's about 80 percent anger. |
| HENRY GELDZAHLER | But there's also humor. |
| JEAN-MICHEL BASQUIAT | People laugh when you fall on your ass. What's humor?[36] |

Near the core, with layers of imposed sociocultural codes stripped away, is where life is intense and graphic but also unstable and macabre. There is only a basic design that is both firm (bone) but fluid (a frenzied "something" explodes from the skeletal figures). Related to this, consider the skull images presented in works such as Basquiat's *Untitled* (1982).[37]

Art critic Jonathan Jones captures something of the skull's energy, the inability to contain through traditional means of denoting space configured—for example, outlines—but also the manner in which the frenetic energy in this painting says something about the condition of certain naming-things within the sociopolitical world of the United States: "Like the work of another heroin user, William Burroughs, his art, with its feeling of being cut and hacked into the canvas rather than daubed, its electric sense of pain in every nerve, shows everyone what's really in their lunch. He serves up American history with all the worms crawling out of it. This painting of a skull is not just about his own morbidity—it's about being killed by America."[38] There is intensity in the eyes of this skull—piercing white dots concentrated on what it views and pulling on the viewer at the same time. The eyes are focused, unlike the wildness marking the rest of the skull. Yet they look to the side, away from the viewer who approaches it head-on. The gaze seems directed at the mass of white paint blurred with shades of pink (and penetrated by a small arrangement of stripes of color emerging from it) along the far side closest to the skull. The skull is distinct from the white mass but connected by an arrangement of thin white lines running from the top of the mass of white to the side of the skull, close to one of the piercing eyes. The two are distinct things, yet connected, engaged, attached by thick white lines that seek to blot out letters (perhaps words) and other markings. There is a roughness but also carefulness in this marking of white over words that does not fully cover a black undercoat suggesting interaction that shifts and changes perception. There is a single and thin black line farther down the image that rests on, but also serves as, a point of connection. This pulsating connection makes for difficult concentration because there is too much activity requiring movement and new thinking. Things, as Basquiat demonstrates, are not distinct in a fixed manner; they interact in both bold and refined ways. Things—whether they be acrylic paint and oil paint, or black and white naming-things—impinge upon each other often in a chaotic fashion that exposes as much as it hides.

The black lines that produce something of an outline for the skull compete and win against the white markings that also try to give some shape to this head, offering some type of framework or border that makes evident the nature of this thing. The skull is an open thing—both defining and being defined by the background. On top of the skull are markings, something resembling a game of tic-tac-toe, providing a calming effect in that the game requires some thought, a stoppage of action long enough to plan and plot moves. Yet this state of reason does not penetrate the skull and so ultimately does not distract from the graphic rage emanating from the skull. In fact, the game might just reflect language games; the relationship between marks that we "read" as words with set meanings is jumbled and manipulated. As Richard Marshall reflects, "To Basquiat the meaning of a word was not necessarily relevant to its usage because he employed words as abstract objects that can be seen as configurations of straight and curved lines that come together to form a visual pattern. The visual and graphic impact of printed letters was sufficient enough to stand alone as an artistic expression."[39] The mouth is open and crowded with marks and colors as if it is about to spew out a verbal dimension of the skull's rage. But the mouth is disassociated from the markings—the words are not clear; they are not fully expressive in a traditional sense. Rather, the chaotic interaction is expressive—with aggressive and "free" lines.

Basquiat paints and draws skulls that have a hint of the African mask. But whereas advocates of primitivism capturing an African aesthetic for the sake of a revitalized West seek to pacify the African mask, Basquiat invests these skulls with wild energy that cannot be tamed. The colors are vibrant, pulsing outside any lines that might serve as boundaries. These skulls have a piercing look that renders the viewer uncomfortable and controlled by the skull. The energy that earlier white artists sought to take away from the African aesthetic as represented, say, by the mask-thing in order to make them tame is reinscribed by Basquiat through his presentation of skull-things. He, and this is also reflected in the urgency of his painting, assumed the tragicomic nature of life, as did characters such as Cross Damon and Bigger Thomas from the work of writer Richard Wright.[40] Basquiat, then, was to the visual arts what Richard Wright was to literature—both maintained a sense of realism, if not absurdist moralism. Both worked from an understanding of the consequences involved in claiming time and space, while recognizing that racial dynamics always inform and shape these decisions made and the content of our life stories.

With Man Ray, for example, the mask is subdued, becoming the thing dominated by the photographer and the white naming-thing holding it.[41] There was an effort to remove the tragic to the extent that it served as a reminder of modernity's failures. Yet with Basquiat this is not possible: only a comparably wild energy can maintain contact with this passion, angst, and discomfort that is the *Untitled* (1982) skull.[42]

*Interplay.*

As wild as he sought to be in thought and action, there are still ways in which Basquiat reflected earlier, modern sensibilities: How could this not be the case considering the influence of figures such as Picasso on his painting? He drew inspiration and ideas from what he labeled the "masters" as well as from other sources of identity discourse that shape our understanding of our embodiment as naming-things. Still, as a racialized naming-thing, he projected them through the turmoil and pleasures of blackened embodiment and folded them upon themselves through a rhythm he associated with the irreverent creativity of jazz.

Basquiat consumed culture—history books, anatomy books, other artists, guide books, and so on—that are symbolic of the constructions of the West and that worried the consumers of African aesthetics.

| HENRY GELDZAHLER | I like the drawing that are just lists of things. |
| JEAN-MICHEL BASQUIAT | I was making one in an airplane once. I was copying some stuff out of a Roman sculpture book. This lady said, "Oh, what are you studying." I said, "It's a drawing."[43] |

He consumed this culture (its dread and possibilities), signified it, and produced an alternate perception of the bodied naming-thing made black. In this regard, he is both scapegoat and conjurer, with the signified and signifier revolving around the category of race as antimeaning. He is both naming-thing involved in a process of naming but, because he consumes the culture, through his art he is also transformed. Others promoted the ordinariness of life but in ways that rendered them extraordinary, markers of something more significant and penetrating behind, underneath, and through the thing—the yearning for grandeur. Basquiat breaks through this, allowing the ordinary to shift locations but remain simply mundane. Take, for example, his *Boxer Rebellion* (1982–1983). While it is much too layered and complex for sufficient discussion here, brief comments give some sense of his naming and use of cultural moments and codes. Framing two boxers, one throwing a punch, is an intense arrangement of words, some crossed out, or with some of the letters blackened. The words "name" boxers ("SUGAR RAY ROBINSON"), body parts (e.g., "ELBOW"), another form of "boxing" (the "CHINESE BOXER REBELLION"), scientific exchanges (i.e., "TECHNOLOGY"), the language of capitalism ("PER CAPITA"), a segment of the creation account from the Hebrew Bible's book of Genesis, beginning with "And the earth was formless . . ."[44] Not all of these markings are in English, as there are words drawn using what appears to be Mandarin in connection to the Chinese Boxer Rebellion. There is also Japanese employed, although the word *Japan* is crossed out (but still visible). These words, drawn from a range of cultural contexts, are distinguished and distinctive to some degree, but mindful of Richard Marshall's observation, there are ways in which Basquiat pulls words from their traditional meanings and makes them speak a different social sensibility. That is to say, the words as things are positioned to interact differently—to suggest a different range of concerns and possibilities by means of which he exposes the conditions of collective life. Cultures collapse onto each other as they collide vis-à-vis language. On some level they are bounded languages—couched within a larger pattern of cultural coded systems meant to keep them intact and "uncontaminated," yet such efforts at safeguarding things are futile. Basquiat, as a naming-thing, claims use of these linguistic codes for his own purposes; they express and explain alternate realities. This is not restricted to codes understood as expressing more secular modes of interaction; the biblical text becomes a thing penetrated, a different set of concerns that grants those theological-religious linguistic sensibilities no more space than their secular rivals. The anti-Christian intent of the Chinese Boxer Rebellion is read with and against the biblical text—one thing (one worldview) is brought into exchange with another (Judeo-Christian sensibilities).

Basquiat merged the visual image and the written text, positioning both with respect to bodies. In this way, he brought into play, challenged, and affirmed the tools of discourse in ways meant to disrupt their unity by changing their content and target. In light of the way power functions even within the realm of cultural aesthetics, Basquiat was consumed in spite of his best efforts to signify and deconstruct.

Significance is not found in the transformation of the ordinary into something else; rather, it is lodged in the ordinary as it is—defiant, boundary questioning, and also docile and proscriptive. In a word, things have significance, impactfulness, as things. From my perspective, this is particularly true with respect to Basquiat's first phase—pieces not easily divested of their intensity are not easily rendered neutral and accessible. The question is this: How are you prepared to view the work of art with respect to the impact of aesthetics on the picture and content of bodied and thought life?[45] What are the ways in which things collide, inform, and shift each other? Art and the viewer are in relationship.

Like others would do after him, Basquiat calls "attention to slippery relationships between revelation and concealment, visibility and invisibility, and presence and absence." In the process there is an act of subversion, "trick and play with audience expectations to challenge tendencies toward objectifying black female and male bodies." Again like others after him, he takes "the juxtaposition of text and image of earlier artists even further to invert power dynamics and foreground the relationship between black bodies and erasure."[46] The sealant of race is ever present, and not even his acceptance in the art world could prevent the impact of racism on his sense of open self as a naming-thing and his sense of belonging to the process of interplay. This, at least in part, accounts for the intensity of his images—the energy of the skulls and the bodies drawn inside out.

Lodged in his paintings over the nine years of his career is a public/private wrestling with embodiment in a troubled world, where identity is unstable, and all has something to do with economics and politics cast within the language of culture. Regarding this, Basquiat, according to Robert Farris Thompson, forced an aesthetic confrontation with the felt nature of urban life. "His," Thompson writes, "is a quest for a sharper, ecumenical assessment of the troubling—yet promising—configurations of our urban destiny and predicament."[47] There is a thickness to this process: Basquiat's work added to the destruction of artistic sensibilities by also critiquing the racial assumptions embedded in both artistic production and the spaces housing this art.

He ripped apart the assumptions of how and what one knows about the nature of interplay between things through the unmasking of blackness as subtext—bodied things inside out, things as both text and context. It had been the case earlier in the twentieth century that Western artists found blackness—particularly Africanness—appealing, but they wanted it sanitized, comforting and comfortable. Basquiat's work signified such safeness, but in an ironic twist he fed off this voyeuristic desire, and the effort to mold his life accordingly was deadly. Perhaps he sought, as Thompson remarked, to achieve a type of existential and ontological wholeness through his work, an identity in opposition to Western desire to rip apart and consume blackness—if quarantining off blackened naming-things for isolated engagement and use could not be managed.[48]

He pulls the bodied naming-thing apart to uncover and discover anew its openness, and in this way he seeks to speak differently the nature of the culturally arranged naming-thing as unfixed and unfinished. In the process, Basquiat does not discount the significance of the "degraded" naming-thing as grotesque in that deconstruction of his own body as naming-thing (e.g., through drug use) has direct impact on what can be captured artistically. All this work, this wildness, entails contradiction—an effort to deny (and in the process reinforce through the romanticizing of the "streets") his middle-class roots. It is both the framework for the artist and the makeup of the artist in some instances. His paintings are deceptive; they are not easy to read or comfortable to feel. They require work, an unraveling of the layers in the same way identities are layered, marking life's meaning from within overlapping realms of interaction and exchange. Blackness as a container for a particular aesthetic many in the Western world considered salvific was presented as a complex signifier—both negative and positive, needed and feared. Basquiat signifies this framework, and rather than examining blackness—outside/in he conceptualizes and presents it inside/out. As Jennifer Clement records in her book *Widow Basquiat: A Love Story*, "Everything was symbolic to him. How he dressed, how he spoke, how he thought, and those with whom he associated. Everything had to be prolific or why do it and his attitude was always tongue-in-cheek. Jean was always watching himself from outside of himself and laughing."[49] By so doing, he also speaks to the fractured and overlapping nature of identity—unfixed, fluid, troubled, thick. "A frequent motif in Basquiat's work—the 'see-through' man—not only responded metaphorically to this period's fascination with expose and destroying people's facades," writes Richard Powell, "but also spoke to the notion that anatomy had a theatrical quality that, when paired with blackness, was a radical attack on society's superficiality and deep-seated racism."[50] That is to say, Basquiat repositions blackened naming-things in a way that pushes against stereotypical discourses by speaking them differently in an energetic and dismissive manner—what some have called Neo-Expressionism.

Created in both his personal and aesthetic choices, "he tried to make people notice him, wake them up, by using a symbol out of context. This occurred in his paintings and in his actions."[51] At times Basquiat approached the Western art world and its "sacred" spaces (e.g., museums) in ways that pull at the diasporic threads of life in the Americas, and in the process shaved away the integrity of these spaces—redirecting their energy and signifying their meaning through what he as a naming-thing can do and produce. "At the museum [MoMA] Jean-Michel takes a bottle of water out of his coat and walks through the halls sprinkling the water here and there around him. 'I'd piss like a dog if I could,' he says, as they wander past paintings by Pollock, Picasso, Kline and Braque. Suzanne [his girlfriend] does not even ask what he is doing. She knows this is one of his voodoo tricks."[52] There is in his response some recognition of the distinctions between himself and these other figures and the manner in which race and class shape the construction and reception of himself as a blackened naming-thing and what it produces. "But, in the end," one writer says, "the differences between Picasso and Basquiat— the different relations they adopt to the ethnographic gaze leveled from the West on traditional African art, the different investments they make in the construction of their own celebrity—are more pronounced than any formal affinities in their work."[53] His action in MoMA tames the impulse of the museum, removing its sanctity and in the process shifting the perception of what can take place in that space. Blackness is not on display as he moves through the halls, but instead blackness taints the space and troubles the racial profile of comfort within a race-based world. And for blacks viewing these same images, there is a different question: Is there anything of me in this? There is a bit of the tragic in this situation, as Michael Harris insightfully notes. Basquiat, Harris reflects, "had to assume a particular social position to play to the bright lights. As happened with the primitivist fascinations in France in the first three decades of the twentieth century, and those in New York, white interest in black expression came at a price for Basquiat. His works were colored by these realities, and his life was stained by them."[54] I believe there are ways in which Basquiat as artist is also trickster, the figure who moves between worlds, crosses ontological and existential geography and in the process allows them to open to new meanings. This involves the forcing of a different set of questions and presuppositions: What is the place of this blackness? What is the reconfiguration of meaning present? What is the materiality of identity over against efforts to fix form and solidify boundaries?

Basquiat calls on the plastic nature of interplay as alternate aesthetic and uses this to tell an existential and ontological story. He signifies the signifier and exposes the complexity (and open nature) of blackened naming-things, a thickness denied by an early appropriation by the likes of Man Ray. As many interpreters have noted, there are ways in which Basquiat seeks to critique Modernist art. The language of colonialism and otherness—with a vocabulary functioning like glue to close off and fix—is signified, shifted, and transformed through a new ownership and use against its use. Yet this process is never complete. Discourse on blackness and power accommodates the change and restores balance through embrace.

Basquiat's aesthetic, as critical as he wanted it to be, promoted a critique of Modernism, but one that the art establishment embraced: the signifier was signified. The basic conceptual paradigms were tweaked, but they persisted nonetheless: "Once the work was done, the dealers became very possessive of it, and tried to control it. Jean [Michel Basquiat] used to say, 'it's like feeding the lions. It's a bottomless pit. You can throw them meat all day long, and they're still not satisfied.'"[55] What is even more telling, however, is the lament Basquiat offered on several occasions: "I wanted to be a star, not a gallery mascot."[56] "Some," says Marc Miller in a 1982 interview with the artist, "saw Basquiat as some sort of primal expressionist." Basquiat responded, "Like an ape? . . . A primate?"[57]

Blackness was consumed, the masked thing—although less passive in construction and placement—could still be used to cover or shift the nature and meaning of aesthetics in relationship to blackness and whiteness. Basquiat sought, it seems, to alter the dynamics of artistic production in relationship to race and class and to do so from within the belly of the beast. But Michel Foucault is correct that the power we seek to fight, to own, to use, is always and everywhere. It cannot be controlled in that manner to the extent it flows in and through us, makes and unmakes us, is constructed by us. The words (and erasures) within Basquiat's paintings speak to the inevitability of discourse and its ability to shape time and space. One sees a graphic example of this in *Pegasus* (1987). From military might as represented in the British airborne forces' use of the winged horse image during World War II to popular culture references, Pegasus has marked a certain mode of might and creativity—for example, a blending of things such as a human and another animal, science and cultural codes, and desire and shortcoming. Basquiat applies the name and its cultural connotations—with perhaps a nod in the direction of the programming system bearing the name that takes in human language and produces code—to a large work consisting of an overwhelming arrangement of words, phrases, and images that provide a geography of expressed meaning. Words and symbols compete for space. They are meaningful to a degree in that they represent something if one isolates them, but they also overlap in significance to the degree that they bleed into each other, sharing space and changing meanings. Some of the words and symbols are crossed out, and in this way they are both present and absent—and they stand out because of the dark and energetic strokes used to subdue them. Yet the black paint in the right corner of the large canvas poses a challenge of space and time. Are the words consuming and thereby changing space, or is the "blank" space of black paint slowly wiping out the cultural codes? In either case, there is contact between expression and a type of silence, between presence and absence, between "something" and "nothing" (both express "things"). Even during this last phase of his life, Basquiat was aware of racial-cultural dynamics related to symbolic forms. There is also something about this painting that speaks to the instability of symbols and codes of the West—their inability to fully capture and contain, to fully inscribe what they encounter.

*Gold Griot* (1984) is marked by interplay of materials—slabs of wood upon which is painted (using acrylic paint and oil stick) a figure with a large and expressive head that is more than skeletal in part because of its aggressive markings. The head is confined within a white outline, but something about the look on its face suggests the confinement is not complete. One thin arm points up and the other down, situating the figure between spaces—or better yet holding together two spaces by occupying a middle location. This being knows something viewers do not and has contact with things that transform. There is gleefulness in the expression—a wide smile full of teeth, a nose with nostrils wide like a deeply satisfying breath is being taken, and almond-shaped eyes (one red and the other white), suggesting a devious contentment. It has only a torso holding it up, with a spine shown inside a dark box, which speaks to the harnessing of language so as to express particular codes. The figure is a bridge of sorts, something along the lines of Eshu, the African god who opens and controls lines of communication between humans and the gods, or the griot, as the title of the work announces, whose stories connect the past and the present.

Basquiat would have certainly encountered cultural codes and stories about such figures during his early years in Brooklyn, and these African ancestral figures that made the trip from Africa to the Americas, and from the Caribbean to North America, would have found the trip from Brooklyn to Manhattan of little challenge. And so Basquiat's awareness of this alternate world would not have faded in Manhattan, where even hip-hop would have encouraged a similar blending of things. But this is a matter of manipulation, not fundamental control. It might be the recognition of this dilemma that marks for him the significance of jazz and the blues, and the legacy of Mississippi (land of the blues) as a location of the tragic nature of suppressed opportunity turned into artistic triumph.

Perhaps his artistic production was Basquiat's effort toward, in Foucault's language, the fostering of spaces for the practice of freedom—or at least spaces of exposure and interplay. Ultimately, artistic expression exposes issues of depth. It provides a means by which to struggle both with and for bodied naming-things and things occupying time and space as well as the sociopolitical, economic, and cultural ramifications of that occupation. It might just be the case that some of art's appeal and terrifying ramifications are played out on the geography of belonging that is, in this case, the blackened naming-thing.

# problem things 8

How does it feel to be a problem?
—W. E. B. DU BOIS, *The Souls of Black Folk*

What did I do to be so black and blue?
—FATS WALLER, "(What Did I Do to Be So) Black and Blue"

Bearden and Basquiat can be said to raise the question of racial stereotyping and "cataloging" as a means by which to foster boundaries and regressive openness, and they do so through the innovative use of biographically informed modalities of artistic production—collage for Bearden and hip-hop-influenced Neo-Expressionism for Basquiat. Furthermore, it is important to note they work in the wake of earlier efforts to frame philosophically and sociologically this process of racialization as fixing. Perhaps the most compelling example of this intellectual exercise is found in the work of W. E. B. Du Bois, who set in motion a diagnosis of black life circumstances with an underlying consideration of naming-thing and thing-thing interaction framed by a cultural climate (as a prophylactic) of disregard.

In this chapter, I highlight a particular text—*The Souls of Black Folk*—not because I want to suggest Du Bois's thinking is not organic and does not change over times. My focus on a single Du Bois volume is not meant to suggest anything along these lines. His corpus is rich and complex, and it demonstrates evolving opinions and theories, which are mindful of shifting sociopolitical circumstances. Yet I limit my attention to this 1903 volume because of the manner in which it outlines a theoretical point of departure for Du Bois regarding the nature and meaning of black being, and it does so in (implicit) conversation with a range of his influences (e.g., William James). The text explicates epistemological and ontological concerns that, while altered in terms of application, continue to inform and influence the conceptual considerations haunting his writings afterward. Still, my concern in interrogating this text involves what it lends readers regarding the nature and meaning of racialized naming-things, not the sociopolitical, intellectual, and economic mechanism one might employ to restructure their relationship to the United States. On this latter point, mechanisms for advancement, Du Bois's thinking differed over time; for instance, he wrestles with the elitism embedded in his early depiction of the "talented tenth." However, I would argue that his sense of a racialized ontology at work in the structuring/restructuring of certain naming-things remained somewhat consistent. That is to say, while the problem of concern to him remains in place, the mechanisms he advances for addressing it shift over time.

*The Souls of Black Folk* entails Du Bois's most widely recognized effort on this score, and that volume begins with a question: "How does it feel to be a problem?"[1] By this question and his explication of it, Du Bois points in the direction of openness denied—to bounded naming-things. It is helpful to keep in mind that before Du Bois described the double consciousness of African Americans, he first announced the cultural climate, or prevailing ethos, shaping the historical moment.[2] "The problem of the Twentieth Century," he writes in the forethought to *The Souls of Black Folk*, "is the problem of the color-line."[3] Reiterated numerous times throughout the book, this short but forceful line captured the racial logic of the post–Civil War United States and shaped the public imagination of and expectations for the nation moving forward.[4] It articulated a sense of bodied experience (i.e., moments of interplay) as wrapped in the garb of racial animosity, and the book's prophetic quality spoke what millions knew but could not articulate safely.

This color-line theory jibed so well with documented activities of a pervasive antiblack racism that it became a frequently employed hermeneutic in both popular and academic analysis. While undeniably impactful and considered by many a complete framing of post-Reconstruction development, what the color-line pronouncement points to, however, is only one dimension of a dualism, what Du Bois references as the "Negro problem." At the start of the first essay in *Souls*, "Of Our Spiritual Strivings," Du Bois reflects,

Between me and the other world there is ever an unasked question: unasked by some through feelings of delicacy; by others through the difficulty of rightly framing it. All, nevertheless, flutter round it. They approach me in a half-hesitant sort of way, eye me curiously or compassionately, and then, instead of saying directly, *How does it feel to be a problem?* they say, I know an excellent colored man in my town; . . . or Do not those Southern outrages make your blood boil? At these I smile, or am interested, or reduce the boiling to a simmer, as the occasion may require. To the real question, how does it feel to be a problem? *I answer seldom a word.*[5]

*How does it feel to be a problem?* With this question, Du Bois highlights the second dimension of the dualism, what I will call the *problem soul*. It is the naming-thing present within a context defined by effort to racially close off and deny active openness; furthermore, the problem soul is marked by a sensibility regarding or posture toward the U.S. cultural climate defined by a vicious logic of racial difference as dangerous.[6] My read of Du Bois suggests not that double consciousness causes the problem soul (as a problem of interplay), but rather it is prior to the Negro problem.[7] The problem soul involves positioning of intent expressed through the African American's existential movement in the world as a troubled and troubling bodied naming-thing trapped by conflicting identities articulated in terms of discourses of boundaries and a certain type of fixity. While important to the larger argument, the problem soul has received limited consideration, and as a consequence our understanding of Du Bois's aim within *Souls*, his most popular text, is truncated.

The Negro problem, framed as a cultural ontology of twoness, is addressed in terms of social, material, and political alterations to public and private life bent on making African Americans whole and functioning citizens—that is, open naming-things.[8] The problem soul, the diagnostic of concern, however, entails a web of psychological, philosophical, social, theological, and affective vantage points constituting a posture that seeks to trouble such violent closing off and reaction against openness. Hence, understanding the problem soul requires a different framing. I suggest adaption of William James's "sick soul" as heuristic for exploring sensitivity to the particular posture toward the world Du Bois intends by the problem soul as marker of interplay fought against. Suggesting the possibility of such a link does not push an unreasonable intellectual connection.[9] To the contrary, Du Bois's "problem" viewed in relationship to James's "sick soul" merely tags a connection that extends beyond more widely recognized overlap. My effort entails unpacking what biographers Arnold Rampersad and David Levering Lewis note in terms of Du Bois's use of the popular psychological category of twoness, which is shadowed by James's "hidden self," or "subconscious." Both the former and the latter escape our full grasp—just as Du Bois's duality avoids our efforts at unification.[10] Ross Posnock puts it well: "With his poetic genius, Du Bois turned skepticism of stable selfhood into an indelible image of the black Americans' anguished psychic striving."[11]

Before moving on, I want to first acknowledge a point that will come up again and that relates to the "anguished striving" noted by Posnock. Simply put, the problem soul, at first read, might be thought to advise a nihilistic or fatalistic turn. However, this is far from what Du Bois intends. Rather than that, Du Bois operates consistent with moralist-absurdist sensibilities later exhibited by writers like Nella Larsen and Richard Wright and theorized by Albert Camus. There is no surrender, no nihilism in statements by Du Bois such as this: ". . . the travail of souls whose burden is almost beyond the measure of their strength, but who bear it in the name of an historic race, in the name of this land of their fathers' fathers, and in the name of human opportunity."[12] The "No!" to demands associated with the cultural climate marking this description of postslavery life is echoed in the "No!" to false promises of redemption recorded by writer Nella Larsen's character Helga Crane in *Quicksand*; in the "No!" to racial terror written by Richard Wright in terms of his life and that of his character Fred Daniels in "The Man Who Lives Underground," and in the perpetual labor of the absurd hero, Sisyphus, endorsed by Camus. This consideration is important because attention to a moralist-absurdist sensibility helps clarify the nature of the problem soul and aids in our surfacing the call for perpetual struggle (i.e., perpetual openness) rather than nihilism central to Du Bois's diagnosis of "strange experience" summed up in *Souls*.[13]

## Double-Consciousness

According to Du Bois, the system of slavery resulted in global cooperation premised on material need and resource, and guided by metaphysical stipulations. One proviso marked Africans as inferior (e.g., fixed and bounded) in every respect, and another extended the correctness of this argument through violent coercion of African Americans into believing themselves inferior (and confined with limited opportunity for interplay).[14] The goal of this debased epistemology and dwarfed ontology is control over docile naming-things, tame minds, and the nation's sociopolitical and economic infrastructure.

Freedom troubles this logic in that it disrupts what were once assumed stable cultural identities by forcing a rethinking of the African American's occupation of time and space. A consequence of this rethinking is double-consciousness—two warring cultural identities African Americans attempt to hold together (as a matter of interaction) in a historical context ill-equipped to grasp and appreciate such complexity.[15] That is to say, against societal wishes, African American naming-things seek interplay between themselves and other things so as to maintain openness over against boundaries limiting interaction on particular sociopolitical and economic fronts.[16] This dilemma is the birth of the existential Negro problem—framed by life within a context of close but troubled proximity without old methods of regulation—played out on geography of entitlement and opportunity, marred by exclusionary borders.

In the essay "Of the Dawn of Freedom," Du Bois offers a question capturing this problem: "What shall be done with Negroes?"[17] First addressed in an expansive and systematic manner through the Freedmen's Bureau, the answer to that nagging question involved judicial structures, economic opportunity, political involvement, educational organizations, and social maneuvering.[18] This approach entailed an assumption that double-consciousness is addressed best through integration and material intervention—thereby tackling the basis of disregard, countering assertions of inferiority, and opening access to "life, liberty, and the pursuit of happiness." Nonetheless, the failure of this tactic is clear in that for so many the African American had not been reconstituted but simply and inconveniently repositioned. In a word, the formerly enslaved were visible in an altered way, but this did not constitute a substantial change in sentiment toward them. "For this much all men know," writes Du Bois, "despite compromise, war and struggle, the Negro is not free."[19] He outlines this situation by vivid sociological and historical narratives regarding life in particular regions of the nation where he believed the Negro problem most graphic.[20]

Effort to foster a "better and truer self" produces frustration in that it involves what Du Bois references as the "contradiction of double aims."[21] Appealing to a religious vocabulary, he expresses these wasted efforts as "wooing false gods and involving false means of salvation."[22] There is a relationship here to tragic-soul life by means of which Du Bois presents, through the musical form of the spirituals and religious rituals, an African American theological response to these existential conditions.[23] Impact, if any, is short-lived, as Du Bois hints at through the fiction undergirding the spirituals.[24] Creating synergy between past and present, these songs wish for a future that does not come. Hence, they are for Du Bois sorrow songs, hauntingly beautiful sorrow songs. The spiritual communities in which these songs were housed primarily and the ministers who led those communities failed to impact the cultural climate that suffocated their aspirations. While Du Bois might have known something of the genre before this transformation, he knew nothing of their context of creation—nothing of the hush arbors, nothing of the traumas of enslavement that provided the affective quality of the narratives, and he believed little of the theological assumptions embedded in their lyrical content. What he did know and what he did experience is this: each attempt to demand something of the world is met with frustration, and so the Negro problem persists.

What should be done with the Negro presupposes a prior consideration: How does it feel to *be* a problem? It is with respect to this question that Du Bois presents the problem soul, which, again, is conditioned, informed, and shaped by a particular cultural climate, or what Du Bois references as a "new philosophy of life" associated with the technologies and strategies of racial deep disregard.[25] It is this philosophy that articulates the "soul-life" of the nation in which by definition African Americans participate.[26]

## Sick Soul

As claimed earlier, William James's description of the sick soul lends itself to framing the problem soul. In suggesting this exploration, I am concerned to apply this category beyond the world he describes, beyond his framing of religion, and beyond the individual concerns that mark *The Varieties of Religious Experience*.[27] In appealing to James's sick soul within this larger context, my aims are to highlight the details of this posture named the problem soul, and thereby capture something of its sensibility and the cultural climate of exclusion it stands against.

I imagine this language will hit some ears wrong. Perhaps it is too clinical, suggesting illness of some sort. However, while to limit the analysis to clinical and medical diagnosis would miss the point, Du Bois does suggest the psychological as a dimension of the situation he describes, and James proposes a philosophical reading. One hears this, for instance, in his naming of the most widely borrowed notion from *Souls* (double-consciousness), which entails Du Bois suggesting African Americans suffer from cultural personality dissociation—or a type of metaphysical and cultural disorder, perhaps cultural schizophrenia, or even a type of cultural dissociative identity disorder. Yet this rendering of the situation, the historical moment, is tied to sociological, historical, and cultural consideration and pronouncements. Using a heuristic of the sick soul, against what might be initial resistance on the part of those who are more comfortable with a type of heroic quality lodged in a sense of tragedy overcome in Du Bois, allows for a different range of questions, a different sense of the problem plaguing Du Bois, and the connection of this problem to death.

Prior to the sick soul, James described a healthy-mindedness marked by optimism regarding circumstances, seeing them as generally good despite all. This stance takes two forms. The first, which is involuntary, defines an immediate emotion of happiness regarding the conditions of life. The second is systematic healthy-mindedness and entails conceptualization of life in a general sense as good.[28] Despite what the term "healthy-minded" might suggest, it is a narrow approach that works with a limited range of experiences.[29] As Charles Taylor notes, the terminology used by James—"morbid," "sick," and "healthy"—suggests a preference for the "healthy-mindedness." However, this is not the case. "James," Taylor writes, "identifies with the sick here. Not just that this is where he classes himself, without, of course, explicitly saying so . . . but also in that he sees the sick as being more profound and insightful."[30] As a religious attitude, healthy-mindedness is practiced as we, according to James, "divert our attention from disease and death as much as we can; and the slaughter-houses and indecencies without end on which our life is founded are huddled out of sight and never mentioned, so that the world we recognize officially in literature and in society is a poetic fiction far handsomer and cleaner and better than the world that really is."[31] Therefore, it is a willful determination to bracket off what is unpleasant and to present the world through a hermeneutic of harmony and comfort. For the healthy-minded, through the exercise of a childlike happiness, the world is projected, as one needs it to be—marked by progression that is not inevitable but that is harnessed to a deep sense of possibility. James finds examples of healthy-mindedness in "New Thought" camps known to highlight the good by preaching potentiality and possibility while, in his words, "deliberately minimizing evil."[32] The healthy-minded, in a religious sense, experience conversion as the once born—an easy attention to happiness and goodness.

Over against this posture is one in which evil is recognized and confronted—to the extent evil is understood as being constitutive of the world. The soul that views evil as pervasive and fundamental is the sick soul. It is

chapter eight

sensitive to the troubling reality of the universe and our relationship to it. *In other words, it is content to be open to entanglement with and interplay between things.* And in a philosophical sense, it offers a deeper knowledge of existence as porous. Despite the tone of this description, James highlights a positive dimension to the perspective offered by the sick soul. The lucidity, a penetrating and guiding awareness, marking it is not to be dismissed and should be valued over against the "fragile fiction" embraced by the healthy-minded—that is, a fiction of unity or wholeness with clear borders that mark off certain dimensions of engagement with things.[33] (Think in terms of my depiction in earlier chapters of theistic approaches meant to close off naming-things.) The sick soul, unlike the more restricted view of the healthy-minded, probes the world and recognizes that "the self is a battle-ground."[34] Still, this is no reason to turn away and take an easier path. "Let us not simply cry out, in spite of all appearance," cautions James, "'Hurrah for the Universe!—God's in Heaven, all's right with the world.' Let us see rather whether pity, pain, and fear, and the sentiment of human helplessness may not open a profounder view and put into our hands a more complicated key to the meaning of the situation."[35] Framed in terms of the individual and her contact with the world, the healthy-minded seeks a sustainable happiness in the face of its contradiction, while the sick soul finds no benefit in such a delusion and does not seek a "higher unity."[36] The sick soul knows, in James's words, "back of everything is the great specter of universal death." What appears good is equally and quickly matched by its negation.[37]

This is not to suggest sick souls are without the possibility of conversion—of a turn toward closure desired. Those deeply sensitive to a world of suffering can be twice born, that is, they can change to a different perspective on engagement with the world—one marked by consciousness affording new consideration of the good and happiness as bound to fixity outside "penetration" by the Divine. However, conversion is a mere possibility not a probability, because the sick soul need not surrender or collapse in the face of misery.[38] As James remarks, some will not be converted because they are never so "exhausted with the struggle of the sick soul" that they give up in the face of crisis.[39] Some have, James proclaims, "drunk too deeply of the cup of bitterness ever to forget its taste."[40] Furthermore, there is an extreme pessimism that can prevent conversion due to a "pathological melancholy."[41] This is a psychological sense of loss blocking optimism, whereby "the subject of melancholy is forced in spite of himself to ignore that of all good whatever. For him it may no longer have the least reality."[42]

The sick soul as a heuristic sheds light on the problem soul, but the two are far from identical. For example, while James speaks of figures such as Tolstoy living in a universe "two stories deep," by which he means a response to and interplay with the universe that entails embrace of good within the shadow of a persistent sadness, the moralist-absurdist tendencies of Du Bois suggest even this stance as a surrender to illusion and a denial of the persistent effect of disregard that overwhelms all else. As witness to this, one need only call to mind the figure John, found in chapter 13 of *Souls*, who returns home from college with lucidity regarding the plight of African Americans, only to be met by a persistent disregard from whites and resistance from his community, which selects religious delusion over mature analysis and confrontation. In the end, neither his lucidity nor the religious *encasement* chosen by the African American community provides protection from the racial dynamics in the town.[43]

For James, religious conversion, as one way of addressing the sick soul, involves a binding of the once "divided self"—a resolution, we might say, of doubleness, through the centrality of certain ideals once neglected.[44] If conversion is substantial resolution—wholeness away from openness—*Souls* rejects its likelihood. Instead, Du Bois proclaims that the two warring ideals defining double-consciousness never merge successfully; a truer self never develops, but instead a "longing," a "wish" for meaning as wholeness, might endure. There is a clear goal—"to be a co-worker in the kingdom of culture, to escape both death and isolation"—but it remains unfulfilled in that openness, the porous nature of things, prevents such escape—always life *and* death.[45]

The problem-soul posture shares with the sick-soul personality a vision of the world that lacks easy comfort vis-à-vis distinction and boundaries between things, and this way attention to James helps to clarify the perception of the world as marked by racial disregard Du Bois seeks to highlight through the problem soul. This positioning against the world in and of itself has not fostered a negative response in that for critics such as Cornel West proper perspective does not involve denial of the tragic quality of life. To the contrary, it is vital; however, what West finds missing is a creative tension between the tragic and the comic. Du Bois's perception of the human condition is lacking because he does not consider sufficiently the current context in which even "ultimate purpose and objective order" are called into question, and he does not fully grasp what West calls the "sheer absurdity of the human condition."[46] West assumes a type of fatalism in Du Bois stemming in part from his failure to engage adequately—instead of paternalistically and dismissively—

the life and resource of the larger African American community. He is outside the circle of concern, so to speak, and therefore lacks a robust safeguard. Without "ritual, cushioned by community or sustained by art," West cautions, "we are urged toward suicide or madness."[47] Yet this community is not foreign to Du Bois. More to the point, however, this "community," complete with the resources West names, has also produced redemptive-suffering models of response to the absurdity of life that challenge persistent struggle and instead promote a radical sense of the future that easily sacrifices the present and "kills," so to speak, the possibility of a robust anthropology by diminishing human responsibility and accountability in the world as well as by giving misery high status. The ritual and artistic expression within African American communities, as Du Bois knows, is not always inclined toward self-care and collective advancement.

On closer inspection, the underlying issue for West seems not a lack of attention to the absurdity of the world—or a disciplined diagnosis of the historical moment. Instead, he challenges what he perceives as Du Bois's failure to find comfort and resolution within the collective life of the "least of these."[48] Du Bois, if one ignores changes to his thinking and reflects only on his early work, appears elitist and "exceptionalist" in orientation, and this "inability to immerse himself fully in the rich cultural currents of black everyday life" constitutes the issue because without this immersion a sense of the tragicomic quality of life is impossible to grasp.[49] Hence, reflecting on his early thinking in isolation, a turn to classical education was betrayed by the theory of the talented tenth; economic inclusion was marred by the tenacious nature of white supremacy; cultural production as Du Bois presented it within his early career failed to do more than offer an apology for African American genius; and political participation was short-circuited by an Enlightenment worldview championing yet another form of elitism as the "impulsive and irrational masses" were guided into public life by their superiors.[50]

I argue, however, that the cultural world of "everyday" interactions is not foreign to Du Bois and that the elitism critiqued by West is later challenged by Du Bois himself; the difference with West is Du Bois's unwillingness to see in this resource a sustainable aid.[51] This disagreement notwithstanding, even limited attention to West's critique points in the direction of the sensibility I want to highlight. While not framing absurdity in the moralist-absurdist manner I have in mind, West does promote implicitly the utility of this vocabulary in connection to Du Bois's perspective in *Souls*.

## Problem Soul

Consideration of the Negro problem, particularly in theological terms, entails a sense of hope funneled through faith in cosmic assistance, while the problem soul connotes "a hope not hopeless but unhopeful."[52] Du Bois mentions this unhopeful posture in relationship to death as physical demise, but it is just as applicable to the depth of disregard—or ontological irrelevance—also marking encounter with the cultural climate associated with the world.[53] To be unhopeful within this cultural climate raises the question of pain and suffering, but not as a matter of theodicy. Rather, the problem-soul posture rejects grand unity of purpose, and this entails a stance much more in line with a Camusian sense of struggle (as interplay) and life without appeal. Paul Taylor points toward this sense of struggle without resolution in Du Bois prior to his departure for Ghana: "Du Bois offered to a friend what we might take as his final assessment of the prospects of social justice. 'Chin up and fight on,' Du Bois says, 'but realize that American Negroes can't win.'"[54] Sharing West's desire to avoid passivity or fatalism, Taylor makes an effort to recast this statement not as a general denouncement of struggle as having a useful outcome; rather, he reads it as an endorsement of pan-African striving for justice as opposed to the more geographically limited push for civil rights in the United States. Taylor argues, yes, Du Bois says *American* Negroes can't win, but he doesn't say Negroes (as a global population) can't win. The more expansive framing of the global African American community involves rejection of America as the standard and embrace of pan-African allegiances—a different type of interplay to be sure.[55]

Beside the mode of revision offered by Paul Taylor, melancholy as response to loss is a manner in which some have attempted to capture the tone of Du Bois's diagnosis.[56] Jonathan Flatley, for whom it can be a positive, argues melancholy is produced for Du Bois through white supremacy. Flatley discusses melancholia in relationship to Du Bois as a means of disclosure—a look into the sources of melancholia thereby producing a historical sense of the source of loss and an interest in the world. Yet I am not convinced this is the best way to frame the problem soul. What would constitute the prior thing, an initial situation, against which the new situation is measured? Loss involves a change in posture, mood, and perception of experience premised on something desired and once present, now gone and therefore mourned. What Du Bois articulates has little if anything to do with properly or improperly addressing loss.

If anything, the African American is culturally constituted by a mode of misplaced nostalgia, consistent with the manner in which Camus captures U.S. self-understanding more broadly. As such, African Americans, at least as culturally or discursively constructed, are without a capacity for loss. The assumed sense of longing or loss is better described as existential disruption—affective, geographical, and physical ramifications tied to the failure of Reconstruction. Du Bois does not point to an original moment of wholeness, a location once beyond the grasp of racial disregard, a space set aside and set apart. No, he poses the question of unendingly warring identities within a cultural climate of violent difference, shaped by a vivid awareness of absurdity, akin to this consideration marking out naming-things set apart as thing-things: What do things of history lose or gain?

It is true the spirituals, or sorrow songs, as Du Bois names them, hint at what may be thought of as a sense of longing. Of course, there is individual loss through the tactics of white supremacy and Jim Crow, but even this is not connected to a remembered past of equality in the United States that is longed for. Jim Crow over against enslavement produces not melancholy but a deep sense of racial disregard as already and always, speaking not to loss but to the overwhelming presence of white supremacy impinging on every dimension of collective life. Furthermore, religious melancholy, as James defines lost meaning, does not apply either. Melancholy as a mode of personal sin or as fear generated by the radical evil marking the world as lacking grand significance and devoid of meaning—presented in a "modern style," as Charles Taylor frames it—does no better a job of capturing the sensibility of the problem soul.[57] These two—personal sin and fear—suggest longing for an alternate, a different relationship to the world that is missing but plausible. This is more consistent with what was said in the second chapter regarding Yates's reading of Bakhtin through a Christian theological hermeneutic which privileged (over against degradation as Bakhtin understands it) wholeness and boundaries. Yet by means of the posture known as the problem soul, personal sin is moot, and fear is an intimate dimension of disregard. There is no ritualization of loss and no effort to end openness.[58] Available to the problem soul are only thought and habits of revolt without resolution—a resolve only to recognize the absurdity of encounter with the world—while maintaining an interplay with/between things.

Charles Long might be said to come closest to offering a useful way to position Du Bois in relationship to melancholia. In his 1975 William James Lecture, Long reflects on *Varieties* and questions the ability of James's "once born" and "twice born" framework to, as he puts it, bear "the weight of the cultural experiences of the Americas, much less the experience of human-kind."[59] The values and meanings accorded life within a context of racial disregard require recognition of a different source for the "twice born" soul. It is this different source Long means to address through his discussion of the negative element of religious experience. Moreover, through religious experience the oppressed push back toward "primordial experience and histories" that critique modernity and its metaphysical categories used to re-create the "other." This second creation, or reinvention, is for Long what Du Bois intends by double-consciousness.

Furthermore, unlike the dread experienced by James and his father, the dread Du Bois chronicles in the essay "On the Faith of the Fathers" might be said to involve reevaluation of, or better yet, the compromised stability of this second creation opening the possibility of a prior meaning—as the persistent separateness of conflicting identities impinges.[60] Religious experience within the context of a new formulation of community addresses a sense of first creation—the self prior to the logic of modern racial disregard—as a "new form of human consciousness." And the political struggles within these newly formed communities speak to the forging of space in which to exercise this new consciousness regarding openness—the porous quality of interaction.[61] It is a crawling back for Long, away from the second creation to a first creation—which is loss of destructive significations of identity and meaning. This loss, then, is rejection of the second creation, the modern articulation of limited metaphysical black worth.

Despite Long's modifications, a feeling of loss assumes an integrity of past experience foreign to African Americans as a consequence of antiblack racism and its structuring of discourse. Perhaps this is why the Cargo cults to which Long points entail unfulfilled resolution sought through material acquisition. The religion of the oppressed, as I read Long, offers conversion—one grounded in the historical consequences of American culture, but conversion nonetheless. Yet for Du Bois, there is no possibility of conversion; there is no salvation (i.e., a reliable end to openness and interplay), not even the type to which Long points. And as described in *Souls*, the religion of African Americans involves not a crawling back but rather an embrace of the second creation, an unwillingness to confront structures of disregard but instead a thinking theologically about second creation as a mode of theodicy resolved through address of personal sin and the mysteries of God's will. Herein closure is sought to the degree that only divine presence penetrates the naming-thing:

all interplay is of limited worth when one considers the interplay with the Divine.

On the microlevel, with the death of Du Bois's son, there is a poetic quality offered through personal pain and angst that lends a softer meaning to the misery of disregard. Du Bois says, "I saw his breath beat quicker and quicker, pause, and then his little soul leapt like a star that travels in the night and left a world of darkness in its train."[62] Still, this brief glimpse of transcendence through removal from the cultural climate by means of death is more often silenced by Du Bois the scientific thinker, who, as he acknowledges, "longs for work" and who "pant[s] for a life full of striving."[63] With this example in place, what James says about evil is applicable. The normal arrangements of life are filled "with moments in which radical evil gets its inning and takes its solid turn."[64] However, as Du Bois outlines the cultural climate, and the ongoing push to render black naming-things fixed and bounded—marginalized and limited—this "turn" seems perpetual.

# epilogue

## CONFRONTING EXPOSURE, OR
## A PSYCHO-ETHICAL RESPONSE TO OPENNESS

This book was to pick up the study of religion where *Terror and Triumph: The Nature of Black Religion* ends. To be precise, I intended it as an extension of *Terror and Triumph*'s theory of relational centralism applied to a wider range of cultural production.[1] Through that approach I meant to urge scholarly understanding of the relationship between religion and culture beyond exploration of dominant theological symbols embedded in culture, beyond the assumption that religion must constitute a *unique* mode of thought or experience, and beyond a narrow range of cultural resources. It was intended to bring greater depth and richness to the study of religion and to understandings of culture—its origins, impact, and longevity—as well as the "things" populating cultural worlds.[2]

This book was to frame cultural "assemblies" in a manner consistent with what I labeled my theory of religion (i.e., religion as the quest for complex subjectivity—a process of meaning making). The rationale was simple: the relationship between religion and cultural production, for example, has been a source of much fruitful discussion. In recent years important books have effectively shifted attention to the connection (making more readily recognizable appropriate subfields) between cultural production and religion. In part this has involved an underlying rationale that the religious is where you find it, so to speak. In other words, the religious is embedded and encoded in the cultural workings of human life. And while these books are vital, my volume was to provide a more expansive investigation than is offered in many of them in that it would not assume a framing of the religious determined and defined in terms of institutional forms, doctrines, or theological vocabulary of particular traditions.

## Prequel: From Complex Subjectivity to Religion as a Technology

I soon realized the project I intended to write required a theoretical step I had not yet made.[3] *Terror and Triumph* outlined a response to particular modalities of dread resulting from effort to fix black bodies. It is not a theory of religion; rather, it is a theory of ethical formulation—a psycho-ethical response to what religion exposes in relationship to certain modalities of disregard. Time to reflect on *Terror and Triumph* and what it proposed, sparked in part by conversation with colleagues, students, and friends, brought me to a realization: While *Terror and Triumph* maintains a sense of the religious as a means of "doing" something against the belittling of collective and individual markers of humanity, this sensibility and ethical frame did not constitute a theory of religion. I needed, then, to go behind *Terror and Triumph*'s ethical impulse. And so the book could not be as initially outlined; it had to be a prequel—the theory of religion *Terror and Triumph* assumed. That book, *Terror and Triumph*, in a way, worked backward—and in the process assumed what I now make explicit.[4]

As argued throughout these pages, religion as a technology, in relationship to strategies such as art, exposes naming-things and thing-things as porous—open and thereby allowing interplay. This realization flies in the face of normative theological narratives of wholeness or fixity made possible through "true" boundaries. And as was discussed in part 3, certain populations of naming-things are discursively warped and culturally marked off so as to maintain the illusion of being closed off. Still, such efforts fall short, and as one might imagine, this realization is not without its trauma—a type of destabilization that does not go unaddressed. This claim highlights the materiality of this fixing in terms of an effort to render vertical, to draw from Bakhtin, things' relationship to other things.

While it is a mislabeling of religion to call it a response to this situation of openness, its work does promote responses. That is to say, porousness is tackled in a variety of ways: hide the problematic (rituals of affirmation); cover the problematic through moral and ethical pronouncements; embrace the problematic as theologically necessary; ignore the problematic as a matter of blind faith. Much of what is produced in light of these possibilities involves an effort to fill the openings, to stabilize boundaries, and to assert the integrity and distinctiveness of things. All of this, as should be clear at this point, I find problematic.

In the final pages of this volume, I propose an alternate psycho-ethical (or affective-active) response to the openness of things illustrated through a Camusian moralist sensibility and a caustic framing of absurdity as, perhaps, an artistic rendition of the catchphrase "Shit happens."[5] Camus's stating of the case regarding the "absurd man" offers applicable insight. "For the absurd man," he reflects, "it is not a matter of explaining and solving, but of experiencing and describing."[6] Even more to the point, he reflects directly on art and the absurd: "The absurd work requires an artist conscious of these limitations and an art in which the concrete signifies nothing more than itself. It cannot be the end, the meaning, and the consolation of a life."[7] The nature and meaning of the absurd, and its connection to religion as a technology, as I want to understand and employ it involves to some degree a sense of limitations and possibilities. But this is not the agape love–driven "impossible possibility" of neoorthodox thinkers, such as Reinhold Niebuhr, resolved through divine intervention—for example, God filling the gaps as the human languishes between history and eternity, between her capacities and the restraints of her nature.[8] Such thinking promotes a theory (and practice) of religion very different from what I work to theorize and follow in this book.

Religion as I have theorized it actually ends where their "hope against hope" begins. That is to say, religion as a technology—a method or what might be called a technique of exposure—affords perspective or at best recognition of circumstances along the lines of what Camus labels "lucidity" or awareness. Hope, I argue, involves not simple recognition of circumstances but also—and this is an important distinction—reflection on more appropriate arrangements of circumstances.[9] In this way, hope involves "vertical" thinking that frames and privileges particular outcomes as not simply plausible but possible through proper orientation and a defined posture—submissive to the Divine and defiant toward the world.

## The Deception of Closure

Even when seeking to do otherwise, as in the case of Yates discussed in chapter 2, many of the dominant narratives regarding openness cast it as a problem to solve. In fact, it is depicted as a problem that can be solved through a range of prescribed patterns of thinking and doing that tend to pull away from the world and the more "unpleasant" realities and functions of life in the world. However, moralism points out the fictive nature of such psycho-ethical responses.[10] Collision between naming-things and other things does not entail a firm epistemological structuring of being. And more to the point, such structuring is not my interest here, nor does Camus offer it to readers. Rather, interplay points to unanswered questions—tension between naming-things and other things. This is not a mode of transgression of boundaries because the boundaries are a fiction to begin with. Offered by moralism simply is recognition of porousness and a naming of ongoing penetration or presence of things in each other, or, as I have referenced through the book, in Camus's terminology, "their presence together." Anything else might be a deception.

Herein, psycho-ethical response as "rebellion, without claiming to solve everything, can at least confront its problems."[11] To continue thinking with Camus, this is not to end absurdity as a marker of openness, nor to control openness, but rather it is a process of "holding" things close. Over against this process, the effort to end absurdity and thereby close things off vis-à-vis "unity" is a futile attempt to banish the angst caused by the threat of the unknown. It is futile in that complexity in the form of contradiction is a defining element of absurdity.[12] While Camus makes this assertion concerning the nature of absurdity as a "rule of life" marked by contradiction within a philosophical discussion of murder and suicide, I think the general epistemological point extends beyond that particular context.[13] Think in terms of his reflections on Sisyphus published just a little earlier than his reflections on the "rebel." In both the case of the former and the nameless latter figure, absurdity is characterized by effort but a lack of resolution—a denial of assertion or "unity." Regarding Sisyphus, he writes, "the lucidity that was to constitute his torture [the awareness of his eternal plight] at the same time crowns his victory."[14] There is no transcendence, not even the pretense of transcendence—that is, as a closing off of that which is porous and penetrated.

This thinking is a substantial difference in that normalizing narratives—such as theological systems of tradition—work to enhance distinction by painting it as having a transcendent quality. Take, for example, the story of Job from the Hebrew Bible. This is a narrative about the relationship of naming-things to thing-things along a negative loop. Thing-things—whether created by naming-things or not—impinge upon Job and damage his existential and ontological sense of bodied integrity. Whether the loss of his children (naming-things) when the house—a thing—collapses on them, or the loss of wealth captured by possession of things, or the betrayal of his naming-thing through illness, this story centers on the destruction or contamination of things as a marker of existential and ontological separation.

> Thy sons and thy daughters were eating and drinking wine in their eldest brother's house and, behold, there came a great wind from the wilderness, and smote the four corners of the house, and it fell upon the young men, and they are dead.[15]

> But put forth thine hand now, and touch his bone and his flesh, and he will curse thee to thy face. And the LORD said unto Satan, behold, he is in thine hand; but save his life. So went Satan forth from the presence of the LORD, and smote Job with sore boils from the sole of his foot unto his crown.[16]

The resolution to the narrative of Job, to the extent there is one, centers on naming-thing epistemological uncertainty as acquiescence to divine prerogative. Such surrender is matched by existential renewal to the extent theological dissonance is eased through availability of other things—such as new wealth. Anchoring resolution in this case is the proper ordering of naming-things, thing-things, and the cosmic "THING" called God. Camus seems aware of this deception, and the notion of ongoing rebellion speaks to this. Bodied naming-things crave a unity that does not exist, and so the illusion of the unity must be created and protected. Camus points to a determined lucidity regarding our existence, while the rest are details we construct.[17]

## Camus and Openness

The psycho-ethical impulse in the book of Job is controlled if not neutralized through contentment with "life without appeal" despite whether such a life is actually possible or not. (If nothing else, this psycho-ethical response is a soft and muted assumption.) In what Job is granted there is appeal—but the appeal is to the subject's subjectivity over against the object and the abject between them. This is to suggest there is "ground" so to speak upon which to stand distinct. It is to attempt resolution through surrender of "one of the terms of the opposition"—in this case a surrender of some subjectivity for the sake of the subject. Yet contrary to this, Camus seeks revolt, not aspiration. Abjection speaks, I argue, to the residue of aspiration. "That revolt is the certainty of a crushing fate, without the resignation that ought to accompany it."[18] Such thinking asserts, at least softly, a comfort with porous things presented to the world. Hence, it is a mode of naming by naming-things without the fallback of wishing for more stability and boundaries held with true integrity. With abjection, vulnerability is a negative, a threat. But for Camus, vulnerability speaks to our existential condition and relationship to the world—a world that impinges and enters us, that we impinge upon and enter. Still, this interplay does not manifest answers to our questions of existence posed by this arrangement of things. The narratives we often tell ourselves in the context of this silence constitute an effort to fortify ourselves. However energetic the telling, they, to a large degree, are pointless in that these narratives produce nothing that did not exist without them.

I see in this perception of the naming-thing's interplay with thing-things something of what Camus notes as the "triumph of the carnal" without grand "consolation" to be found or created.[19] Differentiation is at the end fictional, which leaves lines of "distinction" porous and always compromised. Hence, there is art.

This is the reason for art; if differentiation, meaning, subjectivity, and other tropes for wholeness were possible, the world would be "clear, art would not exist."[20] To explicate what I have in mind, I return to W. E. B. Du Bois, Nella Larsen, Richard Wright, and Orlando Patterson.

### The Value of Openness

While absurdity and the challenge of the open-bodied naming-thing perverted with boundaries of social difference (e.g., race) informs *The Souls of Black Folk*, it is presented graphically much later in *Dusk of Dawn*, where Du Bois writes:

> It is as though one, looking out from a dark cave in a side of an impending mountain, sees the world passing and speaks to it; speaks courteously and persuasively, showing them how these entombed souls are hindered in their natural movement, expression, and development; and how their loosening from prison would be a matter not simply of courtesy, sympathy, and help to them, but aid to all the world. One talks on evenly and logically in this way, but notices that the passing throng does not even turn its head, or if it does, glances curiously and walks on.[21]

For Richard Wright, it is not a cave but rather the underworld, the sewer. Still, the sentiment is the same. In the short story "The Man Who Lived Underground," the sewer is where the protagonist finds himself after a confrontation with the police reinforces his status as problem thing.[22] From the sewer, he sees but is not seen; he discovers and observes the behavior of those who live above him; and in the process he recognizes the futility of their endeavors and the pervasive misery that marks their lives. Du Bois notes the cave as a tomb, and Fred Daniels, the protagonist in Wright's story, sees and feels death around him—from the baby floating by, to the work of the funeral parlor, the dead animals in the butcher shop, and the suicide of the security guard. What humans seek, they cannot have. This is evident for Daniels as he watches people in a type of church worship service also familiar to Du Bois (and Nella Larsen for that matter). Observing them was painful, more penetrating than the ache of his body because he knew what they refused to acknowledge. "A deeper pain," Wright narrates, "induced by the sight of those black people groveling and begging for something they could never get churned in him."[23] There is no comfort, no assurances offered.

Lucidity, like other conceptual maps offered in *Souls*, is doubled. In addition to lucidity regarding the workings of the world in general, Du Bois also alludes to lucidity in terms of a type of clairvoyance allowing African Americans to see both their context and that of whites. The latter is a deep observation. The most telling presentation of this lucidity is in "The Souls of White Folk," an essay in *Darkwater: Voices from within the Veil* (1920). There he writes, "I see these souls undressed and from the back and side. I see the working of their entrails. I know their thoughts and they know that I know. . . . And yet as they preach and strut and shout and threaten, crouching as they clutch at rags of facts and fancies to hid their nakedness, they go twisting, flying by my tired eyes and I see them ever striped—ugly, human."[24] Rejection of a source of appeal deconstructs the workings of the "religion of whiteness" and exposes its human inner workings.[25] A theodical formulation of collective life advantaging whiteness is replaced with an anthropodicy of fragility. Du Bois concludes, "We looked at him clearly, with world-old eyes, and saw simply a human thing weak and pitiable and cruel, even as we are and were. These super-men and world-mastering demi-gods listened, however, to no low tongues of ours, even when we pointed silently to their feet of clay."[26]

Nella Larsen's central character in the novel *Quicksand*, Helga Crane, consistent with a moralist posture toward the trauma of effort to close off openness through coding of gender and race, finds strength in the awareness of the absurd. "Never could she," Larsen acknowledges to the reader, "recall the shames and often the absolute horrors of the black man's existence in America without the quickening of her heart's beating and a sensation of disturbing nausea. It was too awful. The sense of dread of it was almost a tangible thing in her throat."[27] Nausea for Larsen does not connote merely a biological discomfort, but rather there are larger considerations tied to metaphysics. Crane names the absurd. I want to frame this naming in terms of Camus, who understands a similarity between Jean-Paul Sartre's sense of nausea and what he, Camus, means by absurdity. Think of Crane's response to others and herself in light of Camus's framing. He writes, "This discomfort in the face of man's own inhumanity, this incalculable tumble before the image of what we are, this 'nausea' as a writer of today calls it, is also the absurd."[28] There is no grand unity capable of providing meaning within a cold world. "The cruel, unrelieved suffering had beaten down her protective wall of artificial faith in the infinite wisdom, in the mercy, of God," writes Larsen. "For had she not called in her agony on Him? And he had not heard. Why? Because, she knew now, He wasn't there. Didn't exist."[29] But what is sacrificed in order to pretend an answer when none is given by the world, when there is no God to aid the inquiry?

Crane is open and lucid to life marked only by confrontation and a "No!" to her circumstances—that is, societal efforts to close and fix her. This is her situation—her entanglement in a cultural climate of contempt presenting a world that is foreign, hostile, violent, death dealing. In her words, "only scorn, resentment and hate remained—and ridicule. Life wasn't a miracle, a wonder. It was, for Negroes at least, only a great disappointment. Something to be gotten through as best one could. No one was interested in them or helped them. God! Bah!"[30] Her family, her community, and her country offer Crane rest, not resolution—no sustainable respite from the threat of death. "We see," writes Kristin Lattany, "that America is not a glamour queen but a grisly skeleton, her only product death . . . her only lessons how to kill and how to die."[31] Nonetheless, for Larsen through Crane (and Du Bois before her) the ever-present threat of death does not stimulate a sense of melancholy. Instead, death is simply a dimension of what it is to live within the context of the cultural climate of the post–Civil War United States. All this Du Bois captures with the question "How does it feel to be a problem?" and Larsen with a proclamation—"God! Bah!"[32]

Deeply aware of the manner in which the physical can betray—things, including our bodies, can forsake us, and life can entail a challenging quality—Du Bois, Wright, and Larsen respond to (but cannot undo) the threat of death. Du Bois, particularly in terms of double-consciousness, can tend to romanticize this body—highlighting its "dogged strength" over against the destructive qualities of the cultural climate. Still, he recognizes with nineteenth-century religious leader the Reverend Alexander Crummell and Burghardt, his son, the fragility of embodied bodies.[33] The body, a compromised form, is subject to death—the final moment of interplay as the naming-thing is dissolved and returned to the world as "food" for other things—and the problem soul never loses sight of this. Awareness of circumstances in the world helps to avoid what Daniels laments as he views—unobserved by them—people in a movie theater. Watching them laugh at the screen, he recognizes they are unaware of the manner in which they mock themselves—"shouting and yelling at the animated shadows of themselves."[34] To the extent they lack awareness, they are "children, sleeping in their living and awake in their dying."[35] All Daniels encounters as well as the items he steals offer life no meaning. In his hands, money becomes wallpaper, watches wall ornaments, and diamonds floor covering in his hole below the surface. Life, death, and the material trail between them do not constitute a relationship to the world, certainly not one offering resolution or final comfort.[36] While not exactly "sleeping in [her] living and awake in [her] dying," Crane does wrestle with metaphysical and existential dilemmas posed by the intertwined structures of being and not being.[37] That is to say, both Crane and Daniels, like Du Bois, are sensitive to physical demise ("sleeping in their living") as well as metaphysical death ("awake in their dying")—or ontological irrelevance—tied to the cultural climate guiding the historical moment.

Traditional framings of religion as "something" worth speaking and doing, and its theological probing of the world, for Larsen through Crane, Wright through Daniels, and for Du Bois through at least the story of John, offer nothing final. Theological arguments do not wrestle meaning from a silent world and do not offer a way to close off naming-things from the world. Instead, religion as a "some*thing*" prompts what Wright calls "eternity anxiety." The secret to existence, despite the efforts of the religious folks encountered, is not found in the workings of relationship to a cosmic *something*. John, facing those in his church, knows this, and the religious leadership of even a cultural giant like Crummell fares no better.[38]

One might think of the situation this way: the wish against wishes found in some spirituals—at least as they have come to us—is quickly countered by the response of the blues. Both speak a word regarding relationship—connection between questioning humans—that acknowledges the individual but in association with others also confronting (and confronted by) the world. This, one could say, is small and cold comfort.[39] Life is drowned in suffering, and it is marked by interplay—at times uncomfortable but always unavoidable.[40] Crane, who is slowly dying as she gives life to child after child, Wright's hunger unfulfilled in a hostile world, and Camus's championing of the absurdist elucidate Du Bois's diagnosis discussed in chapter 8.

## Embracing Openness

In Camus's narration, as Sisyphus prepares to continue his unending task of rolling his stone as punishment from the Greek gods, he reaches a point at which the stone is rolling down the hill and he is turning to follow it so as to undertake his task yet again. He knows the labor ahead of him and its perpetual nature, but this does not break him; rather, this awareness is his resolve and fixes his posture toward the cultural climate marking his existential situation. Sisyphus's stance and the posture called the problem soul are similar. He has his gods to challenge through his persistence, although this does nothing to change his lot; he gains no quarter in the process. The lucidity, the awareness of his condition and the nature of his relationship to what is beyond him, speaks the problem. It is his posture toward the world. In the telling, both Camus and Du Bois are sure.

This posture is not limited to the challenge of socially coded open-bodied naming-things within a given geography, as some might read my attention to the contextual arrangements of openness in the United States. Mindful of this, I end with some attention to Orlando Patterson's *The Children of Sisyphus*.[41] With this novel, one gets Camusian moralism tied to grotesque realism through the travails of the various characters—residents of the "Dungle," which is an area of Jamaica marked by refuge and open-bodied naming-things exposed to and exposed by waste out of which they crave life. In a word, something of this book has the energy, the presence, of the carnivalistic impulse described by Bakhtin. The situation for these garbage dwellers is horizontal—no time or resource for vertical thought and endeavors. They are grounded in the filth the city would like to deny. They are marked out by a degrading quality that pulls nutrition and vitality from relationship to despised thing-things of the world.

As one of the garbage men responsible for bringing city waste to the Dungle reflects, they were "creatures" that "weren't human. If anyone told him that they were human like himself he would tell them that they lied."[42] This was not because he, as a bodied naming-thing, was not open, because he was—all are. No, he reacted to the values embedded in life with trash and needed to distance himself in order to maintain the illusion that he, as a naming-thing, was private and not exposed publicly to the piled waste of life. Shit ties together the people of the Dungle and the land. The naming-thing to thing-thing, naming-thing to naming-thing, and thing-thing to thing-thing connections are constituted by social engineering and cultural placement of shit out of sight. Yet something of the interplay was intriguing; it pulled at him:

> When he had almost reached the road the garbage-man, under some strange impulse, looked back at the scene he had just left. Something about it frightened him. There was, he imagined, a freakish infernal beauty in the oddly graceful way the mounds of filth undulated towards the unseen shore, in the way the sea murmured and sighed and lashed the shore at intervals with the breaking crack of a crocodile's tail, in the way the crystal blueness of the frightfully near horizon rose sheet behind the debris as if in flight from the menace of the sea.[43]

Bodied naming-things are open and troublingly so. They are penetrated by their surroundings, consumed by and consuming of the waste around them.

The world, as Bakhtin might observe, is defined by bodied presence and activities. There is no distinction to be made in that life, or better yet, the circumstances of life, are horizontal. The grotesque reigns for those with grotesque bodies—those who are constructed within the troubled and troubling world of the Americas. As I have remarked numerous times in this book, the marginalized are often projected as shit.[44] One gets a sense of this in what Dinah encounters after she has departed from the Dungle to live with her new man. In a scene as she is leaving their room to clean the chamber pot, Patterson writes, "In a moment she felt as if they had stripped her of all her being and was tearing it to pieces, searching into every last crevice of it, as if it was the muck the garbage-cart deposited at the Dungle."[45]

Like Sisyphus, residents of the Dungle struggle to move. Sisyphus was punished to struggle eternally, but the shit of the Dungle held the residents bound. For instance, Dinah wanted to exit the Dungle even if it meant cruelly leaving her son behind just as Helga Crane, from Larsen's *Quicksand*, wanted to leave the preacher's house—and in so doing free herself from the pull of the children consuming her, forget the hateful neighbors, and push beyond the circumstances that destroyed her. In either case, unlike Sisyphus, we cannot even imagine them happy, because certain grotesque bodies are so heavily coded with social trappings that the pull on them eventually kills them, or at least compromises them severely.[46] Dinah is pulled back into the Dungle and lives there until her death; for Crane, the naming-thing/thing-thing interplay when coded by race, gender, class, and spirituality create obligation and connections that shape and determine a psycho-ethical loop of terror. Crane plans her move away from the interplay of other naming-things—children—who impinge upon her. However, as Larsen writes, "hardly had she left her bed and become able to walk again without pain, hardly had the children returned from the homes of the neighbors, when she began to have her fifth child."[47]

To attempt closure of these bodies is to render them stable and workable within the larger framework of social logic. This is the case with Dinah's purification—when she is bathed and her body anointed with oil—or when the purifying blood of a pigeon is poured on her and it "was like a razor gliding through her flesh. For one long, excruciating moment she was sure that it was her own blood that flowed."[48] In more charismatic traditions, the role of religious ritual is not to close off the body, but rather to restrict its openness and its receptivity to divine presence only. That is to say—"in the world but not of it"—cosmic forces penetrate the open-bodied naming-thing, and through this penetration safeguard it from impact by other forces. It becomes a new bodied thing by means of which its material nature and connection to the world is downplayed by a new cosmic state of being—"behold old things have passed away, all things become as new" or "put on the full armor of God."[49] This armor, however, serves only to block the body, to hide it and deny it—and in so doing to deny the supple nature of life.

This does not mean within the Dungle that open-bodied naming-things necessarily surrender to the absurdities of life coded by social signifiers that attempt to fix bodies and reduce openness. Some in the Dungle turn to Rastafarianism, but even this more humanistic tradition begs the question of life's parameters and prospects: Is there life without appeal, and how does one live it? For those in the Dungle, yes, life is possible, but it is a life of justified punishment until God says otherwise. This is the delusion of a distinct future. It is a redemptive suffering formulation premised on a life in/on/of shit. Obeah here in the Dungle, as in Christianity in Wright and Larsen, is projected as a means by which to close off the body—to end its openness—through cosmic strategies of disappearance entailed by a particular ritualization of naming-thing/thing-thing interplay. In this case, site-specific dirt "out of place" and out of its original "time" shift nature and meaning—or close the naming-thing to objects and assumed technologies of contact. But, like Christianity, it fails in this regard. The question is this: What is made of that radical openness?

For Wright, Larsen, Patterson, and Camus, it is a life of struggle, but lucidity prevents the assumption that there is merited suffering—for example, painful attempts at closure—premised on a cosmic logic. According to these four, there is no grand unity around which such logic can rest. Perpetual struggle to remain open is the victory. The celebration and perseverance of degraded life, to borrow again from Bakhtin, is this moralist impulse.

These texts taken together and read through moralism offer a moral-ethical response to openness. The response is lucidity—awareness of circumstance and resistance to effort to close off the body. "To perceive the truth of existence," a character in *The Children of Sisyphus* announces, "is to perceive an unutterable tragedy."[50] But it is a tragedy only if one assumes bodied naming-things should be sheltered from impingement, as if well-being is premised on wholeness and completeness.

# notes

INTRODUCTION

1  In *Terror and Triumph: The Nature of Black Religion* (Minneapolis: Fortress Press, 2003), I argued that religion is a quest for complex subjectivity. It is a response to the fundamental questions of human existence: Who are we? What are we? Why are we? When are we? It is a quest, I noted, but one that is unfulfilled and that gives rise to a perpetual rebellion against efforts to deform and dehumanize. The epilogue provides more information concerning the move from religion as a quest for complex subjectivity to religion as a technology.

2  Thank you to one of my project reviewers for these: Susan George, *Religion and Technology in the 21st Century: Faith in the E-World* (Hershey, PA: Information Science Publishing, 2006); Jacques Ellul, *The Technological Society* (New York: Knopf, 1964). My goal here is not to provide a discussion of work related to technology and religion, but rather to simply point out examples of how my efforts in this book differ from much of what constitutes the academic discussion of technology and religion. In doing so, I want to provide a sense of how readers might contextualize my theory of religion.

3  George, *Religion and Technology*, vi–ix.

4  See George, *Religion and Technology*, chapter 1. The distinction holds true in various ways regarding other texts related to religion and technology: Brenda E. Brasher, *Give Me That Online Religion: Churches, Cults and Community in the Information Age* (San Francisco: Jossey-Bass, 2000); David F. Noble, *The Religion of Technology: The Divinity of Man and the Spirit of Invention* (New York: Penguin, 1999); Scott Midson, *Cyborg Theology: Humans, Technology*

*and God* (London: I. B. Tauris, 2017); Nancey Murphy and Christopher C. Knight, eds., *Human Identity at the Intersection of Science, Technology and Religion* (New York: Routledge, 2010); Jeremy Stolow, ed., *Deus in Machina: Religion, Technology, and the Things in Between* (New York: Fordham University Press, 2013); Sam Han, *Technologies of Religion: Spheres of the Sacred in a Post-Secular Modernity* (New York: Routledge, 2016).

5 George, *Religion and Technology*, ix.

6 George, *Religion and Technology*, chapters 5–9.

7 George, *Religion and Technology*, xi–xii.

8 Regarding this he writes, "Technique certainly began with the machine. It is quite true that all the rest developed out of mechanics; it is quite true also that without the machine the world of technique would not exist. But to explain the situation in this way does not at all legitimize it. It is a mistake to continue with this confusion of terms, the more so because it leads to the idea that, because the machine is at the origin and center of the technical problem, one is dealing with the whole problem when one deals with the machine. . . . Technique has now become almost completely independent of the machine, which has lagged far behind its offspring" (Ellul, *Technological Society*, 3–4).

9 Robert K. Merton, foreword to Ellul, *Technological Society*, vi.

10 Ellul, *Technological Society*, xxvi.

11 Ellul, *Technological Society*, 14–15, 22. Ellul also offers a third division related to economic techniques dealing with labor and the arrangement of related plans (22).

12 Ellul, *Technological Society*, 4–12. I also share with Ellul a reluctance to offer resolutions, to propose a fix to the dilemma to which this book points. On this reluctance, Ellul says, "In this study no solution is put forward to the problems raised. Questions are asked, but not answered. I have indeed deliberately refrained from providing solutions. . . . I do not say that no solutions will be found; I merely aver that in the present social situation there is not even a beginning of a solution, no breach in the system of technical necessity" (xxxi). It is in relationship to a similar perspective that I employ the thought of Albert Camus and W. E. B. Du Bois.

13 Ellul, *Technological Society*, 33.

14 Ellul, *Technological Society*, 34.

15 Ellul, *Technological Society*, 34–36.

16 He sees a relationship between scientific investigation—particularly as reflected in the eighteenth and nineteenth centuries—and technique, which subordinates the former to the latter.

17 Ellul, *Technological Society*, 48–49.

18 Ellul, *Technological Society*, 49.

19 Ellul, *Technological Society*, 128.

20 See Ellul, *Technological Society*, chapter 5.

21 It differs in terms of disciplinary locations for each as well as having little concern for the larger debate regarding the positive or negative connotation of machines and machinery within sociopolitical and economic realms, and finally without playing technology off modalities of humanism as a foil.

22 Michel Foucault, *Technologies of the Self: A Seminar* (Amherst: University of Massachusetts Press, 1988), 16–49, 18; Foucault, *Discipline and Punish: The Birth of the Prison* (New York: Vintage, 1995). A detailed discussion of Foucault's formulation and use of the hermeneutical method of technology is beyond the scope of this book. For information on the development of Foucault's thinking on technology, see, for example, Michael C. Behrent, "Foucault and Technology," *History and Technology: An International Journal* 29, no. 1 (2013): 54–104. Behrent notes that as of the 1970s Foucault used technique and technology interchangeably, although, he argues, there remained nuanced distinctions between the two. When I use the two terms, I mean in both cases the method noted above, while recognizing that religion in this function is a basic feature of our social arrangements.

23 Foucault, *Technologies of the Self*, 18.

24 Related to this, power dynamics are most explicitly addressed in the final section of the book.

25 Foucault, *Technologies of the Self*, 18.

26 Foucault, *Technologies of the Self*, 19.

27 Pierre Bourdieu, *The Field of Cultural Production* (New York: Columbia University Press, 1993); Bourdieu, *Outline of a Theory of Practice* (New York: Cambridge University Press, 1977).

28 Gilles Deleuze and Félix Guattari develop the idea of the assemblage in *A Thousand Plateaus: Capitalism and Schizophrenia* (Minneapolis: University of Minnesota Press, 1987). For secondary commentary, see, for instance, Thomas Nail, "What Is an Assemblage," *Substance* 46, no. 1 (2017): 21–37; Jane Bennett, *Vibrant Matter: A Political Ecology of Things* (Durham, NC: Duke University Press, 2010), chapter 2.

29 Foucault, *Technologies of the Self*, 45.

30 At most the religion as a technology urges lucidity or awareness of our human condition(s) and our place within such condition(s).

31 It is possible that my effort to provide clarification will enhance the understanding of certain dimensions of my argument (e.g., what I do not mean by religion as technology) while confusing others (e.g., the structures and sensibilities serving as a precondition for my theorization of religion—or a full explication of what this theory of religion contains). Questions remain. As a consequence, additional work after this book will require more attention to this dimension of my theory.

32 See, for example, Talal Asad's discussion and critique of transhistorical and universalizing definitions of religion: *Genealogies of Religion: Discipline and Reasons of Power in Christianity and Islam* (Baltimore: Johns Hopkins University Press, 1993), chapters 1–2. While a full engagement with Asad is beyond

the scope and purpose of this book, I do want to note that my thinking on religion entails recognition of its constructed nature and its ties to the conceptual category of a certain intellectual geography. Investigation of the implications of these disciplinary (e.g., anthropological) realities is interesting but extends beyond the presentation of religion necessary for this particular project.

33 "Genealogies of Religion, Twenty Years On: An Interview with Talal Asad," *Bulletin for the Study of Religion* blog, https://bulletin.equinoxpub.com/2015/11 /genealogies-of-religion-twenty-years-on-an-interview-with-talal-asad.

34 It does this in relationship to the body and "thing." Readers should keep in mind that I am not concerned with defining the human—what constitutes the human; rather, my focus is narrower than that. I am interested in the body. In addition, I am interested in better understanding the "things" used within the context of artistic production and utilized in the work of religion.

35 I am not concerned with the biological "origins" or workings of this technology called religion, but rather in how it has been arranged and deployed and in how it has functioned.

36 I say this in part in conversation with and in response to a depiction of Albert Camus's categorization of religion over against personal existence and rebellion as suggesting "some positive value" that is not "given." In outlining *The Rebel*, Herbert Read says it is the "trick played by religion or philosophy" to offer these values as given. See Albert Camus, *The Rebel: An Essay on Man in Revolt* (New York: Vintage International, 1991), vii. This also points to my disagreement with Danto regarding art as "embodying meaning."

37 Examples include David Morgan, *The Sacred Gaze: Religious Visual Culture in Theory and Practice* (Berkeley: University of California Press, 2005); Morgan, *The Embodied Eye: Religious Visual Culture and the Social Life of Feeling* (Berkeley: University of California Press, 2012); Colleen McDannell, *Material Christianity: Religion and Popular Culture in America* (New Haven, CT: Yale University Press, 1995); Bruce David Forbes and Jeffrey H. Mahan, eds., *Religion and Popular Culture in America* (Berkeley: University of California Press, 2000); Gordon Lynch, Jolyon Mitchell, and Anna Strhan, eds., *Religion, Media and Culture: A Reader* (New York: Routledge, 2012); Kathryn Lofton, *Oprah: The Gospel of an Icon* (Berkeley: University of California Press, 2011); Lofton, *Consuming Religion* (Chicago: University of Chicago Press, 2017); David Chidester, *Authentic Fakes: Religion and American Popular Culture* (Berkeley: University of California Press, 2005).

38 There is some repetition in this introduction regarding the nature and function of religion. However, I believe this is necessary in order to reinforce my movement beyond my earlier thinking and to make clear the way in which religion operates implicitly throughout the book.

39 As will become clear, religion as a technology not only tells us something about the interaction of things, but it can also use art as a way to address or "manage" the openness of things exposed through this interrogation.

40 Rosi Braidotti, *The Posthuman* (Malden, MA: Polity Press, 2013), 2.

41 Braidotti, *Posthuman*, 3.

42 Braidotti, *Posthuman*, 37. While I am opposed to Enlightenment notions of humanism for reasons including the manner in which it supported tragic ideologies and practices of racial disregard, I have spent some of my professional life rethinking humanism in the form of an African American humanism that, I believe, short-circuits many of the most significant problems reflected in earlier modalities of European humanisms. See, for example, Pinn, *African American Humanist Principles: Living and Thinking Like the Children of Nimrod* (New York: Palgrave Macmillan, 2004); Pinn, *Humanism: Essays on Race, Religion and Cultural Production* (London: Bloomsbury Academic, 2015).

43 See Julia Kristeva, *Powers of Horror: An Essay on Abjection* (New York: Columbia University Press, 1982).

44 This is not to suggest a departure from my ethical realism related to the human presented in my work on humanism. See Pinn, *African American Humanist Principles*; Pinn, *The End of God-Talk: An African American Humanist Theology* (New York: Oxford University Press, 2012); Pinn, *Humanism*.

45 I find this definition of humanist thought too tied to an uncritical embrace of Enlightenment optimism. And in this way, it fails to account for disregard and belittlement used to establish the hierarchy of being upon which it draws; instead, it projects metaphysics of the human being that is false as such. I find no need to articulate the value of human life along these lines, and instead I am content to think about the human in relationship to other life forms—the human tied and dependent always on other modalities of life. And in this mutuality is embedded a recognition that agency is not a defining characteristic of the human thing. So we think and experience the human as unique because we approach life forms from our vantage point, but the human is dependent upon the activities and impingements of other life forms.

   Agency is a shared reality of things. Even when human, naming-thing, create or construct this is not without the resistance of those things employed. For example, the heat of the flame not only shapes and melds things as desired but also destroys; the working of wood demands careful effort, or it resists through breakage, and other animal naming-things resist human command. (Keep in mind that refusal to be used or work as intended is a mode of resistance.)

46 To talk about the subject along the lines preferred by liberation theologians, for instance, is to cover this confluence with nostalgia for the pretense of bounded agents "liberated" into a transformed world. Certainly this is one way to read the nature of personhood and liberation within the work of figures such as James H. Cone (e.g., *A Black Theology of Liberation* [Maryknoll, NY: Orbis Books, 1986]); Dwight N. Hopkins (e.g., *Being Human: Race, Culture, and Religion* [Minneapolis: Fortress Press, 2005]); Kelly Brown Douglas (e.g., *Stand Your Ground: Black Bodies and the Justice of God* [Maryknoll, NY: Orbis Books, 2015]).

47 Karen Barad raises interesting questions concerning what has been the assumed significance of discourse and language in ways that have downplayed

the importance of things themselves. See Barad, "Posthumanist Performativity toward an Understanding of How Matter Comes to Matter," *Material Feminisms*, ed. Stacy Alaimo and Susan J. Hekman (Bloomington: Indiana University Press, 2008), 120–54.

48 One might think about this in terms of animacy, although my concern here isn't the function of the human process of naming but rather a way of thinking through the presence of various things without a hierarchical emphasis. Readers interested in thinking through the concept of naming-things in relationship to the linguistic framing of animacy should see, for example, Mel Y. Chen, *Animacies: Biopolitics, Racial Mattering, and Queer Affect* (Durham, NC: Duke University Press, 2012), chapter 1. It is particularly intriguing to read Chen in relationship to chapters 7–8 and the epilogue in this volume.

49 Bennett, *Vibrant Matter*, viii.

50 Bennett, *Vibrant Matter*, 4.

51 Bennett says, concerning her project, "My claims here are motivated by a self-interested or conative concern for human survival and happiness: I want to promote greener forms of human culture and more attentive encounters between people-materialities and thing-materialities" (*Vibrant Matter*, x). Bennett, for example, does not assume that such effort ultimately solves the problem, but for her the conceptual shift points to the value of things in such a way as to point out the ways in which we live "in a knotted world of vibrant matter, to harm one section of the web may very well be to harm oneself" (13).

52 Paul Rekret argues that new materialism fails to give adequate attention to the sociopolitical contexts in which the separation of mind and matter takes place. While new materialism rejects this distinction through its ontological turn, Rekret argues this failure hampers its ability to maintain its position. See Rekret, "The Head, the Hand, and Matter: New Materialism and the Politics of Knowledge," *Theory, Culture and Society* 35, no. 7–8 (2018): 49–72.

53 I would suggest that injustice is not so logical and the desire to uphold perceived social advantage is often expressed at a group's own peril. Think, for example, of working-class whites voting for Donald Trump.

54 See notes 37 and 41. In addition to texts noted elsewhere in this introduction, for information on new materialism see, for example, Rick Dolphijn and Iris van der Tuin, *New Materialism: Interviews and Cartographies* (London: Open Humanities Press, 2012); Estelle Barrett and Barbara Bolt, eds., *Carnal Knowledge: Towards a "New Materialism" of the Arts* (London: I. B. Tauris, 2013); Vicki Kirby, *What If Culture Was Nature All Along* (Edinburgh: University of Edinburgh Press, 2017); Elizabeth Grosz, *The Incorporeal: Ontology, Ethics, and the Limits of Materialism* (New York: Columbia University Press, 2017; Catherine Keller and Mary-Jane Rubenstein, eds., *Entangled Worlds: Religion, Science, and New Materialisms* (New York: Fordham University Press, 2017).

55 Diana Coole and Samantha Frost frame attention to materiality in this way: "It is now time to subject objectivity and material reality to a similarly radical reappraisal. Our respective researches have prompted our own interests in

changing conception of material causality and the significance of corpo-
reality, both of which we see as crucial for a materialist theory of politics
or agency. We now advance the bolder claim that foregrounding material
factors and reconfiguring our very understanding of matter are prerequisites
for any plausible account of coexistence and its conditions in the twenty-first
century." Coole and Frost, "Introducing the New Materialism," in Coole and
Frost, *New Materialisms*, 2.

56 Camus's notion of the absurd lends itself to the interplay I have in mind: "the
absurd has meaning only in so far as it is not agreed to. . . . A man who has become conscious of the absurd is forever bound to it." Albert Camus, *The Myth
of Sisyphus and Other Essays* (New York: Vintage International, 1991), 30, 31.

57 Hence, it is that which underlies the psycho-ethical impulse highlighted in
my earlier work. The earlier theoretical work allowed ethics to bleed into my
theorization—a holdover perhaps from my work as a constructive theologian.

58 This turn to Camus provides a useful way to connect this thinking about
the nature and meaning of religion to a process of a complex arrangement of
"doing"—or ethics, not simply what one "ought" to do but what this doing
won't achieve (i.e., what cannot be done).

59 See Pinn, *Terror and Triumph*.

60 Mikhail M. Bakhtin, *Rabelais and His World* (Bloomington: Indiana University
Press, 1984).

61 While some boundaries are meant to safeguard against particular forms of
abuse—such as laws against physical violence or sexual assault—they have not
functioned fully and consistently in a way that actually safeguards those most
vulnerable. This is in part due to the manner in which even these boundaries
are tainted by embedded notions of disregard.

62 Stelarc, a science-inspired performance artist, provides an intriguing depiction of the body—what he calls "an evolutionary architecture." He explores
modification of the body vis-à-vis technology that forces a rethinking of the
nature and meaning of body over against machine as well as requiring an
altered theorization of flesh. In this way, he uses IT as a method of fostering alternate conceptions of embodiment, and by extension the nature and
meaning of the embodied human. See, for example, "Zombies, Cyborgs
and Chimeras: A Talk by Performance Artist, Prof Stelarc," YouTube video,
August 5, 2014, https://www.youtube.com/watch?v=TqtiM1hK6lU.

63 The religion as a technology's interrogation of human experience points out
death, but not as an isolated "something" or situation; instead, it is already
always attached to the devices of its exploration—the body and objects. The
religion as a technology in essence uncovers death in all its multidimensional
modalities and representations.

64 My focused attention on the material body is not meant to suggest there is
only the physical body. My previous work argues against this reductive approach, and at least one chapter in this volume—dealing with Du Bois and
the problem soul—at least hints at the affective and constructed realm(s)

of the body. Yet my argument is that it is the physical, material body that is more rarely centered in the study of religion, and so I work to view the theorization of religion from its vantage point so as to fill a gap rather than based on the assumption that it is only the physical/material that "matters."

65  I would argue that Marcella Althaus-Reid's indecent theology is an example of a theological text pushing against easy closure and advocating for openness as an erotic quality. See Althaus-Reid, *Indecent Theology: Theological Perversions in Sex, Gender and Politics* (New York: Routledge, 2000).

66  In understanding ritualization in this manner, I am referencing the thinking of Ronald Grimes and others in ritual studies. See, for example, Grimes, *The Craft of Ritual Studies* (New York: Oxford University Press, 2013).

67  Bakhtin, *Rabelais and His World*.

68  For background information and artistic context on Angelbert Metoyer, see his website: https://www.angelbertmetoyer.com.

69  Dominique Laporte, *History of Shit* (Cambridge, MA: MIT Press, 2000).

70  See, for example, W. E. B. Du Bois, *The Suppression of the African-Slave Trade to the United States of America, 1638–1870* (1896); Du Bois, *The Philadelphia Negro: A Social Study* (1899); Du Bois, *Black Reconstruction: An Essay toward a History of the Part Which Black Folk Played in the Attempt to Reconstruct Democracy in America, 1860–1880* (1935); Du Bois, *Darkwater: Voices from within the Veil* (1920); Du Bois, *Dusk of Dawn: An Essay toward an Autobiography of a Race Concept* (1940).

71  W. E. B. Du Bois, *The Souls of Black Folk* (New York: Vintage Books/Library of America, 1990).

72  Works discussed include Camus, *Myth of Sisyphus and Other Essays*; Camus, *Rebel*; Nella Larsen, *Quicksand*, in *Quicksand and Passing* (New Brunswick, NJ: Rutgers University Press, 1986); Richard Wright, *Native Son* (New York: Harper Perennial Modern Classics, 2005); Richard Wright, *Black Boy (American Hunger): A Record of Childhood and Youth*, 60th anniversary ed. (New York: HarperCollins, 2005); Richard Wright, "The Man Who Lived Underground," in *Eight Men: Short Stories*, 3rd ed., by Richard Wright (New York: Harper Perennial Modern Classics, 2008); Orlando Patterson, *The Children of Sisyphus: A Novel* (Boston: Houghton Mifflin Company, 1964).

73  As the epigraph at the start of the introduction suggests, one could also explore openness through the writings of Alice Walker in addition to Larsen and Wright, for whom connectedness and interplay are dominant motifs. However, something of the absurdist moralism would be lost with Walker. There is in her work a sense of the tragicomic nature of life; however, I read her as still committed to the idea of resolution. This is my read, for example, of *Anything We Love Can Be Saved: A Writer's Activism* (New York: Random House, 1997), as well as *Living by the Word: Selected Writings, 1973–1987* (San Diego: Harcourt Brace Jovanovich, 1988). And whether it is human centered or not (there is something humanistic about much of her writing), I want to tame this appeal to resolution through the absurdist moralist take on the psycho-ethical impulse. In this way, I want to maintain the tragicomic

quality of life as already and always—and without "appeal" to conceptual frameworks of substantive transformation.

## 1. THINGS

1 Daniel Miller, introduction to *Materiality*, ed. Daniel Miller (Durham, NC: Duke University Press, 2005), 5; Daniel Miller, *Material Culture and Mass Consumption* (Oxford: Blackwell, 1987).

2 Ian Hodder labels this the "thingness of things." See Hodder, *Entangled: An Archaeology of the Relationships between Humans and Things* (Malden, MA: Wiley-Blackwell, 2012), 32.

3 Hodder, *Entangled*, 7.

4 The economic and political ramifications of bodiness are even stronger in my more liberation theology–related work in large part because a theologizing of socioeconomic and political circumstances is the raison d'être of black liberation theology.

5 It is not a pressing concern here, but the formal question of distinction between things and objects is resolved in this project, to the extent it surfaces, by means of two notions: (1) the human is a body-thing in relationship to thing-things. A twofold epistemology of thingliness is thereby constituted through the idea of multidirectional relationship, and much of this is worked out through moralistic awareness and lucidity, as described in this and the next chapter. For brief discussions of subject-object in material studies, see, for example, Michael Rowlands, "A Materialist Approach to Materiality," in Miller, *Materiality* (Durham, NC: Duke University Press, 2005), 72–87; Webb Keane, "Signs Are Not the Garb of Meaning: On the Social Analysis of Material Things," in Miller, *Materiality*, 182–205; and Christopher Pinney, "Things Happen: Or, From Which Moment Does That Object Come," in Miller, *Materiality*, 256–72.

6 Rowlands, "Materialist Approach to Materiality," 72–87.

7 Hodder, *Entangled*, 7.

8 This should not be read as even a passive endorsement of the objectification of African Americans or others as consistent with who they are.

9 Peter Schwenger, "Words and the Murder of the Thing," in *Things*, ed. Bill Brown (Chicago: University of Chicago Press, 2004), 138.

10 John Frow, "A Pebble, a Camera, a Man Who Turns into a Telegraph Pole," in Brown, *Things*, 355.

11 Bill Brown, *A Sense of Things: The Object Matter of American Literature* (Chicago: University of Chicago Press, 2003), 4.

12 Hodder, *Entangled*, 49.

13 I am not a Heidegger scholar, nor am I a phenomenologist. I make only mention here of Heidegger's work on things in order to attempt to briefly acknowledge a long-standing tradition of thinking about things. Readers will note (and some undoubtedly will find it problematic) that I give no real

consideration to primary materials related to things authored by philosophers such as Heidegger—although he has provided philosophical commentary on the nature and meaning of things (e.g., in *Being and Time*)—or, in France, Maurice Merleau-Ponty (e.g., in *Phenomenology of Perception* and *The Visible and the Invisible*). This is because I am less interested in presenting or refining a theory of things as related to phenomenology of things, and I am more interested in an engagement and practice of things as presented by those who have developed thing theory and applied it to various areas of the humanities and social sciences.

Hence, I find the texts and authors discussed more useful in light of my particular intentions and my concern to think about the nature of religion through a more multidisciplinary approach. For instance, Bjørnar Olsen (*In Defense of Things: Archaeology and the Ontology of Objects* [Lanham, MD: Rowman and Littlefield, 2010], 70n16) remarks that one can think about Heidegger's take on things as being first concerned with the relevance of a thing for humans. My interest in thinking about things in relationship to religion as a technology through art is concerned on one level with this take on things because art involves the placement and manipulation of things. Still, I find attention to Camus and thing theory over against Heidegger useful in that I am also concerned with the question of what else there might be to say or understand about things. In short, my concern is restricted for the most part to things within the context of artistic production as opposed to a sweeping discussion of things in a more general sense, which accounts for my selection of conversation partners.

14 Something about this idea and this phrasing might bring to mind Heidegger's *Dasein* ("being there") and "being-in-the-world." However, I make this argument not in light of his phenomenology and existentialism but instead in light of Camus's moralism, which I believe challenges some of the intellectual infrastructure of existentialism—at least as it is presented within the context of France—and in light of how figures such as Sartre read Heidegger. My interrogation of the nature and meaning of religion to the extent it concerns itself with the body-thing in relationship to thing-things framed by circumstances (world) prompts a concern with what this situation means, what it produces, and for that particular set of concerns I find Camus of particular importance.

15 On this topic, see, for instance, Olsen, *In Defense of Things*.

16 Raymond Malewitz, *The Practice of Misuse: Rugged Consumerism in Contemporary American Culture* (Stanford, CA: Stanford University Press, 2014), 2–3. I do not have the same economic and political concerns as Malewitz does in framing his rugged consumerism, but there are insights in this volume regarding materiality and materials that I find useful as I think through my particular concerns with things and religion.

17 This is related to what Malewitz notes as "misuse" and, with his economic and political interests (explored primarily through literature and theater),

discusses within the context of what he calls "rugged consumerism." He gives the example of Apollo 13 astronauts needing to reconfigure and "misuse" equipment in order to develop a system that would reduce carbon dioxide levels. What this gets at is the ability of body-things to manipulate and alter things in order to create new things for use. "For the rugged consumer," he writes, "the desired outcome of creative misuse is a renaturalized world in which artificial objects become raw materials for postproduction reproduction" (23). This, it appears, highlights the flexible utility and purpose of things that is not my primary concern. What I have in mind might not be considered repurposing because it raises questions concerning the nature of purpose and how it is represented and displayed. I am more interested in the way artistic creation and placement of things raises questions concerning the nature of things and by extension the nature and meaning of body-things. That is to say, I am interested in what the creation/placement of things within art says about things as things over against their physical utility. Such questions become a "tool," so to speak, of religion as a technology. See Malewitz, *Practice of Misuse*, chapter 1.

18 Antony Hudek, ed., "Introduction//Detours of Objects," in *The Object* (Cambridge, MA: MIT Press, 2014), 16–17.

19 Bill Brown, "Thing Theory," *Critical Inquiry* 28, no. 1 (2001): 1–22.

20 Hudek, "Introduction//Detours of Objects," 17.

21 Arthur Danto, *Beyond the Brillo Box: The Visual Arts in Post-Historical Perspective* (New York: Farrar, Straus and Giroux, 1992), 136.

22 My interest here, which of course is not the only approach to the general topic of the theory of religion, is with the naming—naming that moment in which religion as a technology is applied and interplay between types of things is exposed.

23 This is not a necessary limitation—as if only the human bodied naming-thing matters—but I find it a useful restriction. I want to acknowledge a more expansive category for naming-things, as one might find in work related to transhumanism, posthuman studies, animal studies, or material studies, while framing this project in terms of openness related to only one of the many types of agential "naming" things. (See my comments on posthumanism and new materialism in the introduction.)

24 My goal, as my particular use of thing theorists will make clear, is not the presentation of a thing theory. Instead, thing theory, in conjunction with other theoretical frameworks, affords a range of questions and considerations that help me better frame my own questions and concerns regarding bodies, things, and religion as a technology.

25 Frow, "Pebble, a Camera, a Man," 361.

26 This sense of a moralistic sensibility over against an existentialist sensibility marks my turn to Albert Camus in much of my recent work, including this book. This moralist posture toward the world is played out in both his fiction and nonfiction. It certainly informs the books found in the notes for this

chapter and the next (*The Rebel* in particular). However, I would also like to call attention to the manner in which his journalistic writings speak to this moralistic perspective. For an example of this, see Camus, *Algerian Chronicles* (Cambridge, MA: Harvard University Press, 2013). In his depictions of human suffering, structural injustice, colonialism, and war, one gets a sense of the moralist's challenge to existentialist notions of agency and freedom, in part through his aggressive turn to absurdity and love.

27  Future work might necessitate a turn, for example, to Merleau-Ponty's *Phenomenology of Perception*, as some I have been in conversation with have suggested, by means of which to interrogate the dynamics of that body-encountering world (a body he suggests is not simply an object). However, my first effort is to frame this moment of contact through the earthiness of moralism in that it also contains more than an explicit assertion already regarding the religious connotations of this contact without presupposing an answer—this is found in the question of life without appeal. This is not to say that Merleau-Ponty promotes thinking along religious lines that involves endorsement or theological assumption. Rather, mine is the argument that moralism's logic is consistent with my objectives as they currently stand.

28  Frances S. Connelly, introduction to *Modern Art and the Grotesque*, ed. Frances S. Connelly (New York: Cambridge University Press, 2003), 15. See my comments concerning Julia Kristeva and my project found in the introduction, where I also provide a rationale for my turn to Bakhtin over against other thinkers such as Kristeva and Georges Bataille.

29  Rina Arya is correct to warn against too "open" a use of the term *abject*. As she notes, it is not simply a feeling of disgust, nor is it simply a signifier for shit and other things frowned upon. Rather, the abject has to do with boundaries between the subject and other "things." The inadequacy of boundary stirs up abjection as a sociocultural process by which to protect or keep "clean" the individual. Abjection is a response to the ever-present subject's connection and response to the abject. The relationship of the body-thing to shit plays off this sense of the abject, but the abject/abjection is not restricted to this example. See Rina Arya, *Abjection and Representation: An Exploration of Abjection in the Visual Arts, Film and Literature* (New York: Palgrave Macmillan, 2014).

30  Mikhail M. Bakhtin, *Rabelais and His World* (Bloomington: Indiana University Press, 1984); James Luther Adams, Wilson Yates, and Robert Penn Warren, eds., *The Grotesque in Art and Literature: Theological Reflections* (Grand Rapids, MI: Wm. B. Eerdmans, 1997). In this text, I am most interested in Yates's "An Introduction to the Grotesque: Theoretical and Theological Considerations," which in its scope and detail provides something of a theoretical framing for the overall project. In addition to this turn to Bakhtin, Ola Sigurdson argues there are ample examples of the grotesque within the Christian tradition from which one can draw. See Ola Sigurdson, *Heavenly Bodies: Incarnation, the Gaze, and Embodiment in Christian Theology* (Grand Rapids, MI: Wm. B. Eerdmans, 2016). Sigurdson argues that within the Christian tradition even

the historical and felt presence of God is framed by the grotesque (493). In this there is also a turn to a modified Bakhtinian sense of the grotesque, but like with Yates, it is sanitized by the needs of Christian logic: "The point of the grotesque as a theological category is not to deny the genuine insights of the theological tradition, but rather to attempt, like Barth, to reach a more critical view of these conceptions on the basis of the cross" (503). What I find problematic with Yates's discussion applies here as well. The appeal in this book to a theologized sense of the demonic takes away from the sense of the grotesque I want to follow in that it troubles—casts as negative—the openness, the multiple sides of the body to the extent it limits description to theologized language of good and evil. It also highlights the individualization of the body. What this book calls the grotesque regarding Julian and others, I argue is better described as the suffering body, the body in pain seeking wholeness—not the open body content in itself. Talk of a healing function for the grotesque betrays all this I critique.

31 I have no argument with much of what Yates writes regarding Bakhtin's framing of the grotesque as a positive assessment of life, one that, through carnival for example, celebrates much of what social norms despise.

32 Yates, "Introduction to the Grotesque," 40.

33 Yates, "Introduction to the Grotesque," 47.

34 I am unable to provide images in the text. However, photographs of the exhibits are available at https://kunsthalcharlottenborg.dk/da/udstillinger/tori-wraanes and https://kunsthalcharlottenborg.dk/en/exhibitions/ovartaci-2.

35 Kunsthal Charlottenborg Exhibit, viewed on November 9, 2017.

36 Museum of Contemporary Art Kiasma, "ARS17—Ed Atkins," YouTube video, May 9, 2017, https://www.youtube.com/watch?v=F3vDyaZXx28. A portion of the audiovisual is available at Erich Mülla, "Ed Atkins—Ribbons, 2014," YouTube video, January 11, 2015, https://www.youtube.com/watch?v=3EkqVWXBVOQ.

37 Ed Atkins, "Ribbons," a 2014 installation (channel 4:3 in 16.9 HD video with three-channel surround soundtracks). Louisiana Museum, "Being There," Copenhagen, viewed on November 11, 2017. The quoted text is drawn from the statement provided by the museum in relationship to the Atkins project.

38 Yates, "Introduction to the Grotesque," 49.

39 A turn to the grotesque (through Nietzsche) is also found in African American constructive theology. See, for example, Victor Anderson, *Beyond Ontological Blackness: An Essay on African American Religious and Cultural Criticism* (New York: Continuum, 1995).

40 Yates, "Introduction to the Grotesque," 47.

41 Yates, "Introduction to the Grotesque," 51.

42 Yates, "Introduction to the Grotesque," 52.

43 Yates, "Introduction to the Grotesque," 52.

44 Coco Fusco, *The Bodies That Were Not Ours: And Other Writings* (London: Routledge, 2001), 42.

45  See, for instance, Deuteronomy 23:11–15.
46  Bakhtin, *Rabelais and His World*, 318.
47  This is Yates's thinking, but I argue that it is also present in the work of other theologians who frame life in terms of the "image of God." See, for example, M. Shawn Copeland, *Enfleshing Freedom: Body, Race, and Being* (Minneapolis: Fortress Press, 2010); James H. Evans, *We Have Been Believers: An African-American Systematic Theology* (Minneapolis: Fortress Press, 1992). The same could be said of theologians such as Karl Barth and Jürgen Moltmann.
48  Bakhtin, *Rabelais and His World*, 363–68.
49  Bakhtin, *Rabelais and His World*, 10.
50  Bakhtin, *Rabelais and His World*, 10.
51  Bakhtin, *Rabelais and His World*, 19.
52  Bakhtin, *Rabelais and His World*, 281.
53  Bakhtin, *Rabelais and His World*, 322.
54  Bakhtin, *Rabelais and His World*, 19–20; emphasis added.
55  Bakhtin, *Rabelais and His World*, 26.
56  Bakhtin, *Rabelais and His World*, 317. While not my primary concern, it is worth noting that this interplay has affective markers to the degree that urinating involves discomfort and relief, and the same can be said for defecating. This link between two responses speaks to the manner in which defecating involves both a leaving the open naming-thing and an entering into the world of a new thing-thing (335).
57  Still, there is a romanticization element in Bakhtin that I resist: "Cosmic terror is the heritage of man's ancient impotence in the presence of nature. Folk culture did not know this fear and overcame it through laughter, through lending a bodily substance to nature and the cosmos; for this folk culture was always based on the indestructible confidence in the might and final victory of man" (Bakhtin, *Rabelais and His World*, 336n9).
58  Bakhtin, *Rabelais and His World*, 335.
59  Connelly, introduction to *Modern Art and the Grotesque*, 2, 4, 5.
60  These images are part of the Yoko Ono exhibit at Kunsthal Charlottenborg, "Transmission," which I viewed on November 9, 2017. See https://kunsthalcharlottenborg.dk/en/exhibitions/yoko-ono-transmission/.
61  The connection between a "banquet" and a toilet, I argue, speaks well to the carnivalistic impulse highlighted by Bakhtin.
62  Related to this, I appreciate Kirsten A. Hoving's pronouncement: "As the traditional site of the grotesque, the body and its norms were the starting point for the blurring of distinctions between things, leading to misshapenness, and even to complete disintegration." Kirsten A. Hoving, "Convulsive Bodies: The Grotesque Anatomies of Surrealist Photography," in Connelly, *Modern Art and the Grotesque*, 221.
63  Nella Larsen, *Quicksand*, in *Quicksand and Passing* (New Brunswick, NJ: Rutgers University Press, 1986); Richard Wright, *Native Son* (New York: Harper Perennial Modern Classics, 2005).

64 In future work I will take up the issue of African American moralism using Du Bois, Larsen, Wright, and several others. In so doing, I will read African American thinkers-activists with and over against Albert Camus.

65 For additional information on Nella Larsen, see George Hutchinson, *In Search of Nella Larsen: A Biography of the Color Line* (Cambridge, MA: Belknap Press of Harvard University Press, 2006); Thadious M. Davis, *Nella Larsen, Novelist of the Harlem Renaissance: A Woman's Life Unveiled* (Baton Rouge: Louisiana State University Press, 1994); and Charles R. Larson, *Invisible Darkness: Jean Toomer and Nella Larsen* (Iowa City: University of Iowa Press, 1993).

66 For more information on Wright, see, for example, Hazel Rowley, *Richard Wright: The Life and Times* (New York: Henry Holt and Co., 2001); Michel Fabre, *The World of Richard Wright* (Jackson: University Press of Mississippi, 1985); Fabre, *The Unfinished Quest of Richard Wright*, 2nd ed. (Urbana: University of Illinois Press, 1993); Virginia Whatley Smith, ed., *Richard Wright: Writing America at Home and from Abroad* (Jackson: University Press of Mississippi, 2016); Abdul R. JanMohamed, *The Death-Bound-Subject: Richard Wright's Archaeology of Death* (Durham, NC: Duke University Press, 2005).

67 Richard Wright, *Eight Men: Short Stories*, 3rd ed. (New York: Harper Perennial Modern Classics, 2008).

68 Richard Wright, *Black Boy (American Hunger): A Record of Childhood and Youth*, 60th anniversary ed. (New York: HarperCollins, 2005); Wright, *Native Son*.

69 Paul Gilroy, "Introduction to the Harper Perennial Edition," in Wright, *Eight Men*, xiii.

70 Gilroy, "Introduction to the Harper Perennial Edition," xv.

71 Richard Wright, "The Man Who Lived Underground," in Wright, *Eight Men*, 20.

72 Wright, "Man Who Lived Underground," 21.

73 Wright, "Man Who Lived Underground," 25.

74 Wright, "Man Who Lived Underground," 32–33.

75 Wright, "Man Who Lived Underground," 33–34.

76 Keep in mind Bakhtin's perception of the mouth as of great importance for the grotesque body as an opening to the world.

77 Bakhtin, *Rabelais and His World*, 20; Wright, "Man Who Lived Underground," 30.

78 Wright, "Man Who Lived Underground," 31.

79 Wright, "Man Who Lived Underground," 32.

80 Wright, "Man Who Lived Underground," 84.

81 Larsen, *Quicksand*, 113.

82 Larsen, *Quicksand*, 113.

83 Larsen, *Quicksand*, 121.

84 Nella Larsen's concern with sexuality in *Quicksand* can be read as a racialized-gendered presentation of the grotesque body—the open body. However, I am most concerned with Helga Crane from the point of her turn to the church in that it is the most graphic depiction in the novel of the open body—the penetrated and penetrating body.

## 2. THE ART OF PLACEMENT

1 Robert C. Fuller, *Spirituality in the Flesh: Bodily Sources of Religious Experience* (New York: Oxford University Press, 2008), 7.

2 Hans Belting, *An Anthropology of Images: Picture, Medium, Body* (Princeton, NJ: Princeton University Press, 2011), 11.

3 Belting, *Anthropology of Images*, 3, 5.

4 Belting, *Anthropology of Images*.

5 Belting, *Anthropology of Images*, 37.

6 I draw from the work of Jean-Pierre Warnier, "Inside and Outside: Surfaces and Containers," in *Handbook of Material Culture*, ed. Christopher Tilley, Webb Keane, Susanne Kuechler-Fogden, Mike Rowlands, and Patricia Spyer (Thousand Oaks, CA: Sage Publications, 2006), 186–95. However, it is important to note that my approach to the body is not anthropological in nature and is not Warnier's thinking on the body. I do not share Warnier's take on defining the techniques of the body used to present itself over against an ability to actually know the body as such. Yet there is some overlap in terms of a shared interest in the nature and presentations of subjectivity.

7 Warnier, "Inside and Outside," 186.

8 Bill Brown, "Thing Theory," *Critical Inquiry* 28, no. 1 (2001): 4.

9 Brown, "Thing Theory," 4.

10 Arthur Danto, *What Art Is* (New Haven, CT: Yale University Press, 2013), 128.

11 Arthur Danto, *The Abuse of Beauty: Aesthetics and the Concept of Art*, 21st ed. (Chicago: Open Court, 2003), 139–42.

12 Danto, *Abuse of Beauty*, 142.

13 Danto, *What Art Is*, xii.

14 I offer here what might be an obvious point of clarification. My concern is not with what is labeled "religious art," in that it assumes the conclusion, assumes the meaning, which intends a particular outcome. It assumes, first, that religion is a something—that religion is established in light of rituals, deeds, creeds, etc.

15 Barbara Johnson, *Persons and Things* (Cambridge: Harvard University Press, 2008), 61.

16 Ian Hodder, *Entangled: An Archaeology of the Relationships between Humans and Things* (Malden, MA: Wiley-Blackwell, 2012), 41.

17 Arthur Danto, *Remarks on Art and Philosophy* (Mount Desert Island, ME: Acadia Summer Arts Program, 2014), 21–141.

18 Danto, *Remarks on Art and Philosophy*, 23.

19 Danto, *Remarks on Art and Philosophy*, 29.

20 Danto, *Abuse of Beauty*, 4–5.

21 In earlier work I brought Danto's philosophy of art at the end of art into religious studies and constructive/humanist theology so as to "find" cartographies of religion, and I concerned myself with the manner in which the very question of a difference between the box in the store and Warhol's box provides a way of gauging the structuring of the religious. I framed it in terms of

the "stuff" of religious traditions and to what it might point—the stuff behind the stuff. Such a question and answer points in the direction of things. In this project, I have related questions with which to contend.

22  Danto, *What Art Is*, 28.

23  Danto, *What Art Is*, 36.

24  As will become clear in later chapters, art as such and religion as a technology are in my mind probed by an awareness that something must be said about the absurd as Camus hauntingly explores and explains it—"the desperate encounter between human inquiry and the silence of the universe." The concept of the absurd and its contextualization as the silence of absurdity hold me in certain ways and by extension my theory of religion; and as a consequence, the uncertainty demanded has some bearing on what religion probes and what art can offer regarding that probing. In this way, my discussion of religion as a technology and artistic expression is tied to my interest in the moralist position and its target called absurdity (more on that later). I use Camus to soften some of the optimism of Danto, for example, and to better ground the un/certainty over against meaning endemic to this technology of religion's engagement with art and overall project. Camus does not negate the need to act, to do, but rather questions the plausibility of success. Obligation and opportunity are not removed for him by absurdity, but rather the ramifications of our push, our "No!" to the absurd are limited in impact and scope.

25  Albert Camus, *The Rebel: An Essay on Man in Revolt* (New York: Vintage International, 1991), 82.

26  Camus, *Rebel*, 253.

27  Danto, *What Art Is*, 19.

28  Danto, *What Art Is*, 49.

29  Danto, *What Art Is*, 49.

30  Danto, *What Art Is*, 38.

31  Albert Camus, *The Myth of Sisyphus and Other Essays* (New York: Vintage International, 1991), 53–54.

32  Stephen Greenblatt, "Resonance and Wonder," in *Exhibiting Cultures: The Poetics and Politics of Museum Display*, ed. Ivan Karp and Steven D. Lavine (Washington, DC: Smithsonian Institution Press, 1991), 42–67.

33  Greenblatt, "Resonance and Wonder," 49–51.

34  Being mindful of Camus's cautions, this potentiality is of limited consequences. What I propose, if anything, is only small comfort—not hope—in the same way a time/space for arranging the stuff of life provides something of a reprieve for the figure fixated on order, but it is not a final resolution by any means.

35  The Cameron notion of the gallery as temple is referenced in Steven D. Lavine and Ivan Karp, "Introductions: Museums and Multiculturalism," in Karp and Lavine, *Exhibiting Cultures*, 3; Carol Duncan, "Art Museums and the Ritual of Citizenship," in Karp and Lavine, *Exhibiting Culture*, 90, 91.

36 *Member: Pope.L, 1978–2001*, Museum of Modern Art, New York City, viewed on January 3, 2019. For additional information on Pope.L, see, for example, Nathan Taylor Pemberton, "Crawling through New York City with the Artist Pope.L," *New Yorker*, November 22, 2019, https://www.newyorker.com/culture/culture-desk/crawling-through-new-york-city-with-the-artist-pope-l?verso=true; Adrian Heathfield, Adrienne Edwards, Andre Lepecki, Malik Gaines, Martha Wilson, Naomi Beckwith, Thomas Lax, et al., *member: Pope.L 1978–2011* (New York: Museum of Modern Art, 2019); Mark H. C. Bessire, ed., *William Pope.L: The Friendliest Black Artist in America* (Cambridge, MA: MIT Press, 2002).

37 Daniel Miller, *Stuff* (Malden, MA: Polity Press, 2010), 53.

38 Elaine Heumann Gurian discusses some of the pedagogical and experiential limitations to gallery display imposed by "producers of exhibitions." See Gurian, "Noodling Around with Exhibition Opportunities," in Karp and Lavine, *Exhibiting Culture*, 176–90. Of course, there are race, gender, and sexuality considerations related to the production of exhibits and access to space that merit consideration. Those are beyond the focus of this particular book, but those interested in such considerations should see, for instance, Lonnie G. Bunch III, *Call the Lost Dream Back: Essays on History, Race and Museums* (Washington, DC: American Library Association Editions, 2011); Amy K. Levin, ed., *Gender, Sexuality and Museums: A Routledge Reader* (New York: Routledge, 2010).

39 Svetlana Alpers, "The Museum as a Way of Seeing," in Karp and Lavine, *Exhibiting Culture*, 27.

### 3. ARTISTIC EXPRESSION OF TRANSIENCE

1 Metoyer's family's history is in Louisiana and Texas, tied to landownership and business success.

2 For information on Houston's Project Row House, see https://projectrowhouses.org.

3 Deborah M. Colton, introduction to *Angelbert Metoyer: Babies Walk on Water: Present, Future, and Time Travel*, by Angelbert Metoyer (Houston: Deborah M. Colton Gallery, 2013), 1.

4 In an email exchange on April 18, 2016, he listed the following as his influences: "People, Jesse Lott, Ornette Coleman, and Anthony Braxton."

5 Email exchange with Angelbert Metoyer, April 18, 2016.

6 In conversation, Metoyer raised the question of whether or not his work had an Afrofuturistic "feel" to it because of its attention to the past/present/future in ways that pull on science (particularly physics), African American cultural forms that speak to history as a fluid concept, and so on. Metoyer, *Babies Walk on Water*, and the corresponding gallery show (November 16, 2012–January 26, 2013) serve as an example of this Afrofuturistic sense of time and space. For information on Afrofuturism, see Ytasha L. Womack, *Afrofuturism: The World of Black Sci-Fi and Fantasy Culture* (Chicago: Lawrence

Hill Books/Chicago Review Press, 2013); Alondra Nelson, ed., "Afrofuturism," special issue, *Social Text* 20, no. 2 (2002); Mark Dery, ed., *Flame Wars: The Discourse of Cyberculture* (Durham, NC: Duke University Press, 1994); Reynaldo Anderson and Charles E. Jones, eds., *Afrofuturism 2.0: The Rise of Astro-Blackness* (Lanham, MD: Lexington Books, 2016); Mark Bould and Rone Shavers, eds., "Afrofuturism," special issue, *Science Fiction Studies* 34, no. 2 (July 2007).

7   This exhibit took place at the University of Texas Warfield New Gallery, May 12–December 12, 2016.

8   A shorter and revised version of this statement was found on the wall of the gallery space housing the exhibit.

9   Hans Belting, *An Anthropology of Images: Picture, Medium, Body* (Princeton, NJ: Princeton University Press, 2011), 37.

10  Useful discussions of Vodou include Karen McCarthy Brown, *Mama Lola: A Vodou Priestess in Brooklyn*, updated and expanded ed. (Berkeley: University of California Press, 2001); Maya Deren, *Divine Horsemen: The Living Gods of Haiti* (New Paltz, NY: McPherson, 1983); Leslie Gérald Desmangles, *The Faces of the Gods: Vodou and Roman Catholicism in Haiti* (Chapel Hill: University of North Carolina Press, 1992).

11  See W. E. B. Du Bois, "Of Our Spiritual Strivings," in Du Bois, *The Souls of Black Folk* (New York: Vintage Books/Library of America, 1990).

12  These and other interrogations of thing-things in this chapter and much of the larger text are inspired by my reading of thing theorists such as Bill Brown. See, for instance, Brown, "Thing Theory," *Critical Inquiry* 28, no. 1 (2001): 1–16; Brown, *A Sense of Things: The Object Matter of American Literature* (Chicago: University of Chicago Press, 2003).

13  Albert Camus, *The Myth of Sisyphus and Other Essays* (New York: Vintage International, 1991), 97.

14  This is something along the lines of what historian of religions Charles Long discussed in terms of "crawling back through history" to our first creation. The distinction here is that I do not intend to suggest there is such a point of origin, but rather just greater clarity concerning what we are not. See Charles H. Long, *Significations: Signs, Symbols, and Images in the Interpretation of Religion* (Minneapolis: Fortress Press, 1986).

15  Camus, *Myth of Sisyphus*, 97–98.

16  I find something of this sentiment expressed by Metoyer in conversation. With Camus, I think it plays out in the story "The Artist at Work," in Camus, *Exile and the Kingdom* (New York: Vintage Books, 1991), 110–58.

17  Brown, "Thing Theory," 2.

18  Ian Hodder, *Entangled: An Archaeology of the Relationships between Humans and Things* (Malden, MA: Wiley-Blackwell, 2012), 38.

19  Hodder, *Entangled*, 58.

20  Brown, "Thing Theory," 4–5.

21  Marcel Duchamp, "The Creative Act," Session on the Creative Act, Convention of the American Federation of Arts, Houston, Texas, April 1957, included

as the appendix to Calvin Tomkins, *Duchamp: A Biography* (New York: Henry Holt and Co., 1996), 510.

22 John Frow, "A Pebble, a Camera, a Man Who Turns into a Telegraph Pole," in *Things*, ed. Bill Brown (Chicago: Chicago University Press, 2004), 353–54, 357–58.

23 Eric N. Mack's exhibit *Lemme Walk across the Room* at the Brooklyn Museum of Art used textiles (e.g., shirts and pieces of fabric) to force a similar recognition—the points of contact and impact between bodied naming-things and other things. For Mack, the arrangement of these items in the main hall of the museum allowed for interaction with viewers—a performance of artistic space as dependent on viewers as on artistic "objects." The location of pieces within this exhibit encouraged movement but also disallowed movement to the extent that pieces of fabric hung and draped across rope produced soft barriers that made viewers mindful of their bodies through imposed limitations, while also pointing out the fabricated nature of these restrictions. I viewed the exhibit on April 20, 2019.

24 Arthur Danto, *What Art Is* (New Haven, CT: Yale University Press, 2013), 14.

25 Email exchange with Angelbert Metoyer, April 18, 2016. I have edited the presentation of our conversation to clear up prose so as to move the conversation from a casual email exchange to book form.

26 *Sankofa* is a Ghanaian word indicating "Go back and get it," suggesting the importance of the past for a proper working present and future. It is typically symbolized as a bird with its head turned backward, as if its moving forward is guided by its gaze to what is behind it.

27 He first discussed "Artworld" as a way of philosophically working through the impact of Andy Warhol's 1964 exhibit on his thinking. See Arthur Danto, "The Artworld," *Journal of Philosophy* 61, no. 19 (October 1964): 571–84.

28 Email exchange with Angelbert Metoyer, April 18, 2016.

29 Quoted in Michael Agresta, "Angelbert Metoyer at Co-Lab Projects," *Arts + Culture*, November 10, 2015, http://artsandculturex.com/life-machine (accessed July 2018).

30 Belting, *Anthropology of Images*, 10.

31 Belting, *Anthropology of Images*, 9.

32 Steven Psyllos, "Angelbert Metoyer," in Metoyer, *Babies Walk on Water*, 4; emphasis added.

33 Email exchange with Angelbert Metoyer, April 18, 2016.

34 Belting, *Anthropology of Images*, 17.

35 Although I draw from Arthur Danto's philosophy of art as opposed to other possibilities, I have in mind the line from John Dewey's *Art as Experience*: "If there is justification for proposing yet another philosophy of the esthetic, it must be found in a new mode of approach. . . . But, to my mind, the trouble with existing theories is that they start from a ready-made compartmental-ization, or from a conception of art that 'spiritualizes' it out of connection with the objects of concrete experience" (Dewey, *Art as Experience* [New York: Minton, Balch and Co., 1934], 11).

36  Dewey, *Art as Experience*, 108.

37  Email exchange with Angelbert Metoyer, April 18, 2016. While there are significant differences and contrasting perspectives, there is something of Metoyer's intent in the words of John Dewey regarding art. "The work of art," Dewey notes, "is complete only as it works in the experience of others than the one who created it" (Dewey, *Art as Experience*, 106).

38  Email exchange with Angelbert Metoyer, April 18, 2016.

39  Hodder, *Entangled*, 3, 4.

40  Heather Pesanti, "Strange Pilgrims," in *Strange Pilgrims* (Austin: University of Texas Press, 2015), 11.

41  Barbara E. Johnson, *Persons and Things* (Cambridge: Harvard University Press, 2008), 63. Here Johnson is providing her take on Heidegger's work related to things.

42  This statement should remind readers of the work done by Julia Kristeva related to the abject and abjection.

43  See, for instance, Metoyer, *Babies Walk on Water*.

44  Albert Camus, *The Rebel: An Essay on Man in Revolt* (New York: Vintage International, 1991), 260.

45  Works by philosopher of art Arthur Danto are helpful with respect to the metaphysical content and considerations of the visual arts. See, for instance, Danto, *After the End of Art* (Princeton, NJ: Princeton University Press, 1998); Danto, *The Transfiguration of the Commonplace: A Philosophy of Art* (Cambridge: Harvard University Press, 1983).

46  See Marcus J. Guillory, "The Meta: On the Artwork of Angelbert Metoyer," in *I—AoI (LU—X project)* (Houston: Angelbert's Imagination Studios, 2008), 49–50.

47  Dewey, *Art as Experience*, 214.

48  Colton, introduction to Metoyer, *Babies Walk on Water*, 1.


4. THE "STUFF" OF PERFORMANCE

1  Anthony B. Pinn, *The New Disciples: A Novel* (Durham, NC: Pitchstone Publishing, 2015), 215–16.

2  See Matthew Akers, dir., *Marina Abramovic: The Artist Is Present* (Music Box Films, 2012). The impact of Abramovic's work is far reaching, and this includes a turn toward conscious performance art in hip-hop culture. I have in mind Jay Z's video for the song "Picasso Baby." I would also suggest that many of the videos produced in relationship to Missy Elliot involve a blending of a surrealist aesthetic with a performance art quality. For an example of this, see Missy Elliott and Da Brat, "The Rain (Supa Dupa Fly)," YouTube video, October 26, 2009, https://www.youtube.com/watch?v=hHcyJPTTn9w. In a way that Metoyer would appreciate there is also an Afrofuturistic quality to some of her work, including Missy Elliott and Da Brat, "Sock It 2 Me," YouTube video, October 26, 2009, https://www.youtube.com/watch?

v=9UvBX3REqSY. Margarita Simon Guillory has done intriguing work on Missy Elliot. See "Intersecting Points: The 'Erotic as Religious' in the Lyrics of Missy Elliot," *Culture and Religion* 10, no. 1 (March 2009): 81–96, reprinted in *The Hip Hop and Religion Reader*, ed. Monica R. Miller and Anthony B. Pinn (New York: Routledge, 2015).

3  Amelia Jones, "The Now and the Has Been: Paradoxes of Live Art in History," in *Perform, Repeat, Record: Live Art in History*, ed. Amelia Jones and Adrian Heathfield (Chicago: Intellect Books/University of Chicago Press, 2012), 11–13. Scholars have connected performance art to a variety of practices, and these practices have been explored from various disciplinary perspectives, including psychology, gender studies, media studies, and anthropology.

4  "Performativity, Cultural-Politics, and the Embodiments of Knowledge: An Interview with Amelia Jones Conducted by Jonathan Harris," in *Dead History, Live Art? Spectacle, Subjectivity and Subversion in Visual Culture since the 1960s*, ed. Jonathan Harris (Liverpool: Liverpool University Press, 2007), 91. The essays in this book, including this interview, provide intriguing discussions of what performance art entails and how it has been documented within scholarship.

5  Laurie Carlos, "Introduction: Performance Art Was the One Place Where There Were So Few Definitions," in *Performance: Live Art since 1960*, ed. RoseLee Goldberg (New York: Harry N. Abrams, 1998), 13.

6  I give limited attention to an expansion of this idea later in the chapter when discussing artists such as Ron Athey. On a related note, readers may find the following book interesting: Christopher Braddock, *Performing Contagious Bodies: Ritual Participation in Contemporary Art* (Hampshire, UK: Palgrave Macmillan, 2013).

7  Carlos, "Introduction: Performance Art Was the One Place," 30.

8  Allan Kaprow, "The Real Experiment," in *Essays on the Blurring of Art and Life*, by Allan Kaprow, ed. Jeff Kelly (Berkeley: University of California Press, 1993), 202.

9  Kaprow, "Real Experiment," 201.

10  Kaprow, "Real Experiment," 205.

11  Lynn MacRitchie, "Introduction: The Sincerity of Events," in *A Split Second of Paradise: Live Art, Installation and Performance*, ed. Nicky Childs and Jeni Walwin (London: Rivers Oram Press, 1998), 21.

12  The definition of performance art is widely debated within the literature. Numerous configurations have been considered, but as far as I can tell there is a shared sense of the body as important within "performance" art despite disagreement over its more detailed intents and forms. Within this chapter, how performance art is defined entails a very limited concern in that I provide a definition in terms of parameters simply through the rather fixed range of artists discussed.

    During an earlier period (some of which is covered earlier in this volume), the context justified the argument that the gallery place involved a conscious manipulation of time and space for the purpose of particular and orchestrated modalities of exploration. The naming-thing came into contact with thing-things in ways that raised questions concerning the significance and agency of both. However, there were still assumptions of distinction—at least some distinction—that performance art is out to destroy.

13 There is no "outside" in that even the writing of this chapter (and the next) involves performance on my part—a relationship between body-thing and thing-things—that is meant to reflect upon the performance art of others through the illusion of reification long enough to see this art without seeing it. There is no way around, at least in the context of this text, participation in performance—an embodied naming-thing/thing-thing interaction that speaks to the mutability of both for the purpose of exploration and, as I suggest throughout this book, moralistic awareness and lucidity of circumstances.

14 Henry M. Sayre, *The Object of Performance: The American Avant-Garde since 1970* (Chicago: University of Chicago Press, 1989), 2.

15 RoseLee Goldberg, *Performance Art: From Futurism to the Present* (New York: Thames and Hudson, 2001), 131.

16 Goldberg, *Performance Art*, 7–9.

17 Laurie Anderson, foreword to Goldberg, *Performance*, 6.

18 Anderson, foreword to Goldberg, *Performance*, 34.

19 Andrew Quick, "Taking Place: Encountering the Live," in *Live: Art and Performance*, ed. Adrian Heathfield (London: Tate Publishing, 2004), 93.

20 Anna Dezeuze, "Do-It-Yourself Artworks': A User's Guide," in Harris, *Dead History, Live Art?*, 187–207.

21 Goldberg, *Performance Art*, 147.

22 Clifford Owens, "Notes on the Crisis of Black American Performance Art (2003)," in *Radical Presence: Black Performance in Contemporary Art*, ed. Valerie Cassel Oliver (Houston: Contemporary Arts Museum Houston, 2013), 36.

23 For a discussion of performance art in relationship to art history and to temporality and repetition or capture, see Jones and Heathfield, *Perform, Repeat, Record*.

24 Nick Stillman, "Clifford Owens," in BOMB; *New Art Publications*, no. 117 (Fall 2011): 56.

25 Marvin Carlson, *Performance: A Critical Introduction*, 2nd ed. (New York: Routledge, 2004), 110–11.

26 I highlight the twentieth century, but Marvin Carlson notes that more recent developments, what he labels "avant garde" performance art, are tied to a longer history of performance that merits consideration for context. See Carlson, *Performance*, chapter 4.

27 Carlson, *Performance*, 104–5.

28 Jens Hoffmann and Joan Jonas, "Entrance: On Performance (and Other Complications)," in Hoffman and Jonas, *Art Works: Perform* (New York: Thames and Hudson, 2005), 11.

29 Gavin Butt's edited volume on art criticism and the place of the critic in that work is interesting in light of my phrasing above—"of most interest to me"—in

that it provides context and offers a way of thinking about my concern and my relationship to my discussion of performance art and the other developments discussed in this book. Butt, ed., *After Criticism: New Responses to Art and Performance* (Malden, MA: Blackwell, 2005).

30 Dominic Johnson, *The Art of Living: An Oral History of Performance Art* (New York: Palgrave Macmillan, 2015), 3.

31 MacRitchie, "Introduction: The Sincerity of Events," 28. For a concise discussion of the history of this art movement, see Goldberg, *Performance Art*.

32 Readers should not assume that my comment entails an embracing of redemptive suffering strategies. I remain opposed to them in all their forms. Here I am simply describing the use of the naming-thing by a particular genre of artists, and I do so without theological judgment.

33 Camus experienced the early phase of performance art. For instance, RoseLee Goldberg tells the story of Camus's presence at Yves Klein's exhibit *The Void*, in which the actual exhibit space was blank and the color blue appeared on the exterior of the gallery and the doors, the principle being the "real" blue was present in the impression—the life—brought into the gallery space. In response, in the guest book, Camus wrote, "With the void, a free hand." See Goldberg, *Performance Art*, 145. Scholars also note thematic connections with existentialism in performance art as it emerged in the years after World War II.

34 Albert Camus, *The Myth of Sisyphus and Other Essays* (New York: Vintage International, 1991), 120–21.

35 Dominic Johnson, "Intimacy and Risk in Live Art," in Deirdre Heddon and Jennie Klein, eds., *Histories and Practices of Live Art* (Houndmills, UK: Palgrave Macmillan, 2012), 136.

36 Examples of Athey's work, such as *St. Sebastian* and *Body Art*, are available on YouTube. The commentary provided with the *Body Art* performance on YouTube is particularly helpful in that it places his work within the context of traditional Pentecostal penetration by the Holy Spirit. See also an interview with Athey: Walker Art Center, "In Conversation: Ron Athey," YouTube video, April 8, 2015, https://www.youtube.com/watch?v=zURUN4GdXBo.

37 *Marina Abramovic: The Artist Is Present*. MoMA, 2010. It involved eight hours each day for almost three months—sitting across from attendees, looking at them as they looked at her.

38 For a short, interesting essay on how "live art" (and by extension performance art) wrestles with time, see Beth Hoffmann, "The Time of Live Art," in Heddon and Klein, *Histories and Practices of Live Art*, 37–64.

39 Sayre, *Object of Performance*, 4.

40 See the poster for the film *Marina Abramovic: The Artist Is Present*: https://www.imdb.com/title/tt2073029/.

41 See Orlan's website, http://www.orlan.eu/, and Stuart Jeffries, "Orlan's Art of Sex and Surgery," *The Guardian*, July 1, 2009, https://www.theguardian.com/artanddesign/2009/jul/01/orlan-performance-artist-carnal-art. Amelia Jones, "Survey," in *The Artist's Body*, ed. Tracey Warr (New York: Phaidon, 2006),

32. For examples of Orlan's work as related to the commentary above, see diy artem, "ORLAN, Omniprésence, 1993. Extrait," YouTube video, February 14, 2014, https://www.youtube.com/watch?v=jN1teX2xzho. This concern with pain as strategy is central to the novel with which I open this chapter. In that book it is a strategy for interrogating and collapsing theological assumptions regarding righteousness and sin over against a particular mode of humanism. See Pinn, *New Disciples*.

42 Consider this argument in relationship to the work, for example, of Susan Bordo: Bordo, *Unbearable Weight: Feminism, Western Culture, and the Body*, 10th anniversary ed. (Berkeley: University of California Press, 2004); and Bordo, *The Male Body: A New Look at Men in Public and in Private* (New York: Farrar, Straus and Giroux, 2000).

43 Cherise Smith provides an important discussion of the manner in which performance tackles issues related to cultural construction of identity. See Smith, *Enacting Others: Politics of Identity in Eleanor Antin, Nikki S. Lee, Adrian Piper, and Anna Deavere Smith* (Durham, NC: Duke University Press, 2011).

44 Valerie Cassel Oliver, preface to Cassel Oliver, *Radical Presence*, 10.

45 Cynthia Carr, "Talk Show," in *On Edge: Performance at the End of the Twentieth Century*, by Cynthia Carr (Hanover, NH: University Press of New England, 1993), 200–205.

46 Goldberg, *Performance Art*, 210–15.

47 Lea Vergine, *Body Art and Performance: The Body as Language*, 2nd ed. (Milan: Skira, 2000), 289.

48 Valerie Cassel Oliver, "Putting the Body on the Line: Endurance in Black Performance," in Cassel Oliver, *Radical Presence*, 14.

49 Uri McMillan, *Embodied Avatars: Genealogies of Black Feminist Art and Performance* (New York: New York University Press, 2015), 7.

50 See Adina Rivera, "Adrian Piper, Mythic Being 1973," YouTube video, April 30, 2017, https://www.youtube.com/watch?v=jVcXb8En_Tw; Kennedy, Peter, dir., "The Mythic Being." excerpt from *Other Than Art's Sake*, APRAF Berlin, 1973, http://www.adrianpiper.com/vs/video_tmb.shtml; and John B. Bowles, *Adrian Piper: Race, Gender, and Embodiment* (Durham, NC: Duke University Press, 2011).

51 Adrian Piper, "Preparatory Notes on the Mythic Being," quoted in McMillan, *Embodied Avatars*, 125. Also see Adrian Piper, *Out of Order, Out of Sight*, vol. 1, *Selected Writings in Meta-Art 1968–1992* (Cambridge: MIT Press, 1999).

52 John P. Bowles, "'Acting Like a Man': Adrian Piper's Mythic Being and Black Feminism in the 1970s," in *Signs: Journal of Women in Culture and Society* 32, no. 3 (2007): 621.

53 Smith, *Enacting Others*, 727–77.

54 Bowles, "'Acting Like a Man,'" 633.

55 Ken Johnson, "Art in Review; Adrian Piper," *New York Times*, November 17, 2000, http://www.nytimes.com/2000/11/17/arts/art-in-review-adrian-piper.html.

56 Holland Cotter, "Adrian Piper: A Canvas of Concerns—Race, Racism and Class," *New York Times*, December 24, 1999, http://www.asu.edu/cfa /wwwcourses/art/SOACore/piper-art-review.html.

57 Clifford Owens, "Notes on the Crisis of Black American Performance Art," in Cassel Oliver, *Radical Presence*, 36.

58 Christopher Y. Lew, ed., *Clifford Owens: Anthology* (New York: MoMA PS1, 2012), 8; emphasis added.

59 Kara Walker, "Instructions," in Lew, *Clifford Owens: Anthology*, 5.

60 Stillman, "Clifford Owens," 52.

61 Clifford Owens, introduction to Lew, *Clifford Owens: Anthology*, 8.

62 Christopher Y. Lew, "Trust Me: *Anthology* from One Perspective," in Lew, *Clifford Owens: Anthology*, 46. See Clifford Owens, "Anthology (Maren Hassinger) 2011," YouTube video, March 5, 2015, https://www.youtube.com/watch ?v=AojNZxEOnuI.

63 Lew, "Trust Me," 43.

64 Laurie Carlos, "Introduction: Performance Art Was the One Place Where There Were So Few Definitions," in Goldberg, *Performance*, 9.

65 I make these remarks in part through my encounter with the work of Stephen Bayley. See Bayley, *Ugly: The Aesthetics of Everything* (London: Goodman Fiell, 2012).

66 Goldberg, *Performance Art*, 212.

67 Ron Athey is discussed again in the next chapter, which deals with body-thing/thing-thing configurations through body fluids and performance art.

68 For interesting texts related to issues of race and gender in performance art, see Catherine Ugwu, ed., *Let's Get It On: The Politics of Black Performance* (Seattle: Bay Press, 1995); Smith, *Enacting Others*; Cassel Oliver, *Radical Presence*.

69 Still, it must be noted, this takes place within cultural worlds—always within these worlds—that mark bodies in particular ways, allow or force rather body-things to speak certain social structures of place and meaning. See Dominic Johnson, ed., *Pleading in the Blood: The Art and Performances of Ron Athey* (Chicago: Intellect Books/University of Chicago Press, 2013); Johnson, "Perverse Martyrologies: An Interview with Ron Athey," in Johnson, *Art of Living*, 195–218.

70 For a sense of Orlan's thinking on the body, see Science Gallery Dublin, "The Future of the Body with Performance Artist Orlan," YouTube video, July 1, 2014, https://www.youtube.com/watch?v=PjxEWPAnxDc.

71 Kristine Stiles, "Quicksilver and Revelations: Performance Art at the End of the Twentieth Century," in *Performance Artists Talking in the Eighties*, ed. Linda M. Montano (Berkeley: University of California Press, 2000), 481. One could think of early acts as representing protoperformance art. So self-mutilation by Vincent van Gogh—the cutting off of his ear—while associated with other issues that should not be downplayed, also spoke a particular performed message.

72 Guillermo Gómez-Peña, "In Defense of Performance Art," in Heathfield, *Live: Art and Performance*, 78–79.

73 Quoted in Johnson, "Perverse Martyrologies," 195.

74  I saw *Inverted Birth* at Copenhagen Contemporary (Copenhagen, Denmark): http://cphco.org/en/exhibition/bill-viola.

75  Bill Viola, "Inverted Birth," Copenhagen Contemporary program brochure. Installation viewed November 9, 2017.

76  I saw *The Raft* at Copenhagen Contemporary (Copenhagen, Denmark): http://cphco.org/en/exhibition/bill-viola.

77  I viewed this exhibit on March 17, 2019, in London at the Royal Academy of Arts.

78  Goldberg, *Performance Art*, 164–65; and TheMACBelfast, "Meet the Artist: Stuart Brisley Interview," YouTube video, February 9, 2015, https://www.youtube.com/watch?v=t54I3QABGWY.

79  Quoted in Goldberg, *Performance Art*, 145.

80  See, for instance, LagunaArtMuseum, "Chris Burden—Through the Night Softly," YouTube video, October 27, 2011, https://www.youtube.com/watch?v=OB6gg1i2hc8; and *New York Times*, "Shot in the Name of Art | Op-Docs | The New York Times," YouTube video, https://www.youtube.com/watch?v=drZIWs3Dl1k.

81  Carr, *On Edge*, 17; this quotation includes commentary from Burden. For more of Burden's description of his work, see Linda M. Montano, "Chris Burden," in Montano, *Performance Artists Talking in the Eighties*, 343–47.

82  Carr, *On Edge*, 19. Also see Johnson, "Perverse Martyrologies," 195–218.

83  Carlson, *Performance*, 105. Carlson indicates Milan, but the Manzoni website indicates Rome, April 1961.

84  "The Artist's Shit," Piero Manzoni Archive, http://www.pieromanzoni.org/EN/works_shit.htm.

85  Goldberg, *Performance Art*, 128.

86  Marvin Carlson, introduction to Carlson, *Performance*.

87  Ian Hodder, *Entangled: An Archaeology of the Relationships between Humans and Things* (Malden, MA; Wiley-Blackwell, 2012), 94 and 97–98.

88  Tracey Warr, preface to Warr, *Artist's Body*, 12–13.


5. THE ART OF ELIMINATION

1  See, for instance, Associated Press, "A Golden Throne for the Everyman," YouTube video, September 16, 2016, https://www.youtube.com/watch?v=P1voXTXNbj4.

2  Another example was located a few years ago at London's Saatchi Gallery. Terence Koh's *Untitled (Medusa)* is a small box, dark inside with a urinal. In bringing the elimination of body waste into the gallery, a similar presentation of the body as open takes place. See a description of this work at http://www.artnet.com/artists/terence-koh/untitled-medusa-a-xy1OmQnbrh_rFgM5373Uwg2.

3  Quoted in Martin Engler, "Merda d'Artista (Artist's Shit)," in *Piero Manzoni: When Bodies Became Art*, ed. Martin Engler (Frankfurt am Main: Städel Museum, 2013), 194.

4 I restrict my discussion to the use of human waste. Among those who have used animal waste, readers should consider Chris Ofili. See, for example, Coco Fusco, "Captain Shit and Other Allegories of Black Stardom: The Work of Chris Ofili," in *The Bodies That Were Not Ours: And Other Writings*, by Coco Fusco (London: Routledge, 2001).

5 Michael Thompson, *Rubbish Theory: The Creation and Destruction of Value* (New York: Oxford University Press, 1979), 77.

6 For a working theory related to this point, see Thompson, *Rubbish Theory*.

7 Thompson, *Rubbish Theory*, 39.

8 See Gillian Whiteley, *Junk: Art and the Politics of Trash* (London: I. B. Tauris, 2011). Gignac describes his "New York City Garbage" this way: "In 2001, I started selling garbage. 100% authentic New York City Garbage. The trash is hand-picked and arranged in Lucite cubes that are signed, numbered, and dated. Today, more than 1,300 cubes have been sold to over 20 countries." See Justin Gignac, "New York City Garbage," https://www.justingignac.com /nyc-garbage. Also see "Meet the Creatives," accessed July 2019, http://www .meetthecreatives.design/y73tfg259r0I uopuurvcg3gx23bq5h.

9 Ellah Shohat and Robert Stam, "Narrativizing Visual Culture: Towards a Polycentric Aesthetics," in Nicholas Mirzoeff, ed., *The Visual Culture Reader*, 2nd ed. (New York: Routledge, 1998), 52, and quoted in Whiteley, *Junk*, 7.

10 It is interesting to note that the pop-up Unko Museum outside of Tokyo opened recently and is dedicated to "poop." According to reports, roughly 10,000 people visited during its first week of operations.

11 Whiteley, *Junk*, 8.

12 Whiteley, *Junk*, 27.

13 Cattelan is not the only artist to privilege the evacuation of the bowls as having artistic value of some sort. Cornelius Kolig has used human waste, and has exhibited a picture of himself with pants down, book in hand, and appearing to defecate. "Chaos, Excrement and Cats: A Visit to Artist Corne- lius Kolig," *Profil*, October 30, 2013, https://www.profil.at/gesellschaft/chaos -kot-katzen-besuch-kuenstler-cornelius-kolig-368706. Also see Whiteley, *Junk*, 30.

14 One could add to this discussion the recent exhibit by Kara Walker in New York City, at Sikkema Jenkins and Company. Drawing on images that have populated her work for some time—now not as cut-outs but water-color images—one finds, if one looks carefully, the production and consumption of human waste and other body fluids. This to some degree suggests open bodies—as the scenes demonstrate—coded with social markers of difference such as race, gender, and class. Bodies in the various pieces blend together, overlap, bleed through, and so forth. Again, in this way they suggest the possibility of reading through a race-, gender-, class-sensitive framework of the grotesque.

15 Susan Signe Morrison, *Excrement in the Late Middle Ages: Sacred Filth and Chaucer's Fecopoetics* (New York: Palgrave Macmillan, 2008), 140, 146.

16  Morrison, *Excrement in the Late Middle Ages*, 2.

17  David Waltner-Toews, *The Origin of Feces: What Excrement Tells Us about Evolution, Ecology, and a Sustainable Society* (Toronto: ECW Press, 2013), 10.

18  David Waltner-Toews notes, "Like its sibling scat, shit has the same ancient proto-Indo-European root (*skei*) as the word science, with a meaning having to do with separating one thing from another." *Origin of Feces*, 8.

19  *Merriam-Webster.com Dictionary*, s.v. "shit," accessed January 2, 2021, https://www.merriam-webster.com/dictionary/shit.

20  According to Nick Haslam, "Shit is consistently among the two most frequently uttered swear words in English and can be used in a bewildering variety of ways." Haslam, *Psychology in the Bathroom* (New York: Palgrave Macmillan, 2012), 95.

21  This openness and interplay between naming-things and thing-things is depicted in the photography of Thomas Mailaender, who for an exhibit at the Saatchi Gallery in London produced pictures of exposed body parts that are tattooed with other images. These tattoos are not produced with ink and needles but rather through a stencil covering skin that is exposed to the sun. The image appears embedded in sunburned skin. See Saatchi Gallery, "Artist: Thomas Mailaender," http://www.saatchigallery.com/artists/thomas_mailaender_iconoclasts_i.htm.

22  Waltner-Toews, *Origin of Feces*, 4–5.

23  Waltner-Toews, *Origin of Feces*, 27.

24  Waltner-Toews, *Origin of Feces*.

25  Morrison, *Excrement in the Late Middle Ages*, 16, 26.

26  Waltner-Toews, *Origin of Feces*, xix.

27  Morrison, *Excrement in the Late Middle Ages*, 15.

28  Morrison, *Excrement in the Late Middle Ages*, 5.

29  Morrison, *Excrement in the Late Middle Ages*, 19–25.

30  William A. Cohen, "Introduction: Locating Filth," in *Filth: Dirt, Disgust, and Modern Life*, ed. William A. Cohen and Ryan Johnson (Minneapolis: University of Minnesota Press, 2005), x and xi.

31  Mary Douglas, *Purity and Danger* (New York: Routledge, 2002), xvii.

32  Simone Schnall, "The Mind beyond Boundaries: Concluding Remarks," in *Purity and Danger Now: New Perspectives*, ed. Robbie Duschinksy, Simone Schnall, and Daniel H. Weiss (New York: Routledge, 2016), 272–73.

33  As a corrective to Douglas's argument, William Viney argues that waste is also matter "out of time." That is to say, Viney wants to reassess the descriptions of waste that have dominated because of the manner in which they limit our sense of "contingency and flux" that actually marks our relationship to waste. This attention to time also fosters alternate ways of thinking about use and value: "The value of things raises and diminishes according to the work they do or the future imagined for them, in other words, to their potential realized in time." William Viney, *Waste: A Philosophy of Things* (New York: Bloomsbury Academic, 2014), 4.

34  See Rhys Williams, "There's Power in the Dirt: Impurity, Utopianism and Radical Politics," in Duschinsky, Schnall, and Weiss, *Purity and Danger Now*,

69–84. Also see Katie Shepherd, "Portland Police Chief Says Antifa Protesters Used Slingshot to Launch Urine and Feces-Filled Balloons at Riot Cops," *Willamette Week*, June 23, 2017, http://www.wweek.com/news/city/2017/06/23/portland-police-chief-says-antifa-protesters-used-slingshot-to-launch-urine-and-feces-filled-balloons-at-riot-cops; Mark Hay, "A Brief History of People Protesting Stuff with Poop," *Vice*, April 8, 2015, https://www.vice.com/en_us/article/wd7n8z/a-brief-history-of-people-protesting-stuff-with-poop-197; "Venezuela Accuses Faeces-Throwing Protesters of Using 'Chemical Weapons,' Sky News, May 11, 2017, http://news.sky.com/story/venezuela-accuses-faeces-throwing-protesters-of-using-chemical-weapons-10873140; Renée Feltz, "Nato Protester's Prison Term Extended for Throwing Human Waste at Guard," *The Guardian*, April 12, 2016, https://www.theguardian.com/us-news/2016/apr/12/nato-summit-protester-prison-term-extended-jared-chase; "Cape Town 'Poo Wars': Mass Arrests in South Africa," *BBC News*, June 11, 2013, http://www.bbc.com/news/world-africa-22853095.

35 Julia Kristeva, *Powers of Horror: An Essay on Abjection* (New York: Columbia University Press, 1982), 2.

36 Kristeva, *Powers of Horror*, 3.

37 Kristeva, *Powers of Horror*, 3.

38 Kristeva, *Powers of Horror*, 3–4, 9, and 15.

39 Douglas, *Purity and Danger*, 142.

40 Douglas, *Purity and Danger*, 147, 150.

41 See Gay Hawkins, *The Ethics of Waste: How We Relate to Rubbish* (Lanham: Rowman and Littlefield, 2006), 54.

42 Elizabeth V. Spelman, *Trash Talks: Revelations in the Rubbish* (New York: Oxford University Press, 2016), 2. Also see Greg Kennedy, *An Ontology of Trash: The Disposable and Its Problematic Nature* (Albany: State University of New York Press, 2007); and Michael Thompson, *Rubbish Theory: The Creation and Destruction of Value* (New York: Oxford University Press, 1979).

43 Taro Gomi, *Everyone Poops* (St. Louis: Turtleback, 2001). There is also Julie Markes, *Where's the Poop?* (New York: HarperFestival, 2004). These are just two of the numerous books devoted to introducing children to the social world of shit. Evacuating one's bowels is made natural—an intimate dimension of our being as embodied creatures in need of energy to maintain existence, but foreign enough to require explicit consideration and attention within these books. The distinction and disregard for shit is socially constructed in that up to a certain age children demonstrate no aversion to fecal matter. Books such as these naturalize this process in part by socializing the distinctive location and process for removing shit from sight.

44 Dominique Laporte, *History of Shit* (Cambridge, MA: MIT Press, 2000).

45 Rodolphe el-Khoury, introduction to Laporte, *History of Shit*, xi.

46 Constance Classen, David Howes, and Anthony Synnott, introduction to *Aroma: The Cultural History of Smell*, ed. Constance Classen, David Howes, and Anthony Synnott (New York: Routledge, 1994), 3.

47  Laporte, *History of Shit*, 9 and 11.

48  Morrison, *Excrement in the Late Middle Ages*, 2.

49  According to Waltner-Toews, "Our eating and defecating behavior says far more than any voting behavior about what kinds of citizens we are on this planet. This is why fundamentally, shit matters." Waltner-Toews, *Origin of Feces*, 64; also see 87. Also see Morrison, *Excrement in the Late Middle Ages*, 28: "What the world reassures and admires is just dung or filth that which has no true worth in terms of Christianity history," for example, "and is a sign of foulness and perfidy."

50  Ingen Frygt installation, *Value Art* exhibit, Museum of Contemporary Art, Roskilde, Denmark. I viewed this on November 9, 2017.

51  See Haslam, *Psychology in the Bathroom*, 2–3.

52  Rose George, *The Big Necessity: The Unmentionable World of Human Waste and Why It Matters* (New York: Metropolitan Books, 2008), 2.

53  Nick Haslam writes, "As Rozin and Fallon (1987) show, humans have no innate aversion to excrement and only come to acquire a revulsion in early childhood." Haslam, *Psychology in the Bathroom*, 109.

54  George, *Big Necessity*, 3.

55  Dave Praeger, *Poop Culture: How America Is Shaped by Its Grossest National Product* (Los Angeles: Feral House, 2007), 127.

56  Waltner-Toews, *Origin of Feces*, 100, 103–4; Morrison, *Excrement in the Late Middle Ages*, 17.

57  Biblical texts related to feces include Ezekiel 4:12; 4:15; Isaiah 36:12; Psalm 83:10; Zephaniah 1:17; Judges 3:21–22; 2 Kings 9:37; 18:27; Jeremiah 9:22; Deuteronomy 23:12–13; 2 Timothy 3:16; Luke 4:24–27; Philippians 3:8.

58  Morrison, *Excrement in the Late Middle Ages*, 28.

59  Morrison, *Excrement in the Late Middle Ages*, 37, 53.

60  Morrison, *Excrement in the Late Middle Ages*, 130.

61  Laporte, *History of Shit*, 35.

62  Laporte, *History of Shit*, 61.

63  Laporte, *History of Shit*, 63. The biblical-theological references connecting shit to the soul—shitting to spiritual life—continue: "[Psalm 113:] 'Who is like the Lord our God? Who is seated on high? Who looks far down upon the heavens and the earth? He who raises the poor from the dust and lifts the needy from the ash heap, to make them sit with princes, with the princes of his people. . . .'" Here Laporte ends his quoting of the Bible, and says, "He who seizes my soul literally lifts me out of the shit. To him I swear my eternal love. He who lifts me out of the shit will, by definition, discourage me from smelling it. He will not want me to claim that now- distanced pile—it is a repugnant thing, but one that my desperate attempts to flee only confirm as forever mine" (64).

64  For the curious, the makeup of shit is as follows: "Our shit is 75% water. Beyond that, the 150 grams of daily output include an average 10–12 grams of nitrogen, 2 grams of phosphorus and 3 grams of potassium. . . . Our excrement

also includes 8% fiber and 5% fat." Waltner-Toews, *Origin of Feces*, 17, 18. Also see Ralph A. Lewin, *Merde: Excursions into Scientific, Cultural and Socio-Historical Coprology* (London: Aurum, 1999), 79.

65  Laporte, *History of Shit*, 14; Waltner-Toews, *Origin of Feces*, 148.

66  Morrison, *Excrement in the Late Middle Ages*, 25.

67  William James, *The Varieties of Religious Experience: A Study in Human Nature* (New Hyde Park, NY: University Books, 1963), 245–46.

68  James, *Varieties of Religious Experience*, 245–46.

69  Lewin, *Merde*, 146.

70  Laporte, *History of Shit*, 34. Unlike Laporte, I am not concerned with the relationship of shit to economic-political structures such as capitalism. My concern is simply the dimension of his argument that speaks to what shit might suggest regarding the material dimensions of embodied existence, what it might name regarding our relationship to our bodies as open.

71  Laporte, *History of Shit*, 28–32, 98, 102. According to Susan Signe Morrison, "As Victoria Sweet points out, bodies are understood within and reflect the context of the society studying them. For us, the body is analogous to a computer; DNA, like microchip for computers, hardwires our physical and perhaps even behavioral destiny. During the industrial revolution, bodies were seen as machines, but in the Middle Ages, a fundamentally agrarian culture, bodies were seen as plants. This vegetable body has resultant waste—such as semen—to be 'composted' for the engineering of future 'vegetables.'" Morrison, *Excrement in the Late Middle Ages*, 18.

72  Captain John G. Bourke, *Scatalogic Rites of All Nations: A Dissertation upon the Employment of Excrementitious Remedial Agents in Religion, Therapeutics, Divination, Witchcraft, Love-Philters, Etc., in All Parts of the Globe* (Washington, DC: W. H. Lowdermilk & Co., 1891), 12.

73  Cohen, "Introduction: Locating Filth," viii.

74  Praeger, *Poop Culture*, 11.

75  Kristeva, *Powers of Horror*, 17.

76  Petra ten-Doesschate Chu, "Scatology and the Realist Aesthetic," *Art Journal* 52, no. 3 (1993): 41–46.

77  Jeff Persels and Russell Ganim, "Introduction: Scatology, the Last Taboo," in *Fecal Matters in Early Modern Literature and Art: Studies in Scatology*, ed. Jeff Persels and Russell Ganim (Burlington, VT: Ashgate, 2004), xiv.

78  Alison G. Stewart, "Expelling from Top and Bottom: The Changing Role of Scatology in Images of Peasant Festivals from Albrecht Dürer to Pieter Bruegel," in Persels and Ganim, *Fecal Matters in Early Modern Literature and Art*, 119.

79  For example: *I Poop You* gallery show in the San Francisco Bay Area (2013) and *Gold Poo*, spray-painted gold dog feces in Brooklyn. In addition, Tobias Wong made pills that, when ingested, turned feces a glittering gold color; Terence Koh sold "his own gold-painted excrement for $500,000"; and Toronto has a "Poop Café." Gerald Silk, "Myths and Meanings in Manzoni's Merda d'artista," *Art Journal* 52, no. 3 (1993): 65–75.

80  Susan M. Canning, "The Ordure of Anarchy: Scatological Signs of Self and Society in the Art of James Ensor," *Art Journal* 52, no. 3 (1993): 47–53.

81  Jojada Verrips, "Excremental Art: Small Wonder in a World Full of Shit," *Journal of Extreme Anthropology* 1, no. 1 (2017): 19. As another example within the twentieth century, Verrips turns to surrealism: "Two famous surrealists, Salvador Dali and Joan Miro, shocked their colleagues and audiences with the painting 'The Lugubrious Game' (1929) and 'Man and Woman in Front of a Pile of Excrement' (1935). Dali's canvas shows a man who evidently has shit in his pants and has soiled his legs, and Miro's shows exactly what the title says" (24).

82  Verrips, "Excremental Art," 19. Images are available at http://www .gilbertandgeorge.co.uk.

83  According to Petra ten-Doesschate Chu, "Marieluise Jurreit relates several of these performances [by German and Austrian performance artists of the 1960s and early 1970s], such as the one by the Austrian artist Gunter Busch who, on the stage of an auditorium of the University of Vienna, undressed, urinated, drank his urine from his cupped hand, and vomited. He ended his performance by defecating with his back to the audience, then smearing his feces on his naked body while singing the Austrian national anthem." Ten-Doesschate Chu, "Scatology and the Realist Aesthetic," 41.

84  Kristeva, *Powers of Horror*, 53.

85  Kristeva, *Powers of Horror*, 108.

86  Hal Foster et al., "The Politics of the Signifier II: A Conversation on the 'Informe' and the Abject," *October* 67 (1994): 3–21, http://www.jstor.org/stable /778965.

87  Kristeva, *Powers of Horror*, 208.

88  Jan Koenot, "When the Body Speaks Louder Than Words: The Image of the Body as a Figure of the Unknown," in *Fluid Flesh: The Body, Religion and the Visual Arts*, ed. Barbara Baert (Leuven, Belgium: Leuven University Press, 2009), 5.

89  Such a discussion is beyond the scope of this project. However, those interested in the ritual implications of other body fluids should see the following: Lawrence A. Hoffman, *Covenant of Blood: Circumcision and Gender in Rabbinic Judaism* (Chicago: University of Chicago Press, 1996); Nancy Jay, *Throughout Your Generations Forever: Sacrifice, Religion, and Paternity* (Chicago: University of Chicago Press, 1992); Orlando Patterson, *Rituals of Blood: Consequences of Slavery in Two American Centuries* (New York: Basic Civitas, 1998); Blake Leyerle, "Blood Is Seed," *Journal of Religion* 81, no. 1 (2001): 26–48; Dennis J. McCarthy, "The Symbolism of Blood and Sacrifice," *Journal of Biblical Literature* 88, no. 2 (1969): 166–76; Dennis J. McCarthy, "Further Notes on the Symbolism of Blood and Sacrifice," *Journal of Biblical Literature* 92, no. 2 (1973): 205–10; Rachel Adler, "In Your Blood, Live: Re-visions of a Theology of Purity," *Tikkun* 8, no. 1 (1993): 38–42; Jeff Rosen, "Blood Ritual," *New Republic* 207, no. 19 (1992): 9–10; Richard John Neuhaus, "By the Blood of His Cross," *First Things: A Monthly Journal of Religion and Public Life*, May 2000, 66–70.

90  See, for instance, Athey's thinking on blood, life, and art: Ron Athey, "Polemic of Blood," *Walker Reader*, March 19, 2015, https://walkerart.org /magazine/ron-athey-blood-polemic-post-aids-body; and Amelia Abraham, "Ron Athey Literally Bleeds for His Art," *Vice*, September 24, 2014, https:// www.vice.com/en_us/article/vdpx8y/ron-athey-performance-art-amelia -abraham-121. See also Dominic Johnson, ed., *Pleading in the Blood: The Art and Performances of Ron Athey* (Chicago: Intellect Books/University of Chicago Press, 2013).

91  Koenot, "When the Body Speaks Louder Than Words," 16.

92  Also of interest are Serrano's *Body Fluid* and *Shit* series. In general, his early work counterpositions body parts, blooded human bodies, and other animal bodies over against Christian images such as crosses and religious leaders. While these pieces are intriguing, the images pull body fluid from the body—fostering a sense of distance. My concern is maintaining the tension between the body and what it eliminates so as to highlight the body as open. See Serrano's website: http://andresserrano.org.

93  For an interesting historical discussion of the body that relates to the period of St. Augustine, see Caroline Walker Bynum, *The Resurrection of the Body in Western Christianity, 200–1336* (New York: Columbia University Press, 1995).

94  For a discussion of smell as it relates to waste, see Classen, Howes, and Synnott, *Aroma*.

95  *Dali/Duchamp*, Royal Academy of Arts (London), viewed on October 15, 2017.

96  See Praeger, *Poop Culture*, 18–48. Other materials include *Wim Delvoye: Cloaca—New and Improved* (New York: Rectapublishers, 2002); *Wim Delvoye: Studies for Cloaca 1997–2006* (New York: Rectapublishers, 2008). See Nate Freeman, "'Feces Is Very Cosmopolitan': Wim Delvoye on His Notorious 'Cloaca' at the Museum Tinguely in Basel," *Art News*, June 16, 2017, https://www.artnews.com/art-news/market/feces-is-very-cosmopolitan-wim -delvoye-on-his-notorious-cloaca-at-the-museum-tinguelys-retrospective-in -basel-8556.

97  Praeger, *Poop Culture*, 18.

98  Praeger, *Poop Culture*, 151.

99  Verrips, "Excremental Art," 29.

100 Piero Manzoni, *Artist's Shit No. 014*, May 1961, viewable at https://www.moma .org/collection/works/80768.

101 In addition to the sale of shit, of interest is the effort of Stuart Brisley to chronicle "the cultural value" of shit through the creation of his Museum of Ordure. See http://www.ordure.org. Also see Michael Newman, *Stuart Brisley—Performing the Political Body and Eating Shit* (Belfast: Museum of Ordure, 2015).

102 Martin Engler, "The Body, Its Image, Its Actions and Objects: Piero Manzoni and the Biology of Art," in *Piero Manzoni: When Bodies Became Art*, ed. Martin Engler (Frankfurt am Main: Stadel Museum, 2013), 13.

103 This would come to include later in the twentieth century not only the presentation of shit as art, but also the mechanism of removing the residue, the final signs of shit, from the body in the form of toilet paper. Think in terms of ShitBegone toilet paper, which was art sold as a common product related to waste removal: "ShitBegone is mass-produced art appropriated by the artist as a consumer good. You can look at it in a gallery, you can read about it in art magazines, but ultimately it's intended for you to buy in a store and use to wipe your butt. ShitBegone does not fully function as art until it's on a store shelf next to brands evoking teddy bears and fluffy clouds." Praeger, *Poop Culture*, 173.

104 For a discussion of "in" place and "out of" place, see Douglas, *Purity and Danger*. Read this, for example, in relationship to William Ian Miller, *The Anatomy of Disgust* (Cambridge, MA: Harvard University Press, 1997), and also Duschinsky, Schnall, and Weiss, *Purity and Danger Now*.

105 Martin Engler, "Merda d'Artista (Artist's Shit)," in Engler, *Piero Manzoni*, 194.

106 For an interesting discussion of judgment, see Anthony Julius, *Transgressions: The Offences of Art* (Chicago: University of Chicago Press, 2003).

107 For religio-theological interpretations, see, for instance, Dominique Laporte, "Piero Manzoni: Artisan of the Seventh Day," in Engler, *Piero Manzoni*; Stephan de Beer, "Jesus in the Dumping Sites: Doing Theology in the Overlaps of Human and Material Waste," in HTS *Teologiese Studies/Theological Studies* 70, no. 3 (2014): e1–e8; Crispin Paine, "Sacred Waste," *Material Religion* 10, no. 2 (2014): 241–42; Cecelia F. Klein, "Teocuitlatl, 'Divine Excrement': The Significance of 'Holy Shit' in Ancient Mexico," *Art Journal* 52, no. 3 (1993): 20–27; Sally M. Promey, ed., *Sensational Religion: Sensory Cultures in Material Practice* (New Haven, CT: Yale University Press, 2014).

108 While I want to bracket her framing of this process in terms of theological ritualization in the context of "Cuban popular religion" and instead frame this process in terms of my sense of religion as technology, I do find Kristina Wirtz's argument for the "social biography" (476) of waste items and the agency of engagement—over against Mary Douglas's concern of a more structuralist analysis of dirt as struggle against representative social arrangements—compelling. See Kristina Wirtz, "Hazardous Waste: The Semiotics of Ritual Hygiene in Cuban Popular Religion," *Journal of the Royal Anthropological Institute* 15, no. 3 (2009): 476–501.

109 Wirtz is referencing a claim by Daniel Miller (*Material Culture and Mass Consumption* [Oxford: Blackwell, 1987], 1). Wirtz, "Hazardous Waste," 477.

110 Wirtz writes in terms of the "interpenetration" of things, and I find this phrasing useful. Yet it is the spiritualization of this interpenetration that I want to bracket. Wirtz, "Hazardous Waste," 483.

111 Dominique Laporte speaks of Manzoni as losing bits of his body through his work—through breathing into balloons for *Artist's Breath* or in filling cans with his shit. See Laporte, "Piero Manzoni," 142.

112 Stella Santacatterina, "Piero Manzoni," *Third Text* 13, no. 45 (1998), 27.

## 6. PIECES OF THINGS

1 David Marriott, "Corpsing; or, the Matter of Black Life," *Cultural Critique* 94 (Fall 2006): 35.

2 Butler, quoted in Rina Arya, *Abjection and Representation: An Exploration of Abjection in the Visual Arts, Film and Literature* (New York: Palgrave Macmillan, 2014), 72. Coco Fusco makes an interesting statement concerning this process when discussing Chris Ofili's work: "The amount of colonial imagery associating blacks with dirt, waste and excrement is nothing if not staggering, as is the nineteenth-century preoccupation with illness, the association of odor with disease and symbolic rendering of blacks as carriers of dirt, and thus disease, and thus degeneracy." Coco Fusco, *The Bodies That Were Not Ours: And Other Writings* (New York: Routledge, 2001), 42.

3 Marriott, "Corpsing," 35.

4 Arthur Danto, "Postmodern Art and Concrete Selves," in *Philosophizing Art: Selected Essays*, by Arthur Danto (Berkeley: University of California Press, 1999), 134. I highlight this political dimension of art in other essays as well. It is an ongoing theme in my writing on art. See, for instance, Anthony Pinn, et al., "Making Bodies with a Brush Stroke: African American Visual Art and the Re/constitution of Black Embodiment," *Black Religion and Embodiment* (London: Equinox, 2017).

5 Frederick Douglass, *Narrative of the Life of Frederick Douglass, an American Slave* (Boston: Anti-Slavery Office, 1845); Douglass, *Life and Times of Frederick Douglass* (Hartford, CT: Park Publishing Co., 1882); Richard Wright, *Black Boy* (New York: Harper and Brothers, 1945); Harriet Ann Jacobs, *Incidents in the Life of a Slave Girl* (Boston: Published for the author, 1861).

6 Listen to Bessie Smith songs such as "Gimme a Pig Foot and a Bottle of Beer" and "Chicago Bound Blues," and to Billie Holiday tunes such as "God Bless the Child" and "Strange Fruit."

7 Richard J. Powell, *Black Art and Culture in the 20th Century* (New York: Thames and Hudson, 1997), 13.

8 Powell, *Black Art and Culture*, 18.

9 This exhibit presented a compelling depiction of the manner in which African American artists have rethought the raced and classed nature of bodied naming-things. As part of the research for this chapter and the following chapter, I viewed the exhibit at The Broad in Los Angeles (March 30, 2019) and the Brooklyn Museum of Art (October 9, 2018).

10 Powell, *Black Art and Culture*, 159.

11 The performative nature of identity is well-worn territory. See, for instance, Judith Butler, *Gender Trouble: Feminism and the Subversion of Identity* (New York: Routledge, 2006).

12 Powell, *Black Art and Culture*, 151.

13 Michael D. Harris, *Colored Pictures: Race and Visual Representation* (Chapel Hill: University of North Carolina Press, 2003), 2.

14 Harris, *Colored Pictures*, 2–3.

15 Arthur Danto, "Depiction and Description," in *The Body/Body Problem: Selected Essays*, by Arthur Danto (Berkeley: University of California Press, 1999), 98.

16 Arthur Danto, "Art-in-Response," in Danto, *Philosophizing Art*, 59.

17 Hans Belting, *An Anthropology of Images: Picture, Medium, Body* (Princeton, NJ: Princeton University Press, 2011), 40.

18 Elizabeth Grosz, *Becoming Undone: Darwinian Reflections on Life, Politics, and Art* (Durham, NC: Duke University Press, 2011), 189.

19 See Harris, *Colored Pictures*, chapter 6, which deals with inversion of stereotypes.

20 Biographical information on Bearden is not highlighted in this chapter. However, for those interested in a concise presentation of that material, see, for instance, Myron Schwartzman, *Romare Bearden: His Life and Art* (New York: Harry N. Abrams, 1990).

21 Matthew S. Witkovsky, "Experience vs. Theory: Romare Bearden and Abstract Expressionism," in *Black American Literature Forum* 23, no. 2 (1989): 257.

22 Lee Stephens Glazer, "Signifying Identity: Art and Race in Romare Bearden's Projections, *Art Bulletin* 76, no. 3 (1994): 411.

23 Glazer, "Signifying Identity," 412.

24 Glazer, "Signifying Identity," 413.

25 Myron Schwartzman, *Romare Bearden: His Life and Art* (New York: Harry N. Abrams, 1990), 197.

26 Gail Gelburd, *Romare Bearden in Black-and-White: Photomontage Projections, 1964* (New York: Whitney Museum of American Art, 1997), 17–18.

27 Schwartzman, *Romare Bearden*, 230.

28 Witkovsky, "Experience vs. Theory," 277.

29 Glazer, "Signifying Identity," 417.

30 Jae Emerling, "On the Image of Bearden," in *Romare Bearden: Southern Recollections*, by Carla M. Hanzal et al. (Charlotte, NC: Mint Museum, 2011), 65.

31 Schwartzman, *Romare Bearden*, 7.

32 Leslie King-Hammond, "Bearden's Crossroads: Modernist Roots/Riffing Traditions," in Hanzal et al., *Romare Bearden: Southern Recollections*, 87.

33 Ralph Ellison, "The Art of Romare Bearden," in *Going to the Territory* (New York: Random House, 1986), 229.

34 Gelburd, *Romare Bearden in Black-and-White*, 29.

35 Darby English speaks to this point in "Ralph Ellison's Romare Bearden," in *Romare Bearden, American Modernist*, ed. Ruth Fine and Jacqueline Francis (Washington, DC: National Gallery of Art, 2011), 13–25.

36 Robert G. O'Meally, "'We Used to Say Stashed': Romare Bearden Paints the Blues," in Fine and Francis, *Romare Bearden, American Modernist*, 61–87.

37 See Carla M. Hanzal, introduction to Hanzal et al., *Romare Bearden: Southern Recollections*, 21–24.

38 Cornel West, *Prophesy Deliverance! An Afro-American Revolutionary Christianity* (Philadelphia: Westminster Press, 1982).

39 Ralph Ellison, "The Art of Romare Bearden," in Ellison, *Going to the Territory*, 234.

40 Gelburd, *Romare Bearden in Black-and-White*, 29.

41 Robert G. O'Meally provides an intriguing discussion of similar themes in his analysis of Bearden's artistic reflections on *The Odyssey*. See O'Meally, *Romare Bearden: A Black Odyssey* (New York: DC Moore Gallery, 2007).

## 7. "CAPTURED" THINGS

This chapter is a modified version of an essay published as Anthony B. Pinn, "Why Can't I Be Both? Jean-Michel Basquiat and Aesthetics of Black Bodies Reconstituted," *Journal of Africana Religion* 1, no. 1 (2013): 109–32. It is used by permission of The Pennsylvania State University Press.

1 This chapter represents a concern with Basquiat's art that goes back several years and is expressed over several publications. In this regard, it expands some of my existing thinking on his art and, through my concern with thing theory, pushes my reading of his art in new directions.

2 Nicholas Mirzoeff, "Introduction: The Multiple Viewpoint: Diasporic Visual Cultures," in *Diaspora and Visual Culture: Representing Africans and Jews*, ed. Nicholas Mirzoeff (New York: Routledge, 2000), 1–2.

3 See Alain Locke, introduction to *The New Negro: An Interpretation* (New York: Antheum, 1986).

4 Rasheed Araeen, "The Artist as a Post-Colonial Subject and This Individual's Journey towards 'the Centre,'" in *Views of Difference: Different Views of Art*, ed. Catherine King (New Haven, CT: Yale University Press, 1999), 231.

5 Araeen, "Artist as a Post-Colonial Subject," 242.

6 James Putnam, *Art and Artifact: The Museum as Medium*, 2nd ed. (New York: Thames and Hudson, 2009); Ivan Karp and Steven D. Lavine, eds., *Exhibiting Cultures: The Poetics and Politics of Museum Display* (Washington, DC: Smithsonian Institution Press, 1991).

7 Wendy A. Grossman, *Man Ray, African Art, and the Modernist Lens* (Washington, DC: International Arts and Artists; Minneapolis: University of Minnesota Press, 2009), 1–9.

8 Grossman, *Man Ray, African Art*, 81.

9 Grossman, *Man Ray, African Art*, 4.

10 Christoph Grunenberg, "Case Study 1: The Modern Art Museum," in *Contemporary Cultures of Display*, ed. Emma Barker (New Haven, CT: Yale University Press, 1999), 30.

11 See Barker, *Contemporary Cultures of Display*, and Karp and Lavine, *Exhibiting Cultures*.

12 Elsbeth Court, "Case Study 6: Africa on Display: Exhibiting Art by Africans," in Barker, *Contemporary Cultures of Display*, 152.

13 Grossman, *Man Ray, African Art*, 31.

14 Petrine Archer-Straw, *Negrophilia: Avant-Garde Paris and Black Culture in the 1920s* (New York: Thames and Hudson, 2000), 19.

15 Joseph Conrad, *Heart of Darkness* (New York: W. W. Norton and Co., 2005).

16 Archer-Straw, *Negrophilia*, 18.

17  Svetlana Alpers, "The Museum as a Way of Seeing," in Karp and Lavine, *Exhibiting Cultures*, 23–24.

18  Alpers, "Museum as a Way of Seeing," 19.

19  Will Rea, "Finding Your Contemporaries: The Modernities of African Art," in *Identity Theft: The Cultural Colonization of Contemporary Art*, ed. Jonathan Harris (Liverpool: Liverpool University Press, 2008), 137.

20  Alpers, "Museum as a Way of Seeing," 20, 87.

21  Graham Lock and David Murray, introduction to *The Hearing Eye: Jazz and Blues Influences in African American Visual Art*, ed. Graham Lock and David Murray (New York: Oxford University Press, 2009).

22  Thomas McEvilley, "Jean-Michel Basquiat Here Below," in *Dubuffet, Basquiat: Personal Histories* (New York: PaceWildenstein, 2006), 33.

23  McEvilley, "Jean-Michel Basquiat Here Below," 34.

24  McEvilley, "Jean-Michel Basquiat Here Below," 34.

25  McEvilley, "Jean-Michel Basquiat Here Below," 34.

26  Michael D. Harris, *Colored Pictures: Race and Visual Representation* (Chapel Hill: University of North Carolina Press, 2003), 195.

27  Richard J. Powell, *Black Art and Culture in the 20th Century* (New York: Thames and Hudson, 1997), 78–80.

28  Useful materials related to Lorraine Hansberry include Lorraine Hansberry, *A Raisin in the Sun: A Drama in Three Acts* (New York: Random House, 1959); Imani Perry, *Finding Lorraine: The Radiant and Radical Life of Lorraine Hansberry* (Boston: Beacon Press, 2019); Pat McKissack and Fredrick McKissack, *Lorraine Hansberry: Dramatist and Activist* (New York: Delacorte Press, 1994).

29  Henry Geldzahler, "Jean-Michel Basquiat (1983)," in *Making It New: Essays, Interviews, and Talks*, by Henry Geldzahler (New York: Turtle Point Press, 1994), 197.

30  Geldzahler, "Jean-Michel Basquiat (1983)," 199.

31  Gianni Mercurio, ed., *The Jean-Michel Basquiat Show* (New York: Rizzoli International Publications, 2006), 18.

32  For information on Basquiat in relationship to the physicality and representational significance of New York and the New York art world, see the following documentaries: *Jean-Michel Basquiat: The Radiant Child* (Cinedigm, 2008) and *American Masters: Basquiat* (PBS, 2018).

33  Peter Halley, *Peter Halley: Collected Essays, 1981–1987* (Zurich: Lapis Press, 1988), 108.

34  Geldzahler, "Jean-Michel Basquiat (1983)," 200.

35  See Henry David Thoreau, *Walden* (Princeton, NJ: Princeton University Press, 2004), chapter 18.

36  Geldzahler, "Jean-Michel Basquiat (1983)," 205. Read this remark—"People laugh when you fall on your ass. What's humor?—in light of Robert Farris Thompson, "Royalty, Heroism, and the Streets: Jean-Michel Basquiat," in Lock and Murray, *Hearing Eye*, 276.

37  This painting sold for $110.5 million in 2017. At the time, it was the most expensive painting ever sold by an American painter.

38  Jonathan Jones, "Is This Basquiat Worth $100m? Yes—His Art of American Violence Is Priceless," *The Guardian*, May 19, 2017, https://www.theguardian .com/artanddesign/2017/may/19/jean-michel-basquiat-110m-sothebys.

39  Richard D. Marshall, "Jean-Michel Basquiat: Speaking in Tongues," in exhibit catalog, Lugano, Museuo d'Arte Moderna, Jean-Michael Basquiat, 2005, p. 40. Quoted in Sotheby's Contemporary Art Evening Auction: http://www .sothebys.com/fr/auctions/ecatalogue/lot.24.html/2017/contemporary-art -evening-auction-n09761, accessed December 30, 2019.

40  Cross Damon: Richard Wright, *The Outsider* (New York: Harper Perennial Modern Classics, 2008); Bigger Thomas: Richard Wright, *Native Son* (New York: Harper Perennial Modern Classics, 2005).

41  See, for example, "Mother of Pearl Face and Ebony Mask" (1926) at http:// www.manraytrust.com.

42  The following provides the image as well as a story concerning the tremen- dous sum paid for it: Associated Press, "Jean-Michel Basquiat Skull Painting Sells for Record $110.5m at Auction," *The Guardian*, May 18, 2017, https://www .theguardian.com/artanddesign/2017/may/19/jean-michel-basquiat-skull -painting-record-1105m-at-auction.

43  Geldzahler, "Jean-Michel Basquiat (1983)," 203.

44  The Boxer Rebellion was a movement from 1899 to 1901 that fought against Christianity and imperialism.

45  Henry Geldzahler raises this question with respect to the photograph. Geldzahler, "What I Know about Photography," in Geldzahler, *Making It New*, 333.

46  Celeste-Marie Bernier, *African American Visual Arts: From Slavery to the Present* (Chapel Hill: University of North Carolina, 2008), 194.

47  Robert Farris Thompson, "Royalty, Heroism, and the Streets: The Art of Jean- Michel Basquiat," in Lock and Murray, *Hearing Eye*, 254.

48  Phoebe Hoban, *Basquiat: A Quick Killing in Art* (New York: Penguin Books, 1998), 80–81.

49  Jennifer Clement, *Widow Basquiat: A Love Story* (Edinburgh: Payback Press, 2000), 75.

50  Powell, *Black Art and Culture*, 167.

51  Clement, *Widow Basquiat*, 75.

52  Clement, *Widow Basquiat*, 38.

53  Dick Hebdige, "Welcome to the Terrordome: Jean-Michel Basquiat and the 'Dark' Side of Hybridity," in *Jean-Michel Basquiat*, ed. Richard Marshall (New York: Whitney Museum of American Art/Harry N. Abrams, 1993), 62–63.

54  Harris, *Colored Pictures*, 256.

55  Hoban, *Basquiat: A Quick Killing*, 116.

56  Hoban, *Basquiat: A Quick Killing*, 116.

57  Hoban, *Basquiat: A Quick Killing*, 168.

1 W. E. B. Du Bois, "Of Our Spiritual Striving," in *The Souls of Black Folk* (New York: Vintage Books/Library of America, 1990), 1. This essay was first published in *Atlantic Monthly* as "Strivings of the Negro People," August 1897.

2 I am grateful to friends and colleagues who read early versions of this chapter and offered helpful feedback that improved my argument. Thank you, Peter Paris, Jeffrey Kripal, April DeConick, and Mark Ryan. This chapter was first presented as the Annual William James Lecture at Harvard Divinity School, March 2017. A version of that lecture was also given at the American Institute, Oxford University (November 17, 2017), and as the annual American Journal of Theology and Philosophy Lecture held at the American Academy of Religion's 2018 meeting.

3 Du Bois, *Souls of Black Folk*, 3.

4 My goal is not to interrogate, nor describe Du Bois's praxis, but rather to better understand his diagnosis of a problem. For an interesting discussion of the introductory and closing materials of *Souls*, see Shamoon Zamir, "The Souls of Black Folk: Thought and After Thought," in *The Cambridge Companion to W. E. B. Du Bois*, ed. Shamoon Zamir (New York: Cambridge University Press, 2008), 7–36.

5 Du Bois, *Souls of Black Folk*, 7; italics added.

6 Du Bois, *Souls of Black Folk*, 8.

7 Cornel West, *The American Evasion of Philosophy: A Genealogy of Pragmatism* (Madison: University of Wisconsin Press, 1989), 142.

8 Arnold Rampersad notes about Du Bois that "enumeration is crucial to his style." And so there is no reason to believe the importance of duality is limited to double-consciousness. Instead, it is useful to recognize that tension is vital to his presentation: twoness related to consciousness, secular over against religious, liberal arts over against industrial training, and so on. See Rampersad, *The Art and Imagination of W. E. B. Du Bois* (Cambridge, MA: Harvard University Press, 1976), 73; Shamoon Zamir, *Dark Voices: W. E. B. Du Bois and American Thought, 1888–1903* (Chicago: University of Chicago Press, 1995), 116. Such a reading of the category informs, for instance, the thinking of Robert Gooding-Williams, who remarks, "Given his understanding of the Negro problem, we may suppose that Du Bois took 'How does it feel to be a problem?' to be asking 'How does it feel to be excluded from the group life of American society?'" Gooding-Williams, *In the Shadow of Du Bois: Afro-Modern Political Thought in America* (Cambridge, MA: Harvard University Press, 2009), 71.

9 David Levering Lewis, *W. E. B. Du Bois, Biography of a Race: 1868–1919* (New York: Henry Holt and Co., 1993), 96. Lewis also suggests a connection to Goethe and Chesnutt, who make use of a similar construction (282). Shamoon Zamir argues for a Hegelian turn in Du Bois's work, which accounts for the use of twoness. See Zamir, *Dark Voices*. Also see Ross Posnock, "The Influence of William James on American Culture," in *The Cambridge Companion to William James*, ed. Ruth Anna Putnam (New York: Cambridge University Press, 1997),

327–40; and James's discussion of the "Hidden Self" in Robert Richardson, ed., *The Heart of William James* (Cambridge, MA: Harvard University Press, 2010), 79–100.

10  Rampersad, *Art and Imagination of W. E. B. Du Bois*, 74.

11  Posnock, "Influence of William James on American Culture," 338.

12  Du Bois, *Souls of Black Folk*, 14.

13  Like Camus, Du Bois notes hypocrisy, and exposes values that actually promote disregard. Even his attention to the Negro problem speaks to this moralist posture in that it offers a jeremiad—i.e., a clear vision of circumstances and a warning regarding their outcome. *Souls* discusses these circumstances and draws attention to socioeconomic, cultural, and political approaches of redress. In this way, Du Bois calls for consistency between the best of the Reconstruction aims and an ongoing commitment to radical change. West, *American Evasion of Philosophy*, 142.

14  Du Bois, *Souls of Black Folk*, 68–69.

15  Cornel West represents double consciousness as the cause of a problem soul and ultimately critiques it in terms of dissatisfying structures of communal leadership. Others critique him for the inherent limitation of doubleness, which fails to consider the variety of ways in which African Americans are rendered foreign. Gender, sexuality, and a host of other constructions shape our presence in the world, but they are not captured by the black-white dichotomy, which binds Du Bois's souls. Yet this twoness and accompanying insight has served as a signifier for the marginality, the "otherness" of African Americans. Although critiqued, the persistent application of this signifier suggests its utility depends on the intended approach toward otherness.

16  Du Bois, *Souls of Black Folk* says the following on page 72, which speaks to the Negro problem as the context for the earlier narrative he provides regarding the three moments: "Yet after all they are but gates, and when turning our eyes from the temporary and the contingent in the Negro problem to the broader question of the permanent uplifting and vacillation of black men in America, we have a right to inquire, as this enthusiasm for material advancement mounts to its height. . . . Is not life more than meat, and the body more than raiment?" Du Bois is here critiquing the Washingtonian model of education for African Americans.

17  Du Bois, *Souls of Black Folk*, 16.

18  Du Bois, *Souls of Black Folk*, 28.

19  Du Bois, *Souls of Black Folk*, 34.

20  Du Bois, *Souls of Black Folk*: "What is thus true of all communities is peculiarly true of the South, where, outside of written history and outside of printed law, there has been going on for a generation as deep a storm and stress of human souls, as intense a ferment of feeling, as intricate a writhing of spirit, as ever a people experienced. Within and without the somber veil of color vast social forces have been at work—efforts for human betterment, movements toward disintegration and despair, tragedies and comedies in social and economic life, and a swaying and lifting and sinking of human hearts which

have made this land a land of mingled sorrow and joy of change and excitement and unrest" (131–32).

21  Du Bois, *Souls of Black Folk*, 9.
22  Du Bois, *Souls of Black Folk*, 10.
23  Terrence Johnson, *Tragic Soul-Life: W. E. B. Du Bois and the Moral Crisis Facing American Democracy* (New York: Oxford University Press, 2012), 6.
24  Johnson, *Tragic Soul-Life*, 38–39.
25  Du Bois, *Souls of Black Folk*, 143–44.
26  Lewis, *W. E. B. Du Bois, Biography of a Race*, 280.
27  William James, *The Varieties of Religious Experience: A Study in Human Nature* (New Hyde Park, NY: University Books, 1963).
28  James, *Varieties of Religious Experience*, 87.
29  Martin Halliwell, "Morbid and Positive Thinking: William James, Psychology, and Illness," in *William James and the Transatlantic Conversation: Pragmatism, Pluralism, and Philosophy of Religion*, ed. Martin Halliwell and Joel D. S. Rasmussen (New York: Oxford University Press, 2014), 101.
30  Charles Taylor, "Twice-Born," in *Varieties of Religion Today: William James Revisited*, by Charles Taylor (Cambridge, MA: Harvard University Press, 2002), 339.
31  James, *Varieties of Religious Experience*, 90.
32  James, *Varieties of Religious Experience*, 130.
33  James, *Varieties of Religious Experience*, 137.
34  Pericles Lewis, "James's Sick Souls," *Henry James Review* 22, no. 3 (2001): 251.
35  James, *Varieties of Religious Experience*, 135.
36  James, *Varieties of Religious Experience*, 144.
37  James, *Varieties of Religious Experience*, 139.
38  Halliwell, "Morbid and Positive Thinking," 101; Lewis, "James's Sick Souls," 252; Gary T. Alexander, "William James, the Sick Soul, and the Negative Dimensions of Consciousness: A Partial Critique of Transpersonal Psychology, *Journal of the American Academy of Religion* 48, no. 2 (1980): 200.
39  As found in Jill L. McNish, "'Failure, Then, Failure!' Shame and William James's 'Sick Soul,'" *CrossCurrents* 53, no. 3 (2003): 393. A similar sense of exhaustion and surrender marks early African American conversion accounts.
40  James, *Varieties of Religious Experience*, 187.
41  James, *Varieties of Religious Experience*, 144–45.
42  James, *Varieties of Religious Experience*, 145.
43  One could read the story of John as a not-so-subtle critique of higher education as a mechanism for countering racial disregard. What John encounters instead suggests that antiblack racism does not bend to logic and is not subdued by reasonable argument.
44  James, *Varieties of Religious Experience*, 189.
45  Du Bois, *Souls of Black Folk*, 9.
46  Cornel West, "Black Strivings in a Twilight Civilization," in *The Cornel West Reader* (New York: Basic Civitas, 1999), 89.
47  West, "Black Strivings in a Twilight Civilization," 89–90. Arnold Rampersad offers a different perspective. He suggests that Du Bois maintained a certain

mode of optimism over against the pessimism of the masses. Whereas West seems to sense an embedded hopefulness, a strategic optimism premised on the disruptive cultural practices of African Americans, within the larger community of African Americans, Rampersad notes a deep pessimism. See Rampersad, *Art and Imagination of W. E. B. Du Bois*, 86.

48 West, "Black Strivings in a Twilight Civilization," 89–90. Also see, for example, the discussion of the "talented tenth" isolated in Henry Louis Gates Jr. and Cornel West, *The Future of the Race* (New York: Vintage Books, 1996).

49 West, "Black Strivings in a Twilight Civilization," 89. Also see Cornel West, *Prophesy Deliverance! An Afro-American Revolutionary Christianity* (Philadelphia: Westminster, 1982).

50 West, "Black Strivings in a Twilight Civilization," 93.

51 Ultimately, West is concerned with the outcomes of this attachment to community and ritual, whereas I am concerned with the description of a particular posture toward the world as opposed to resolution of the challenges presented by that view.

52 Du Bois, *Souls of Black Folk*, 188.

53 Du Bois, *Souls of Black Folk*, 151.

54 Gerald Horne, 1986, 345, in Paul C. Taylor, "What's the Use of Calling Du Bois a Pragmatist? *Metaphilosophy* 35, nos. 1–2 (2004): 101.

55 Taylor, "What's the Use of Calling Du Bois a Pragmatist?" 101.

56 Jonathan Flatley, *Affective Mapping: Melancholia and the Politics of Modernism* (Cambridge, MA: Harvard University Press, 2008).

57 Charles Taylor, "The Twice-Born," in Taylor, *Varieties of Religion Today*, 340, 342.

58 I find Julia Kristeva's discussion of melancholy more compelling than most accounts, particular the framing of a "living death." Yet its affective and psychological dimensions, for my mind, do not capture Du Bois's sentiment. See Kristeva, *Black Sun: Depression and Melancholia* (New York: Columbia University Press, 1989). Also see Sanja Bahun, *Modernism and Melancholia: Writing as Countermourning* (New York: Oxford University Press, 2014).

59 Charles H. Long, "The Oppressive Elements in Religion and the Religions of the Oppressed," *Harvard Theological Review* 69, nos. 3–4 (1976): 401. This globalizing of the issue is important. Du Bois understood the Negro problem as a localized dimension of a larger world problem. See Du Bois, "The Color Line Belts the World," in *W. E. B. Du Bois: A Reader*, ed. David Levering Lewis (New York: Henry Holt and Co., 1995), 42.

60 See Richard Rorty, "Religious Faith, Intellectual Responsibility, and Romance," in *The Cambridge Companion to William James*, ed. Ruth Anna Putnam (New York: Cambridge University Press, 1997). For what this personal experience of dread might say concerning issues of masculinity and domestic space, see Jessica R. Feldman, "A Shelter of the Mind: Henry, William, and the Domestic Scene," in Putnam, *Cambridge Companion to William James*.

Long, "Oppressive Elements in Religion," 407. This is also not the dread chronicled by Kierkegaard in that he collapses into God in the face of dread and fear, but not so for Du Bois. See, for example, Søren Kierkegaard, *Fear and Trembling* (n.p.: Merchant Books, 2012), and read this against Du Bois, *Souls of Black Folk*, and Du Bois, *Dusk of Dawn: An Essay toward an Autobiography of a Race Concept* (New York: Harcourt, Brace and Co., 1940), for instance.

61 Long, "Oppressive Elements in Religion," 409, 411.

62 Du Bois, *Souls of Black Folk*, 152.

63 Du Bois, *Souls of Black Folk*, 152. A similar and persistent sense of the world as suffering emerges, for example, with Richard Wright through family. "My mother's suffering," he writes in *Black Boy*, "grew into a symbol in my mind, gathering to itself all the poverty, the ignorance, the helplessness, the painful, baffling, hunger-ridden days and hours; the restless moving, the futile seeking, the uncertainty, the fear, the dread; the meaningless pain and the endless suffering." Richard Wright, *Black Boy* (New York: Harper and Brothers, 1945), 111.

64 Quoted in Robert D. Richardson, *William James: In the Maelstrom of American Modernism: A Biography* (Boston: Houghton Mifflin, 2006), 399.

EPILOGUE

1 Anthony B. Pinn, *Terror and Triumph: The Nature of Black Religion* (Minneapolis: Fortress Press, 2003).

2 I initially framed the book in relationship to three tasks pointing to (1) enhancement of the study of religion by expanding the forms of cultural production interrogated; (2) pushing the study of religion's engagement with culture beyond the relationship of organized religious traditions and their cultural signifiers to a more expansive sense of the religious; and (3) contributing to an important and growing discourse on religion and embodiment through a framing of religion and culture in terms of bodies and what bodies construct (and "arrange") in time and space. I believed working toward these three would add greater complexity and richness to the study of religion by highlighting the "ordinary" nature of the religious in relationship to human experience within the context of material history.

3 I understood religion as a quest for complex subjectivity to involve meaning making. In that earlier work, in that phrase "meaning making," what was most important was the meaning. Now the central dimension is "making"— as in the interaction between things.

4 Much of *Terror and Triumph* involves a subtle embrace of dimensions of Camus's sense of the human and/in the world. Here I make this conversation partner an explicit figure.

5 Camus is aware of shit, noting in *The First Man* the impact of its odor: "Camus, *The First Man*: This night inside him, yes these tangled hidden roots that bound him to this magnificent and frightening land, as much to its scorching days as to its heartbreakingly rapid twilights, and that was like a second life, truer perhaps than the everyday surface of his outward life; its history would be told as a series of obscure yearnings and powerful indescribable

sensations, the odor of the schools, of the neighborhood stables, of laundry on his mother's hands, of jasmine and honeysuckle in the upper neighborhoods, of the pages of the dictionary and the books he devoured, and *the sour smell of the toilets at home and at the hardware store*, the smell of the big cold classrooms where he would sometimes go alone before or after class, the warmth of his favorite classmates, *the odor of warm wool and feces that Didier carried around with him*, of the cologne big Marconi's mother doused him with so profusely that Jacques, sitting on the bench in class, wanted to move still closer to his friend . . . the longing, yes, to live, to live still more, to immerse himself in the greatest warmth this earth could give him, which was what he without know-ing it hoped for from his mother" (italics added). This is from the *New York Times Book Review*, and I accessed it as quoted in Gabriel P. Weisberg, "In Deep Shit: The Coded Images of Travies in the July Monarchy," *Art Journal* 52, no. 3 (1993): 36–40.

6  Albert Camus, *The Myth of Sisyphus and Other Essays* (New York: Vintage Inter-national, 1991), 94.

7  Camus, *Myth of Sisyphus*, 97.

8  For Niebuhr's thinking on theological anthropology and issues of justice, see, for example, Niebuhr, *Moral Man and Immoral Society: A Study in Ethics and Poli-tics* (Louisville, KY: Westminster John Knox, 2002); and Niebuhr, *The Nature and Destiny of Man: A Christian Interpretation* (Louisville, KY: Westminster John Knox, 1996).

9  More compelling than Niebuhr for me, although still a perspective I do not embrace, is the thinking of Dietrich Bonhoeffer. While there is still a vertical framing, he does also acknowledge in a more "earthy" and engaged manner the horizontal nature of interplay. What I find most appealing about his work is the much stronger sense of the tragic quality of life and work—reflecting to some extent, although perhaps in a limited way, the realities of the marginal-ized through his involvement with Abyssinian Baptist Church in Harlem. Involvement in/with the world comes with a more significant cost and entails a more "costly" ethical outreach. In a word, he promotes a modality of ethics with dirty hands. See Bonhoeffer, *Letters and Papers from Prison* (New York: Touchstone, 1997); and Bonhoeffer, *The Cost of Discipleship* (New York: Touch-stone, 1995). Mindful of this, I find it less difficult to read Camus and Du Bois theologically in light of Bonhoeffer than in relationship to most theologians/ ethicists.

10  It is not only his nonfiction that speaks to these conceptual frameworks of concern to me. Although not addressed in this chapter, *The Plague* by Camus speaks of the open body—in fact, the book's action is impossible if bodies are not open, are not porous. The rats, the bite of fleas, the presence of blood and other tainted body fluids speaks this openness. However, for Camus in this book, the open body compromised and changed prompts philosophical and theological questions regarding suffering by means of which he interrogates psycho-ethical frameworks for life (or the plague, as the two are the same for

his characters). My primary interest here is not the psycho-ethical response to inadequate philosophical-theological claims regarding suffering, but rather the shit of life, literally the shit of life, marking the presence of open bodies. That is to say, I focus on the naming of that initial moment of contact between body-things and thing-things—and body waste, such as shit, as a mark of this openness—an openness that speaks to the nature of the body and the body as device within religion as a technology.

11 Albert Camus, *The Rebel: An Essay on Man in Revolt* (New York: Vintage International, 1991), 305.

12 Camus, *Rebel*, 8.

13 Camus, *Rebel*, 9.

14 Camus, *Myth of Sisyphus*, 121.

15 Job 1:18–19 (KJV).

16 Job 2:5–7 (KJV).

17 Camus, *Myth of Sisyphus*, 19.

18 Camus, *Myth of Sisyphus*, 54.

19 Camus, *Myth of Sisyphus*, 97.

20 Camus, *Myth of Sisyphus*, 98.

21 W. E. B. Du Bois, *Dusk of Dawn: An Essay toward an Autobiography of a Race Concept* (New York: Harcourt, Brace and Co., 1940), 130–31.

22 This is the second story in the collection titled *Eight Men*. The story was first published in 1942 in the journal *Accent*. A longer version was published two years later in *Cross Section: A Collection of New American Writing*, edited by Edwin Seaver (New York: L. B. Fischer, 1944). The version of the story referenced in this lecture is the 1944 version (pages 58–102).

23 Richard Wright, "The Man Who Lived Underground," in *Eight Men: Short Stories*, 3rd ed., by Richard Wright (New York: Harper Perennial Modern Classics, 2008), 25.

24 W. E. B. Du Bois, "The Souls of White Folk," in *W. E. B. Du Bois: A Reader*, ed. David Levering Lewis (New York: Henry Holt and Co., 1995), 453. Du Bois might be said to turn to the mystical dimensions of capacity—the manner in which the mystical might open the hidden passages marking the subconscious self. This would serve to elevate the "blindness" regarding others noted by William James. See James, "On a Certain Blindness in Human Beings," in *The Heart of William James*, ed. Robert Richardson (Cambridge, MA: Harvard University Press, 2010), 145–63.

25 Du Bois, "Souls of White Folk," 454.

26 Du Bois, "Souls of White Folk," 456.

27 Nella Larsen, *Quicksand*, in Larsen, *Quicksand and Passing* (New Brunswick, NJ: Rutgers University Press, 1986), 82.

28 Camus, *Myth of Sisyphus*, 15. Camus, of course, is referring to existentialist Jean-Paul Sartre's novel *Nausea*.

29 Larsen, *Quicksand*, 130.

30 Larsen, *Quicksand*, 130.

31  Kristin Hunter Lattany, "Off-Timing: Stepping to the Different Drummer," in *Lure and Loathing: Essays on Race, Identity, and the Ambivalence of Assimilation*, ed. Gerald Early (New York: Penguin Press, 1993), 164.

32  Slavery, as sociologist Orlando Patterson has aptly noted, involves a social death—the surrender of will or authority for the sake of physical life. This certainly has shaped the context and content of African American existence in the Americas, but I have in mind a different dimension of this situation. What Patterson describes so vividly entails the existential arrangements of "life," the experience of living within a context of race-based discrimination. One should not ignore ontological considerations—ways in which the very being of African Americans is defined by the presence of demise. An African American body is a social construct meant to signify and speak of the end of being as subject.

33  Materials related to Crummell include Crummell, *Destiny and Race: Selected Writings, 1840–1898* (Amherst, MA: University of Massachusetts Press, 1992); J. R. Oldfield, ed., *Civilization and Black Progress: Selected Writings of Alexander Crummell on the South* (Charlottesville: University of Virginia Press, 1995); Wilson Jeremiah Moses, *Alexander Crummell: A Study of Civilization and Discontent* (New York: Oxford University Press, 1989).

34  Wright, "Man Who Lived Underground," 30.

35  Wright, "Man Who Lived Underground," 30.

36  Wright, "Man Who Lived Underground," 51, 54.

37  W. E. B. Du Bois was familiar with *Quicksand*. In fact, he named it one of the best works of fiction by an African American since Chesnutt. Deborah E. McDowell references this in the introduction to Larsen, *Quicksand and Passing*, ix; Wright, "Man Who Lived Underground," 30.

38  Wright, "Man Who Lived Underground," 60, 61.

39  Robert Zaretsky, *A Life Worth Living: Albert Camus and the Quest for Meaning* (Cambridge, MA: Harvard University Press, 2013), 10, 16.

40  Zaretsky, *Life Worth Living*, 8.

41  Orlando Patterson, *The Children of Sisyphus: A Novel* (Boston: Houghton Mifflin Co., 1965).

42  Patterson, *Children of Sisyphus*, 20.

43  Patterson, *Children of Sisyphus*, 26.

44  Butler quoted in Rina Arya, *Abjection and Representation: An Exploration of Abjection in the Visual Arts, Film and Literature* (New York: Palgrave Macmillan, 2014), 72.

45  Patterson, *Children of Sisyphus*, 71.

46  This is a reference to a line from the short essay on Sisyphus found in Camus, *Myth of Sisyphus*: "One must imagine Sisyphus happy" (119–23).

47  Larsen, *Quicksand*, 135.

48  Patterson, *Children of Sisyphus*, 156–58, 160.

49  2 Corinthians 5:17; Ephesians 6:10.

50  Patterson, *Children of Sisyphus*, 63.

# bibliography

BOOKS AND ARTICLES

Abraham, Amelia. "Ron Athey Literally Bleeds for His Art." *Vice*. September 24, 2014. https://www.vice.com/en_us/article/vdpx8y/ron-athey-performance -art-amelia-abraham-121.

Adams, James Luther, Wilson Yates, and Robert Penn Warren, eds. *The Grotesque in Art and Literature: Theological Reflections*. Grand Rapids, MI: Wm. B. Eerdmans, 1997.

Adler, Rachel. "In Your Blood, Live: Re-visions of a Theology of Purity." *Tikkun* 8, no. 1 (1993): 38–42.

Agresta, Michael. "Angelbert Metoyer at Co-Lab Projects." *Arts and Culture*. November 10, 2015. Accessed July 2018. http://artsandculturex.com/life -machine.

Alaimo, Stacy, and Susan J. Hekman, eds. *Material Feminisms*. Bloomington: Indiana University Press, 2008.

Alexander, Gary T. "William James, the Sick Soul, and the Negative Dimensions of Consciousness: A Partial Critique of Transpersonal Psychology." *Journal of the American Academy of Religion* 48, no. 2 (1980): 191–205.

Althaus-Reid, Marcella. *Indecent Theology: Theological Perversions in Sex, Gender and Politics*. New York: Routledge, 2000.

Anderson, Reynaldo, and Charles E. Jones, eds. *Afrofuturism 2.0: The Rise of Astro-Blackness*. Lanham, MD: Lexington Books, 2016.

Anderson, Victor. *Beyond Ontological Blackness: An Essay on African American Religious and Cultural Criticism*. New York: Continuum, 1995.

Archer-Shaw, Petrine. *Negrophilia: Avant-Garde Paris and Black Culture in the 1920s.* New York: Thames and Hudson, 2000.

Arya, Rina. *Abjection and Representation: An Exploration of Abjection in the Visual Arts, Film and Literature.* New York: Palgrave Macmillan, 2014.

Asad, Talal. *Genealogies of Religion: Discipline and Reasons of Power in Christianity and Islam.* Baltimore: Johns Hopkins University Press, 1993.

Associated Press. "Jean-Michel Basquiat Skull Painting Sells for Record $110.5m at Auction." *The Guardian.* May 19, 2017. https://www.theguardian.com /artanddesign/2017/may/19/jean-michel-basquiat-skull-painting-record -1105m-at-auction.

Athey, Ron. "Polemic of Blood." *Walker Art.* May 19, 2015. https://walkerart.org /magazine/ron-athey-blood-polemic-post-aids-body.

Baert, Barbara, ed. *Fluid Flesh: The Body, Religion, and the Visual Arts.* Leuven, Belgium: Leuven University Press, 2009.

Bahun, Sanja. *Modernism and Melancholia: Writing as Countermourning.* Modernist Literature and Culture. New York: Oxford University Press, 2014.

Bakhtin, Mikhail M. *Rabelais and His World.* Translated by Helene Iswolsky. 1st Midland book ed. Bloomington: Indiana University Press, 1984.

Barker, Emma, ed. *Contemporary Cultures of Display.* Art and Its Histories 6. New Haven, CT: Yale University Press, 1999.

Barrett, Estelle, and Barbara Bolt, eds. *Carnal Knowledge: Towards a "New Materialism" through the Arts.* London: I. B. Tauris, 2013.

Bayley, Stephen. *Ugly: The Aesthetics of Everything.* London: Goodman Fiell, 2012.

Behrent, Michael C. "Foucault and Technology." *History and Technology* 29, no. 1 (2013): 54–104. https://doi.org/10.1080/07341512.2013.780351.

Belting, Hans. *An Anthropology of Images: Picture, Medium, Body.* Translated by Thomas Dunlap. Princeton, NJ: Princeton University Press, 2011.

Bennett, Jane. *Vibrant Matter: A Political Ecology of Things.* Durham, NC: Duke University Press, 2010.

Bernier, Celeste-Marie. *African American Visual Arts: From Slavery to the Present.* Chapel Hill: University of North Carolina Press, 2008.

Bessire, Mark H. C., ed. *William Pope.L: The Friendliest Black Artist in America.* Cambridge, MA: MIT Press, 2002.

Bonhoeffer, Dietrich. *Letters and Papers from Prison.* New York: Touchstone, 1997.

Bonhoeffer, Dietrich. *The Cost of Discipleship.* New York: Touchstone, 1995.

Bordo, Susan. *The Male Body: A New Look at Men in Public and in Private.* New York: Farrar, Straus and Giroux, 2000.

Bordo, Susan. *Unbearable Weight: Feminism, Western Culture, and the Body.* 10th anniversary ed. Berkeley: University of California Press, 2004.

Bould, Mark. "The Ships Landed Long Ago: Afrofuturism and Black SF." *Science Fiction Studies* 34, no. 2 (2007): 177–86.

Bould, Mark, and Rone Shavers, eds. "Afrofuturism." Special issue, *Science Fiction Studies* 34, no. 2 (July 2007).

Bourdieu, Pierre. *The Field of Cultural Production.* Edited by Randal Johnson. New York: Columbia University Press, 1993.

Bourdieu, Pierre. *Outline of a Theory of Practice*. New York: Cambridge University Press, 1977.

Bourke, Captain John Gregory. *Scatalogic Rites of All Nations: A Dissertation upon the Employment of Excrementitious Remedial Agents in Religion, Therapeutics, Divination, Witchcraft, Love-Philters, Etc., in All Parts of the Globe*. Washington, DC: W. H. Lowdermilk and Co., 1891. http://hdl.handle.net/2027/uc1 .32106011901953.

Bowles, John P. "'Acting Like a Man': Adrian Piper's Mythic Being and Black Feminism in the 1970s." *Signs: Journal of Women in Culture and Society* 32, no. 3 (2007): 621–47. https://doi.org/10.1086/510921.

Bowles, John P. *Adrian Piper: Race, Gender, and Embodiment*. Durham, NC: Duke University Press, 2011.

Braddock, Christopher. *Performing Contagious Bodies: Ritual Participation in Contemporary Art*. Hampshire, UK: Palgrave Macmillan, 2013.

Braidotti, Rosi. *The Posthuman*. Malden, MA: Polity Press, 2013.

Brasher, Brenda E. *Give Me That Online Religion*. San Francisco: Jossey-Bass, 2001.

Brown, Bill. *A Sense of Things: The Object Matter of American Literature*. Chicago: University of Chicago Press, 2003.

Brown, Bill, ed. *Things*. Chicago: University of Chicago Press, 2004.

Brown, Bill. "Thing Theory." *Critical Inquiry* 28, no. 1 (2001): 1–22. https://doi.org/10 .1086/449030.

Brown, Karen McCarthy. *Mama Lola: A Vodou Priestess in Brooklyn*. Updated and expanded ed. Comparative Studies in Religion and Society. Berkeley: University of California Press, 2001.

Bunch, Lonnie G., III. *Call the Lost Dream Back: Essays on History, Race and Museums*. Washington, DC: American Library Association Editions, 2011.

Butler, Judith. *Gender Trouble: Feminism and the Subversion of Identity*. New York: Routledge, 2006.

Butt, Gavin. *After Criticism: New Responses to Art and Performance*. New Interventions in Art History. Malden, MA: Blackwell, 2005.

Bynum, Caroline Walker. *The Resurrection of the Body in Western Christianity, 200–1336*. Lectures on the History of Religions. New series no. 15. New York: Columbia University Press, 1995.

Camus, Albert. *Algerian Chronicles*. Cambridge, MA: Harvard University Press, 2013.

Camus, Albert. *Exile and the Kingdom*. New York: Vintage Books, 1991.

Camus, Albert. *The Myth of Sisyphus and Other Essays*. Translated by Justin O'Brien. New York: Vintage International, 1991.

Camus, Albert. *The Rebel: An Essay on Man in Revolt*. New York: Vintage International, 1991.

Canning, Susan. "The Ordure of Anarchy: Scatological Signs of Self and Society in the Art of James Ensor." *Art Journal* 52, no. 3 (1993): 47–53. https://doi.org /10.2307/777368.

Carlson, Marvin. *Performance: A Critical Introduction*. 2nd ed. New York: Routledge, 2004.

Carr, Cynthia. *On Edge: Performance at the End of the Twentieth Century*. Hanover, NH: University Press of New England, 1993.

Cassel Oliver, Valerie, ed. *Radical Presence: Black Performance in Contemporary Art*. Houston: Contemporary Arts Museum Houston, 2013.

CERCL Writing Collective. *Embodiment and Black Religion: Rethinking the Body in African American Religious Experience*. Sheffield, UK: Equinox Publishing, 2017.

Chen, Mel Y. *Animacies: Biopolitics, Racial Mattering, and Queer Affect*. Durham, NC: Duke University Press, 2012.

Chiappini, Rudy, ed. *Jean-Michel Basquiat*. Lugano: Skira; Museo d'Arte Moderna, Citta di Lugano, 2005.

Chidester, David. *Authentic Fakes: Religion and American Popular Culture*. Berkeley: University of California Press, 2005.

Childs, Nicky, and Jeni Walwin, eds. *A Split Second of Paradise: Live Art, Installation and Performance*. New York: Rivers Oram Press, 1998.

Classen, Constance, David Howes, and Anthony Synnott. *Aroma: The Cultural History of Smell*. New York: Routledge, 1994.

Clement, Jennifer. *Widow Basquiat: A Love Story*. Edinburgh: Payback Press, 2000.

Cohen, William A., and Ryan Johnson, eds. *Filth: Dirt, Disgust, and Modern Life*. Minneapolis: University of Minnesota Press, 2005.

Cone, James H. *A Black Theology of Liberation*. Maryknoll, NY: Orbis Books, 1986.

Connelly, Frances S. *Modern Art and the Grotesque*. Cambridge, UK: Cambridge University Press, 2003.

Conrad, Joseph. *Heart of Darkness*. 4th ed. New York: W. W. Norton and Co., 2005.

Coole, Diana H., and Samantha Frost, eds. *New Materialisms: Ontology, Agency, and Politics*. Durham, NC: Duke University Press, 2010.

Copeland, M. Shawn. *Enfleshing Freedom: Body, Race, and Being*. Innovations. Minneapolis: Fortress Press, 2010.

Cotter, Holland. "Adrian Piper: A Canvas of Concerns—Race, Racism and Class." *New York Times*. December 24, 1999. http://www.asu.edu/cfa/wwwcourses/art/SOACore/piper-art-review.html.

Crummell, Alexander. *Destiny and Race: Selected Writings, 1840–1898*. Amherst, MA: University of Massachusetts Press, 1992.

Danto, Arthur. *The Abuse of Beauty: Aesthetics and the Concept of Art*. 21st ed. Chicago: Open Court, 2003.

Danto, Arthur. *After the End of Art*. Princeton, NJ: Princeton University Press, 1998.

Danto, Arthur. "The Artworld." *Journal of Philosophy* 61, no. 19 (1964): 571–84. https://doi.org/10.2307/2022937.

Danto, Arthur. *Beyond the Brillo Box: The Visual Arts in Post-Historical Perspective*. New York: Farrar, Straus and Giroux, 1992.

Danto, Arthur. *The Body/Body Problem: Selected Essays*. Berkeley: University of California Press, 1999.

Danto, Arthur. *Philosophizing Art: Selected Essays*. Berkeley: University of California Press, 1999.

Danto, Arthur. *Remarks on Art and Philosophy*. Edited by Marion Boulton Stroud. Mount Desert Island, ME: Acadia Summer Arts Program, 2014.

Danto, Arthur. *The Transfiguration of the Commonplace: A Philosophy of Art*. Cambridge, MA: Harvard University Press, 1983.

Danto, Arthur. *What Art Is*. New Haven, CT: Yale University Press, 2013.

Davis, Thadious M. *Nella Larsen, Novelist of the Harlem Renaissance: A Woman's Life Unveiled*. Baton Rouge: Louisiana State University Press, 1994.

De Beer, Stephan. "Jesus in the Dumping Sites: Doing Theology in the Overlaps of Human and Material Waste." *HTS Teologiese Studies/Theological Studies* 70, no. 3 (2014): e1–e8. https://doi.org/10.4102/hts.v70i3.2724.

Deleuze, Gilles, and Félix Guattari. *A Thousand Plateaus: Capitalism and Schizophrenia*. Minneapolis: University of Minnesota Press, 1987.

Deren, Maya. *Divine Horsemen: The Living Gods of Haiti*. New Paltz, NY: McPherson, 1983.

Dery, Mark, ed. *Flame Wars: The Discourse of Cyberculture*. Durham, NC: Duke University Press, 1994.

Desmangles, Leslie Gérald. *The Faces of the Gods: Vodou and Roman Catholicism in Haiti*. Chapel Hill: University of North Carolina Press, 1992.

Dewey, John. *Art as Experience*. New York: Minton, Balch and Co., 1934.

Dolphijn, R., and I. van der Tuin, eds. *New Materialism: Interviews and Cartographies*. London: Open Humanities Press, 2012. http://dspace.library.uu.nl/handle/1874/256718.

Douglas, Kelly Brown. *Stand Your Ground: Black Bodies and the Justice of God*. Maryknoll, NY: Orbis Books, 2015.

Douglas, Mary. *Purity and Danger*. New York: Routledge, 2002.

Douglass, Frederick. *Life and Times of Frederick Douglass*. Hartford, CT: Park Publishing Co., 1882.

Douglass, Frederick. *Narrative of the Life of Frederick Douglass, an American Slave*. Boston: Anti-Slavery Office, 1845.

Du Bois, W. E. B. *Black Reconstruction: An Essay toward a History of the Part Which Black Folk Played in the Attempt to Reconstruct Democracy in America, 1860–1880*. New York: Harcourt, Brace and Co., 1935.

Du Bois, W. E. B. *Darkwater: Voices from within the Veil*. New York: Harcourt, Brace and Howe, 1920.

Du Bois, W. E. B. *Dusk of Dawn: An Essay toward an Autobiography of a Race Concept*. New York: Harcourt, Brace and Co., 1940.

Du Bois, W. E. B. *The Philadelphia Negro: A Social Study*. Publications of the University of Pennsylvania. Political Economy and Public Law Series 14. Philadelphia: University of Pennsylvania, 1899.

Du Bois, W. E. B. *The Souls of Black Folk*. New York: Vintage Books/Library of America, 1990.

Du Bois, W. E. B. "Strivings of the Negro People." *Atlantic Monthly*, August, 1987.

Du Bois, W. E. B. *The Suppression of the African Slave-Trade to the United States of America, 1638–1870*. Harvard Historical Studies 1. New York: Longmans, Green and Co., 1896.

Du Bois, W. E. B. *W. E. B. Du Bois: A Reader*. Edited by David Levering Lewis. New York: Henry Holt and Co., 1995.

Du Bois, W. E. B., and Kwame Anthony Appiah. *Dusk of Dawn*. Edited by Henry Louis Gates. New York: Oxford University Press, 2014.

Dubuffet, Jean, and Lawrence Rinder. *Dubuffet, Basquiat: Personal Histories*. New York: PaceWildenstein, 2006.

Duschinsky, Robbie, Simone Schnall, and Daniel H. Weiss, eds. *Purity and Danger Now: New Perspectives*. London: Routledge, 2016.

Ellison, Ralph. *Going to the Territory*. New York: Random House, 1986.

Ellul, Jacques. *The Technological Society*. New York: Knopf, 1964.

Engler, Martin, ed. *Piero Manzoni: When Bodies Became Art*. Frankfurt am Main: Stadel Museum, 2013.

Evans, James H. *We Have Been Believers: An African-American Systematic Theology*. Minneapolis: Fortress Press, 1992.

Fabre, Michel. *The Unfinished Quest of Richard Wright*. Translated by Isabel Barzun. 2nd ed. Urbana: University of Illinois Press, 1993.

Fabre, Michel. *The World of Richard Wright*. Center for the Study of Southern Culture Series. Jackson: University Press of Mississippi, 1985.

Feltz, Renée. "NATO Protester's Prison Term Extended for Throwing Human Waste at Guard." *The Guardian*. April 12, 2016. https://www.theguardian.com/us-news/2016/apr/12/nato-summit-protester-prison-term-extended-jared-chase.

Fine, Ruth, and Jacqueline Francis, eds. *Romare Bearden, American Modernist*. Washington, DC: National Gallery of Art, 2011.

Flatley, Jonathan. *Affective Mapping: Melancholia and the Politics of Modernism*. Cambridge, MA: Harvard University Press, 2008.

Forbes, Bruce David, and Jeffrey H. Mahan, eds. *Religion and Popular Culture in America*. Berkeley: University of California Press, 2000.

Foster, Hal, Benjamin Buchloh, Rosalind Krauss, Yve-Alain Bois, Denis Hollier, and Helen Molesworth. "The Politics of the Signifier II: A Conversation on the 'Informe' and the Abject." *October* 67 (1994): 3–21.

Foucault, Michel. *Discipline and Punish: The Birth of the Prison*. New York: Vintage Books, 1995.

Foucault, Michel. *Technologies of the Self: A Seminar*. Amherst: University of Massachusetts Press, 1988.

Foucault, Michel, Luther H. Martin, Huck Gutman, and Patrick H. Hutton, eds. *Technologies of the Self: A Seminar with Michel Foucault*. Amherst: University of Massachusetts Press, 1988.

Freeman, Nate. "'Feces Is Very Cosmopolitan': Wim Delvoye on His Notorious 'Cloaca' at the Museum Tinguely in Basel." *ARTnews.com* (blog). June 16, 2017. https://www.artnews.com/art-news/market/feces-is-very-cosmopolitan-wim-delvoye-on-his-notorious-cloaca-at-the-museum-tinguelys-retrospective-in-basel-8556/.

Fuller, Robert C. *Spirituality in the Flesh: Bodily Sources of Religious Experiences*. New York: Oxford University Press, 2008.

Fusco, Coco. *The Bodies That Were Not Ours: And Other Writings*. London: Routledge, 2001.

Gates, Henry Louis, Jr., and Cornel West. *The Future of the Race*. New York: Vintage Books, 1996.

Gelburd, Gail. *Romare Bearden in Black-and-White: Photomontage Projections, 1964*. New York: Whitney Museum of American Art, 1997.

Geldzahler, Henry. *Making It New: Essays, Interviews, and Talks*. New York: Turtle Point Press, 1994.

George, Rose. *The Big Necessity: The Unmentionable World of Human Waste and Why It Matters*. New York: Metropolitan Books, 2008.

George, Susan. *Religion and Technology in the 21st Century: Faith in the E-World*. Hershey, PA: Information Science Publishing, 2006.

Glazer, Lee Stephens. "Signifying Identity: Art and Race in Romare Bearden's Projections." *Art Bulletin* 76, no. 3 (1994): 411–26. https://doi.org/10.1080/00043079.1994.10786595.

Goldberg, RoseLee. *Performance: Live Art since 1960*. New York: Harry N. Abrams, 1998.

Gomi, Taro. *Everyone Poops*. Turtleback School and Library ed. St. Louis: Turtleback, 2001.

Gooding-Williams, Robert. *In the Shadow of Du Bois: Afro-Modern Political Thought in America*. Cambridge, MA: Harvard University Press, 2009.

Grimes, Ronald L. *The Craft of Ritual Studies*. New York: Oxford University Press, 2013.

Grossman, Wendy. *Man Ray, African Art, and the Modernist Lens*. Washington, DC: International Arts and Artists; Minneapolis: University of Minnesota Press, 2009.

Grosz, Elizabeth A. *Becoming Undone: Darwinian Reflections on Life, Politics, and Art*. Durham, NC: Duke University Press, 2011.

Grosz, Elizabeth A. *The Incorporeal: Ontology, Ethics, and the Limits of Materialism*. New York: Columbia University Press, 2017.

Guillory, Marcus J. "The Meta: On the Artwork of Angelbert Metoyer." In *I—AoI (LU—X project)*, 49–50. Houston: Angelbert's Imagination Studios, 2008.

Halley, Peter. *Peter Halley: Collected Essays, 1981-1987*. Zurich: Lapis Press, 1988.

Halliwell, Martin, and Joel D. S. Rasmussen, eds. *William James and the Transatlantic Conversation: Pragmatism, Pluralism, and Philosophy of Religion*. New York: Oxford University Press, 2014.

Han, Sam. *Technologies of Religion: Spheres of the Sacred in a Post-Secular Modernity*. New York: Routledge, 2016.

Hansberry, Lorraine. *A Raisin in the Sun: A Drama in Three Acts*. New York: Random House, 1959.

Hanzal, Carla M., et al. *Romare Bearden: Southern Recollections*. Charlotte, NC: Mint Museum, 2011.

Harris, Jonathan, ed. *Dead History, Live Art? Spectacle, Subjectivity and Subversion in Visual Culture since the 1960s*. Liverpool: Liverpool University Press, 2007.

Harris, Jonathan, ed. *Identity Theft: The Cultural Colonization of Contemporary Art*. Tate Liverpool Critical Forum 10. Liverpool: Liverpool University Press, 2008.

Harris, Michael D. *Colored Pictures: Race and Visual Representation*. Chapel Hill: University of North Carolina Press, 2003.

Haslam, Nick. *Psychology in the Bathroom*. New York: Palgrave Macmillan, 2012.

Hawkins, Gay. *The Ethics of Waste: How We Relate to Rubbish*. Lanham, MD: Rowman and Littlefield, 2006.

Hay, Mark. "A Brief History of People Protesting Stuff with Poop." *Vice*. April 8, 2015. https://www.vice.com/en_us/article/wd7n8z/a-brief-history-of-people -protesting-stuff-with-poop-197.

Heathfield, Adrian, ed. *Live: Art and Performance*. London: Tate Publishing, 2004.

Heddon, Deirdre, and Jennie Klein, eds. *Histories and Practices of Live Art*. Hound-mills, UK: Palgrave Macmillan, 2012.

Heidegger, Martin. *Being and Time*. New York: Harper and Row, 1962.

Hoban, Phoebe. *Basquiat: A Quick Killing in Art*. New York: Penguin, 1998.

Hodder, Ian. *Entangled: An Archaeology of the Relationships between Humans and Things*. Malden, MA: Wiley-Blackwell, 2012.

Hoffman, Lawrence A. *Covenant of Blood: Circumcision and Gender in Rabbinic Judaism*. Chicago Studies in the History of Judaism. Chicago: University of Chicago Press, 1996.

Hoffmann, Jens, and Joan Jonas. *Art Works: Perform*. New York: Thames and Hudson, 2005.

Hopkins, Dwight N. *Being Human: Race, Culture, and Religion*. Minneapolis: Fortress Press, 2005.

Hudek, Antony, ed. *The Object*. Cambridge, MA: MIT Press, 2014.

Hutchinson, George. *In Search of Nella Larsen: A Biography of the Color Line*. Cambridge, MA: Belknap Press of Harvard University Press, 2006.

Jacobs, Harriet Ann. *Incidents in the Life of a Slave Girl*. Boston: Published for the author, 1861.

James, William. *The Heart of William James*. Edited by Robert D. Richardson. Cambridge, MA: Belknap Press of Harvard University Press, 2010.

James, William. *The Varieties of Religious Experience: A Study in Human Nature*. Enlarged ed., with appendices and introduction by Joseph Ratner. Gifford Lectures on Natural Religion, 1901–1902. New Hyde Park, NY: University Books, 1963.

JanMohamed, Abdul R. *The Death-Bound-Subject: Richard Wright's Archaeology of Death*. Post-Contemporary Interventions. Durham, NC: Duke University Press, 2005.

Jay, Nancy B. *Throughout Your Generations Forever: Sacrifice, Religion, and Paternity*. Chicago: University of Chicago Press, 1992.

Johnson, Barbara E. *Persons and Things*. Cambridge, MA: Harvard University Press, 2008.

Johnson, Dominic. *The Art of Living: An Oral History of Performance Art*. New York: Palgrave Macmillan, 2015.

Johnson, Dominic. *Pleading in the Blood: The Art and Performances of Ron Athey*. Intellect Live. Chicago: Intellect Books/University of Chicago Press, 2013.

Johnson, Ken. "Art in Review; Adrian Piper." *New York Times*. November 17, 2000. https://www.nytimes.com/2000/11/17/arts/art-in-review-adrian-piper.html.

Johnson, Terrence L. *Tragic Soul-Life: W. E. B. Du Bois and the Moral Crisis Facing American Democracy*. New York: Oxford University Press, 2012.

Jones, Amelia, and Adrian Heathfield, eds. *Perform, Repeat, Record: Live Art in History*. Chicago: Intellect Books/University of Chicago Press, 2012.

Jones, Jonathan. "Is This Basquiat Worth $110m? Yes—His Art of American Violence Is Priceless." *The Guardian*. May 19, 2017. https://www.theguardian.com/artanddesign/2017/may/19/jean-michel-basquiat-110m-sothebys.

Julius, Anthony. *Transgressions: The Offences of Art*. Chicago: University of Chicago Press, 2003.

Kaprow, Allan. *Essays on the Blurring of Art and Life*. Edited by Jeff Kelly. Lannan Series of Contemporary Art Criticism. Berkeley: University of California Press, 1993.

Karp, Ivan, and Steven D. Lavine, eds. *Exhibiting Cultures: The Poetics and Politics of Museum Display*. Washington, DC: Smithsonian Institution Press, 1991.

Keller, Catherine, and Mary-Jane Rubenstein, eds. *Entangled Worlds: Religion, Science, and New Materialisms*. Transdisciplinary Theological Colloquia. New York: Fordham University Press, 2017.

Kennedy, Greg. *An Ontology of Trash: The Disposable and Its Problematic Nature*. SUNY Series in Environmental Philosophy and Ethics. Albany: State University of New York Press, 2007.

Kierkegaard, Søren. *Fear and Trembling*. N.p.: Merchant Books, 2012.

King, Catherine, ed. *Views of Difference: Different Views of Art*. Art and Its Histories 5. New Haven, CT: Yale University Press, 1999.

Kirby, Vicki. *What If Culture Was Nature All Along?* New Materialisms. Edinburgh: Edinburgh University Press, 2017.

Klein, Cecelia F. "Teocuitlatl, 'Divine Excrement': The Significance of 'Holy Shit' in Ancient Mexico." *Art Journal* 52, no. 3 (1993): 20–27. https://doi.org/10.1080/00043249.1993.10791519.

Kristeva, Julia. *Black Sun: Depression and Melancholia*. European Perspectives. New York: Columbia University Press, 1989.

Kristeva, Julia. *Powers of Horror: An Essay on Abjection*. Translated by Leon Roudiez. New York: Columbia University Press, 1982.

Laporte, Dominique. *History of Shit*. Cambridge, MA: MIT Press, 2000.

Larsen, Nella. *Quicksand and Passing*. American Women Writers Series. New Brunswick, NJ: Rutgers University Press, 1986.

Larson, Charles R. *Invisible Darkness: Jean Toomer and Nella Larsen*. Iowa City: University of Iowa Press, 1993.

Lattany, Kristin Hunter. "Off-Timing: Stepping to the Different Drummer." In *Lure and Loathing: Essays on Race, Identity, and the Ambivalence of Assimilation*, ed. Gerald Early. New York: Penguin Press, 1993.

Levin, Amy K., ed. *Gender, Sexuality and Museums: A Routledge Reader*. New York: Routledge, 2010.

Lew, Christopher Y., ed. *Clifford Owens: Anthology*. New York: MoMA PS1, 2012.

Lewin, Ralph A. *Merde: Excursions into Scientific, Cultural and Socio-Historical Coprology*. London: Aurum, 1999.

Lewis, David Levering. *W. E. B. Du Bois, Biography of a Race, 1868–1919*. New York: Henry Holt and Co., 1993.

Lewis, Pericles. "James's Sick Souls." *Henry James Review* 22, no. 3 (2001): 248–58. https://doi.org/10.1353/hjr.2001.0030.

Leyerle, Blake. "Blood Is Seed." *Journal of Religion* 81, no. 1 (2001): 26–48. https://doi
.org/10.1086/490764.

Lock, Graham, and David Murray, eds. *The Hearing Eye: Jazz and Blues Influences in
African American Visual Art*. New York: Oxford University Press, 2009.

Locke, Alain. *The New Negro: An Interpretation*. New York: Antheum, 1986.

Lofton, Kathryn. *Consuming Religion*. Chicago: University of Chicago Press, 2017.

Lofton, Kathryn. *Oprah: The Gospel of an Icon*. Berkeley: University of California
Press, 2011.

Long, Charles H. "The Oppressive Elements in Religion and the Religions of the
Oppressed." *Harvard Theological Review* 69, nos. 3–4 (1976): 397–412.

Long, Charles H. *Significations: Signs, Symbols, and Images in the Interpretation of
Religion*. Minneapolis: Fortress Press, 1986.

Lynch, Gordon, Jolyon P. Mitchell, and Anna Strhan, eds. *Religion, Media and
Culture: A Reader*. New York: Routledge, 2012.

Malewitz, Raymond. *The Practice of Misuse: Rugged Consumerism in Contemporary
American Culture*. Stanford, CA: Stanford University Press, 2014.

Markes, Julie. *Where's the Poop?* New York: HarperFestival, 2004.

Marriott, David. "Corpsing; or, The Matter of Black Life." *Cultural Critique* 94
(Fall 2016): 32–64. https://doi.org/10.5749/culturalcritique.94.2016.0032.

Marshall, Richard, ed. *Jean-Michel Basquiat*. New York: Whitney Museum of
American Art/Harry N. Abrams, 1992.

"Mass Arrests over SA 'Poo Wars.'" *BBC News*. June 11, 2013. https://www.bbc.com
/news/world-africa-22853095.

McCarthy, Dennis J. "Further Notes on the Symbolism of Blood and Sacrifice."
*Journal of Biblical Literature* 92, no. 2 (1973): 205–10. https://doi.org/10.2307
/3262953.

McCarthy, Dennis J. "The Symbolism of Blood and Sacrifice." *Journal of Biblical
Literature* 88, no. 2 (1969): 166–76. https://doi.org/10.2307/3262876.

McDannell, Colleen. *Material Christianity: Religion and Popular Culture in America*.
New Haven, CT: Yale University Press, 1995.

McEvilley, Thomas. "Jean-Michel Basquiat Here Below." In *Dubuffet, Basquiat:
Personal Histories*. New York: PaceWildenstein, 2006.

McKissack, Pat, and Fredrick McKissack. *Lorraine Hansberry: Dramatist and Activist*. New York: Delacorte Press, 1994.

McMillan, Uri. *Embodied Avatars: Genealogies of Black Feminist Art and Performance*.
New York: New York University Press, 2015.

McNish, Jill L. "'Failure, Then, Failure!': Shame and William James's 'Sick Soul.'"
*CrossCurrents* 53, no. 3 (2003): 389–403.

Mercurio, Gianni, ed. *The Jean-Michel Basquiat Show*. New York: Rizzoli International Publications, 2006.

Merleau-Ponty, Maurice. *Phenomenology of Perception*. Abingdon, UK: Routledge,
2012.

Merleau-Ponty, Maurice. *The Visible and the Invisible: Followed by Working Notes*.
Evanston, IL: Northwestern University Press, 1968.

Midson, Scott A. *Cyborg Theology: Humans, Technology and God*. Library of Modern Religion. London: I. B. Tauris, 2018.

Miller, Daniel. *Material Culture and Mass Consumption*. Social Archaeology. Oxford: Blackwell, 1987.

Miller, Daniel, ed. *Materiality*. Durham, NC: Duke University Press, 2005.

Miller, Daniel. *Stuff*. Malden, MA: Polity Press, 2010.

Miller, Monica R., and Anthony B. Pinn, eds. *The Hip Hop and Religion Reader*. New York: Routledge, 2015.

Miller, William Ian. *The Anatomy of Disgust*. Cambridge, MA: Harvard University Press, 1997.

Mirzoeff, Nicholas, ed. *Diaspora and Visual Culture: Representing Africans and Jews*. New York: Routledge, 2000.

Montano, Linda M., ed. *Performance Artists Talking in the Eighties*. Berkeley: University of California Press, 2000.

Morgan, David. *The Embodied Eye: Religious Visual Culture and the Social Life of Feeling*. Berkeley: University of California Press, 2012.

Morgan, David. *The Sacred Gaze: Religious Visual Culture in Theory and Practice*. Berkeley: University of California Press, 2005.

Morrison, Susan Signe. *Excrement in the Late Middle Ages: Sacred Filth and Chaucer's Fecopoetics*. New Middle Ages. New York: Palgrave Macmillan, 2008.

Moses, Wilson Jeremiah. *Alexander Crummell: A Study of Civilization and Discontent*. New York: Oxford University Press, 1989.

Murphy, Nancey, and Christopher C. Knight, eds. *Human Identity at the Intersection of Science, Technology, and Religion*. Ashgate Science and Religion Series. New York: Routledge, 2010.

Nail, Thomas. "What Is an Assemblage?" *Substance* 46, no. 1 (2017): 21–37. https://doi.org/10.3368/ss.46.1.21.

Nelson, Alondra, ed. "Afrofuturism." Special issue, *Social Text* 20, no. 2 (2002).

Neuhaus, Richard John. "By the Blood of His Cross." *First Things: A Monthly Journal of Religion and Public Life*, May 2000, 66–70.

Niebuhr, Reinhold. *Moral Man and Immoral Society: A Study in Ethics and Politics*. Louisville, KY: Westminster John Knox, 2002.

Niebuhr, Reinhold. *The Nature and Destiny of Man: A Christian Interpretation*. Louisville, KY: Westminster John Knox, 1996.

Noble, David F. *The Religion of Technology: The Divinity of Man and the Spirit of Invention*. New York: Penguin, 1999.

Oldfield, J. R., ed. *Civilization and Black Progress: Selected Writings of Alexander Crummell on the South*. Charlottesville: University of Virginia Press, 1995.

Olsen, Bjørnar. *In Defense of Things: Archaeology and the Ontology of Objects*. Archaeology in Society Series. Lanham, MD: Rowman and Littlefield, 2010.

O'Meally, Robert G. *Romare Bearden: A Black Odyssey*. New York: DC Moore Gallery, 2007.

Paine, Crispin. "Sacred Waste." *Material Religion* 10, no. 2 (2014): 241–42. https://doi.org/10.2752/175183414X13990269049563.

Patterson, Orlando. *The Children of Sisyphus: A Novel*. Boston: Houghton Mifflin Co., 1965.

Patterson, Orlando. *Rituals of Blood: Consequences of Slavery in Two American Centuries*. New York: Basic Civitas, 1998.

Pemberton, Nathan Taylor. "Crawling through New York City with the Artist Pope.L." *New Yorker*. November 22, 2019. https://www.newyorker.com/culture/culture-desk/crawling-through-new-york-city-with-the-artist-pope-l.

Perry, Imani. *Looking for Lorraine: The Radiant and Radical Life of Lorraine Hansberry*. Boston: Beacon Press, 2018.

Persels, Jeff, and Russell Ganim. *Fecal Matters in Early Modern Literature and Art: Studies in Scatology*. Studies in European Cultural Transition 21. Burlington, VT: Ashgate, 2004.

Pinn, Anthony B. *African American Humanist Principles: Living and Thinking Like the Children of Nimrod*. New York: Palgrave Macmillan, 2004.

Pinn, Anthony B. *The End of God-Talk: An African American Humanist Theology*. New York: Oxford University Press, 2012.

Pinn, Anthony B. *Humanism: Essays on Race, Religion and Cultural Production*. London: Bloomsbury Academic, 2015.

Pinn, Anthony B. *The New Disciples: A Novel*. Durham, NC: Pitchstone Publishing, 2015.

Pinn, Anthony B. *Terror and Triumph: The Nature of Black Religion*. Minneapolis: Fortress Press, 2003.

Pinn, Anthony B. "'Why Can't I Be Both?': Jean-Michel Basquiat and Aesthetics of Black Bodies Reconstituted." *Journal of Africana Religions* 1, no. 1 (2013): 109–32.

Piper, Adrian. *Out of Order, Out of Sight*. Vol. 1, *Selected Writings in Meta-Art 1968–1992*. Cambridge, MA: MIT Press, 1999.

Powell, Richard J. *Black Art and Culture in the 20th Century*. World of Art. New York: Thames and Hudson, 1997.

Praeger, Dave. *Poop Culture: How America Is Shaped by Its Grossest National Product*. Los Angeles: Feral House, 2007.

Project Row Houses. "Project Row Houses." Accessed May 30, 2020. https://projectrowhouses.org.

Promey, Sally M. *Sensational Religion: Sensory Cultures in Material Practice*. New Haven, CT: Yale University Press, 2014.

Putnam, James. *Art and Artifact: The Museum as Medium*. 2nd ed. New York: Thames and Hudson, 2009.

Putnam, Ruth Anna. *The Cambridge Companion to William James*. New York: Cambridge University Press, 1997.

Rainer, Christian. "Chaos, Kot und Katzen: Besuch bei Künstler Cornelius Kolig." *Profil*. October 30, 2013. https://profil.at/gesellschaft/chaos-kot-katzen-besuch-kuenstler-cornelius-kolig-368706.

Rampersad, Arnold. *The Art and Imagination of W. E. B. Du Bois*. Cambridge, MA: Harvard University Press, 1976.

Rekret, Paul. "The Head, the Hand, and Matter: New Materialism and the Politics of Knowledge." *Theory, Culture and Society* 35, nos. 7–8 (2018): 49–72. https://doi.org/10.1177/0263276418806369.

Richardson, Robert D. *William James: In the Maelstrom of American Modernism: A Biography*. Boston: Houghton Mifflin, 2006.

Rosen, Jeff. "Blood Ritual." *New Republic* 207, no. 19 (1992): 9–10.

Rowley, Hazel. *Richard Wright: The Life and Times*. New York: Henry Holt and Co., 2001.

Saatchi Gallery. "Thomas Mailaender—Artist Profile." *Saatchi Gallery*. Accessed May 30, 2020. https://www.saatchigallery.com/artists/thomas_mailaender_iconoclasts_i.htm.

Santacatterina, Stella. "Piero Manzoni: Art as Reflection on Art." *Third Text* 13, no. 45 (1998): 23–28. https://doi.org/10.1080/09528829808576762.

Sayre, Henry M. *The Object of Performance: The American Avant-Garde since 1970*. Chicago: University of Chicago Press, 1989.

Schwartzman, Myron. *Romare Bearden: His Life and Art*. New York: Harry N. Abrams, 1990.

Sheedy, Matt. "Genealogies of Religion, Twenty Years On: An Interview with Talal Asad." *Bulletin for the Study of Religion*. November 25, 2015. https://bulletin.equinoxpub.com/2015/11/genealogies-of-religion-twenty-years-on-an-interview-with-talal-asad.

Shephard, Katie. "Portland Police Chief Says Antifa Protesters Used Slingshot to Launch Urine and Feces-Filled Balloons at Riot Cops." *Willamette Week*. June 23, 2017. https://www.wweek.com/news/city/2017/06/23/portland-police-chief-says-antifa-protesters-used-slingshot-to-launch-urine-and-feces-filled-balloons-at-riot-cops.

Shohat, Ellah, and Robert Stam. "Narrativizing Visual Culture: Towards a Polycentric Aesthetics." In Nicholas Mirzoeff, ed., *The Visual Culture Reader*, 2nd ed. New York: Routledge, 1998.

Sigurdson, Ola. *Heavenly Bodies: Incarnation, the Gaze, and Embodiment in Christian Theology*. Grand Rapids, MI: Wm. B. Eerdmans, 2016.

Silk, Gerald. "Myths and Meanings in Manzoni's Merda d'Artista." *Art Journal* 52, no. 3 (1993): 65–75. https://doi.org/10.2307/777371.

Simon, Margarita L. "Intersecting Points: The 'Erotic as Religious' in the Lyrics of Missy Elliott." *Culture and Religion* 10, no. 1 (2009): 81–96. https://doi.org/10.1080/14755610902786353.

Sky News. "Venezuela Accuses Faeces-Throwing Protesters of Using 'Chemical Weapons.'" *World News/Sky News*. May 11, 2017. https://news.sky.com/story/venezuela-accuses-faeces-throwing-protesters-of-using-chemical-weapons-10873140.

Smith, Cherise. *Enacting Others: Politics of Identity in Eleanor Antin, Nikki S. Lee, Adrian Piper, and Anna Deavere Smith*. Durham, NC: Duke University Press, 2011.

Smith, Virginia Whatley, ed. *Richard Wright: Writing America at Home and from Abroad*. Jackson: University Press of Mississippi, 2016.

Spelman, Elizabeth V. *Trash Talks: Revelations in the Rubbish*. New York: Oxford University Press, 2016.

Stillman, Nick. "Clifford Owens." *BOMB; New Art Publications*, no. 117 (2011): 50–57.

Stolow, Jeremy. *Deus in Machina: Religion, Technology, and the Things in Between*. New York: Fordham University Press, 2013.

Taylor, Charles. *Varieties of Religion Today: William James Revisited.* Cambridge, MA: Harvard University Press, 2002.

Taylor, Paul C. "What's the Use of Calling Du Bois a Pragmatist?" *Metaphilosophy* 35, nos. 1–2 (2004): 99–114.

Ten-Doesschate Chu, Petra. "Scatology and the Realist Aesthetic." *Art Journal* 52, no. 3 (1993): 41–46. https://doi.org/10.1080/00043249.1993.10791522.

Thompson, Michael. *Rubbish Theory: The Creation and Destruction of Value.* New York: Oxford University Press, 1979.

Thoreau, Henry David. *Walden.* Princeton, NJ: Princeton University Press, 2004.

Tilley, Christopher, Webb Keane, Susanne Kuechler-Fogden, Mike Rowlands, and Patricia Spyer, eds. *Handbook of Material Culture.* Thousand Oaks, CA: Sage Publications, 2006.

Tomkins, Calvin. *Duchamp: A Biography.* New York: Henry Holt and Co., 1996.

Ugwu, Catherine, ed. *Let's Get It On: The Politics of Black Performance.* Seattle: Bay Press, 1995.

Vergine, Lea. *Body Art and Performance: The Body as Language.* 2nd ed. Milan: Skira, 2000.

Verrips, Jojada. "Excremental Art: Small Wonder in a World Full of Shit." *Journal of Extreme Anthropology* 1, no. 1 (2017): 19–46. https://doi.org/10.5617/jea.4335.

Viney, William. *Waste: A Philosophy of Things.* New York: Bloomsbury Academic, 2014.

Walker, Alice. *Anything We Love Can Be Saved: A Writer's Activism.* New York: Random House, 1997.

Walker, Alice. *Living by the Word: Selected Writings, 1973–1987.* San Diego: Harcourt Brace Jovanovich, 1988.

Waltner-Toews, David. *The Origin of Feces: What Excrement Tells Us about Evolution, Ecology, and a Sustainable Society.* Toronto: ECW Press, 2013.

Warr, Tracey, ed. *The Artist's Body.* New York: Phaidon Press, 2006.

West, Cornel. *The American Evasion of Philosophy: A Genealogy of Pragmatism.* Madison: University of Wisconsin Press, 1989.

West, Cornel. *The Cornel West Reader.* New York: Basic Civitas, 1999.

West, Cornel. *Prophesy Deliverance! An Afro-American Revolutionary Christianity.* Philadelphia: Westminster Press, 1982.

Whiteley, Gillian. *Junk: Art and the Politics of Trash.* New York: I. B. Tauris, 2011.

Williams, Robin, and Contemporary Austin. *Strange Pilgrims.* Edited by Heather Pesanti. Austin: University of Texas Press, 2015.

Wirtz, Kristina. "Hazardous Waste: The Semiotics of Ritual Hygiene in Cuban Popular Religion." *Journal of the Royal Anthropological Institute* 15, no. 3 (2009): 476–501. https://doi.org/10.1111/j.1467-9655.2009.01569.x.

Witkovsky, Matthew S. "Experience vs. Theory: Romare Bearden and Abstract Expressionism." *Black American Literature Forum* 23, no. 2 (1989): 257–82. https://doi.org/10.2307/2904236.

Womack, Ytasha L. *Afrofuturism: The World of Black Sci-Fi and Fantasy Culture.* Chicago: Lawrence Hill Books/Chicago Review Press, 2013.

Wright, Richard. *Black Boy.* New York: Harper and Brothers, 1945.

Wright, Richard. *Black Boy (American Hunger): A Record of Childhood and Youth.* 60th anniversary ed. New York: HarperCollins, 2005.

Wright, Richard. *Eight Men: Short Stories.* 3rd ed. New York: Harper Perennial Modern Classics, 2008.

Wright, Richard. *Native Son.* New York: Harper Perennial Modern Classics, 2005.

Wright, Richard. *The Outsider.* New York: Harper Perennial Modern Classics, 2008.

Zamir, Shamoon. *Dark Voices: W. E. B. Du Bois and American Thought, 1888–1903.* Chicago: University of Chicago Press, 1995.

Zaretsky, Robert. *A Life Worth Living: Albert Camus and the Quest for Meaning.* Cambridge, MA: Harvard University Press, 2013.


ARTWORK

"About MoO." Museum of Ordure. Accessed June 2, 2020. http://www.ordure.org.

Basquiat, Jean-Michel. *Untitled.* 1982. Acrylic, oilstick, and spray paint on canvas. Sothebys. http://www.sothebys.com/fr/auctions/ecatalogue/lot.24.html/2017/contemporary-art-evening-auction-n09761.

Charlottenborg, Kunsthal. *Ovartaci and the Art of Madness.* September 2017. Exhibition. Museum Ovartaci, Aarhus, Denmark. https://kunsthalcharlottenborg.dk/en/exhibitions/ovartaci-2.

Charlottenborg, Kunsthal. *Yoko Ono Transmission.* October 2017. Exhibition. Kunsthal Charlottenborg, Copenhagen, Denmark. https://kunsthalcharlottenborg.dk/en/exhibitions/yoko-ono-transmission.

Gignac, Justin. "New York City Garbage." Accessed June 2, 2020. https://www.justingignac.com/nyc-garbage.

Koh, Terrence. *Untitled Medusa.* 2006. Mixed media sculpture, artist's piss, and wiring. Saatchi Gallery, London. http://www.artnet.com/artists/terence-koh/untitled-medusa-a-xy1OmQnbrh_rFgM5373Uwg2.

Lew, Christopher Y., curator. *Clifford Owens: Anthology.* November 2011. Exhibition. MoMA PS New York. https://www.moma.org/calendar/exhibitions/3786.

Mack, Eric N. *Lemme Walk across the Room.* January 2019. Exhibition. Brooklyn Museum, New York. https://www.brooklynmuseum.org/exhibitions/eric_mack.

Manzoni, Piero. *Artist's Shit.* 1960. Mixed media exhibition. Piero Manzoni Archive. http://www.pieromanzoni.org/EN/works_shit.htm.

Metoyer, Angelbert. *Angelbert Metoyer: Babies: Walk on Water: Present, Future and Time Travel.* 2012. Exhibition. Deborah Colton Gallery. http://www.deborahcoltongallery.com/International/exhibition/angelbert-metoyer-babies-walk-water-present-future-and-time-travel.

Metoyer, Angelbert. *Wrestling History: Points along a Journey of Discovery Hidden in the Temple.* May 2016. Exhibition. University of Texas New Gallery, Austin, Texas. https://liberalarts.utexas.edu/public-affairs/news/warfield-center-announces-spring-exhibition-in-the-new-gallery.

Pope.L. *Member Pope.L, 1978–2001*. October 2019. Exhibition. MoMA, New York. https://www.moma.org/calendar/exhibitions/5059.

Serrano, Andres. *Body Fluid Series*. 1986–1990. Photographic exhibition. http://andresserrano.org.

Viola, Bill. *Inverted Birth*. August 29, 2017. Exhibition. Copenhagen Contemporary, Copenhagen, Denmark. https://copenhagencontemporary.org/en/bill-viola.

Wrånes, Tori. *Ældgammel Baby*. September 2017. Exhibition. Kunsthal Charlottenborg. https://kunsthalcharlottenborg.dk/da/udstillinger/tori-wraanes.


AUDIOVISUAL MEDIA

Akers, Matthew, dir. *Marina Abramovic: The Artist Is Present*. Music Box Films, 2012.

Associated Press. "A Golden Throne for the Everyman." YouTube video. September 16, 2016. https://www.youtube.com/watch?v=P1voXTXNbj4.

Curtin University. "Zombies, Cyborgs and Chimeras: A Talk by Performance Artist, Prof Stelarc." YouTube video. August 5, 2014. https://www.youtube.com/watch?v=TqtiM1hK6lU.

diy artem. "ORLAN, Omniprésence, 1993. Extrait." YouTube video. February 14, 2014. https://www.youtube.com/watch?v=jN1teX2xzho.

Elliott, Missy, and Da Brat. "The Rain (Supa Dupa Fly)." YouTube video. October 26, 2009. https://www.youtube.com/watch?v=hHcyJPTTn9w.

Elliott, Missy, and Da Brat. "Sock It 2 Me." YouTube video. October 26, 2009. https://www.youtube.com/watch?v=9UvBX3REqSY.

Kennedy, Peter, dir. "The Mythic Being." Excerpt from *Other Than Art's Sake*. APRAF Berlin, 1973. http://www.adrianpiper.com/vs/video_tmb.shtml.

LagunaArtMuseum. "Chris Burden—Through the Night Softly." YouTube video. October 27, 2011. https://www.youtube.com/watch?v=OB6gg1i2hc8.

MITVBG. "Jay-Z 'Picasso Baby' at the Pace Gallery in New York City." YouTube video. July 10, 2013. https://www.youtube.com/watch?v=p6WpZe093qQ.

Mülla, Erich. "Ed Atkins—Ribbons 2014." YouTube video. January 11, 2015. https://www.youtube.com/watch?v=3EkqVWXBVOQ.

Museum of Contemporary Art Kiasma. "ARS17—Ed Atkins." YouTube video. May 9, 2017. https://www.youtube.com/watch?v=F3vDyaZXx28.

*New York Times*. "Shot in the Name of Art—Op Docs—The New York Times." YouTube video. May 22, 2015. https://www.youtube.com/watch?v=drZIWs3Dl1k.

Rivera, Adina. "Adrian Piper, Mythic Being 1973." YouTube video. April 30, 2017. https://www.youtube.com/watch?v=jVcXb8En_Tw.

TheMACBelfast. "Meet the Artist: Stuart Brisley Interview." YouTube video. February 9, 2015. https://www.youtube.com/watch?v=t54I3QABGWY.

Walker Art Center. "In Conversation: Ron Athey." YouTube video. April 8, 2015. https://www.youtube.com/watch?v=zURUN4GdXB0.

# index

CPSIA information can be obtained
at www.ICGtesting.com
Printed in the USA
LVHW081921250123
737856LV00003BB/686